D0569769

SCIENCE AND CULTURE SERIES
JOSEPH HUSSLEIN, S.J., PH.D., GENERAL EDITOR

GODS OF THE GENTILES

Rev. Leopold J. Czekaj, S.J.

GODS of the GENTILES

NON-JEWISH CULTURAL RELIGIONS OF ANTIQUITY

George C. Ring, S.J., A.M., S.T.D.
Agrégé in Theology of the Gregorian University, Rome
Associate Professor of Apologetics, St. Louis University

The Bruce Publishing Company
Milwaukee

Imprimi potest: P. A. Brooks, S.J., Praep. Prov., Provinciae Missourianae
Nihil obstat: H. B. Ries, Censor librorum
Imprimatur: ✠ Samuel A. Stritch, Archiepiscopus Milwaukiensis
September 28, 1938

Printed in the U. S. A.

TO MY FATHER AND MOTHER
IN AFFECTIONATE MEMORY

PREFACE BY THE GENERAL EDITOR

WE HAVE here an authentic and striking picture of the religions of the great cultural nations of pagan antiquity. The period covered is some three millenniums before the coming of Christ. The center of action is the vast Mediterranean region.

The author's treatment, while strictly scientific and based on extensive historical research, is popular throughout, with touches of a genial humor that not merely relieves our awe of the past but makes us realize the better how truly all mankind is kin. Concentrating moreover on leading features, and frequently massing in a tabular way the less important details, he is able to present his subject in its proper perspective.

The book is in reality a history of the pre-Christian religions that most powerfully influenced the ancient civilizations with which we are historically familiar, and which dominated the world of their day. The Jewish religion, as something distinct and apart, is not considered here.

Every intrusion of religious apologetics has been vigilantly guarded against in this work. Its purpose is to present a purely objective account, colored by no subjective views of the writer. In this he differs widely from the vast majority of historic popularizers in our day, and even from men who otherwise are deserving of real recognition. The author believes that his best service to religion consists in making known the truth, leaving the reader to judge impartially for himself. True religion needs no other vindication.

On that same account his book makes its appeal to all men alike, without respect to creed. Nor is any invective leveled in it against the pagan religions themselves. That, again, was not the author's purpose. He was writing, not with the pen of the theologian, nor yet with the easy-flowing quill of a moralist, but in the attitude of a recorder of facts, merely giving life, color, and action to the resuscitated past.

Overlaid with error and extravagance, corrupted by vice and impurities, the religions of paganism were surely far from commendable. Yet not because of that should we consider them as deprived of every glint of truth or ray of hope, nor were men void of all aspirations after higher things. It is from this point of view that Doctor Ring considers the cults of the ancient world. His treatment is invariably fair, understanding, and illuminative.

While the book has developed out of successive semesters of lectures given in the classroom, and can well be used in courses on the History of Religion as a suitable text, it has now taken on all the features that make of it a captivating volume for popular reading. If the opening chapter offers a slight challenge, owing to the compression of vast periods of history into a comparatively few pages, it serves as an important background to the entire first section. Down into the wide, stoneless, alluvial plain here described, the early descendants of Noe came, as the Scripture records, and began their work of construction, using baked brick, with "slime" for cement. Modern discoveries made in these areas have been of the most fascinating kind confirmative of Scripture details.

Here grew up in course of time the little city-states; here developed the marvelous culture of Sumer and the engineering feats of Accad; here finally arose the mighty walls, the palaces and temples of Babylon and Nineveh that were among the wonders of the world. From this source, too, Egypt is by many held to have derived no little of its earliest culture.

Temples, palaces, and tombs may well be mentioned as symbolizing the earliest civilizations to which our eyes turn as we look into the distant past. Everywhere we still can trace the ruins of mighty edifices of worship on which the nations lavished their material wealth and all the resources of their genius. Here art and architecture could be seen at their best. In Persia, Rome, and Greece, no less than in earlier Sumeria, Babylonia, Assyria, and Egypt, men gave overwhelming evidence of their confidence in the Divine. If Greek religion was deeply penetrated with the influence of poet and artist, yet men never lost their fundamental sense of the need and the truth of religion, however perverted its expression often became. In the Athenian Areopagus St. Paul was able to begin where Paganism had left off, with the proclamation of the "Unknown God" to whom an altar had been erected: "What therefore you worship, without knowing it, that I preach to you."

Timely and interesting, GODS OF THE GENTILES is a work that has been needed and should remain a standard volume.

JOSEPH HUSSLEIN, S.J., PH.D.,
General Editor, Science and Culture Series

St. Louis University,
October 11, 1938

CONTENTS

ILLUSTRATIONS

In the Text

Inserts

PART ONE

RELIGION OF THE ASSYRO-BABYLONIANS

CHAPTER « 1

HISTORIC BACKGROUND

THE Tigris-Euphrates valley forms the eastern horn of what is aptly styled the Fertile Crescent, a name coined for the arable strip of land stretching from Egypt's northern border to the head of the Persian Gulf. From faraway sources in the Armenian highlands two rivers flow through this mountainless land, the Tigris and the Euphrates—the one impetuously, the other languidly—both coursing along in a southeasterly direction for a distance of about eight hundred miles. Anciently a branch of each united above a town known as Lagash, while other branches splayed off to empty separately into the gulf. Today, just south of ruinous Lagash, there is a confluence and the two streams empty through a single mouth.

Such splendid waterways, fertilizing a wide and rich alluvial plain, obviously afforded on their deep stream an easy highway for commerce, offering to the early pioneers one of nature's most cordial invitations to found for themselves here a home and a fatherland. Though the absolute age of man in this region is not at present ascertainable, yet archeology has shown that at the close of the fourth millenium B.C. numerous city-states flourished in that favored stretch of land, now known to us as the Mesopotamian plain.

Chief of the city-states, if we read from north to south, were Ashur, Akkad, Kish, Babylon, Nippur, Lagash, Larsa, Nisin, Ur. The basis of their common culture was Sumerian, the marvelous and extensive discoveries of which have astonished our generation. The Sumerians themselves, however, were possibly not their original founders. Furthermore, any picture

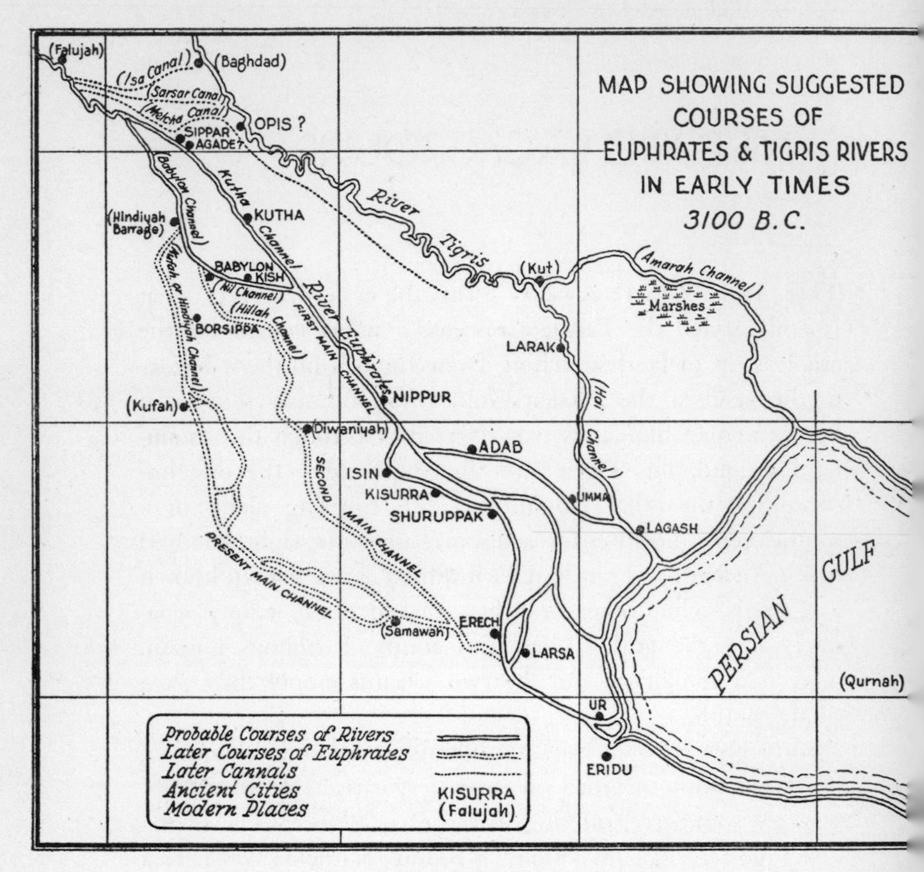

Fig. 1. The Tigris-Euphrates Valley in 3100 B.C.

The head of the Persian Gulf is now about one hundred and seventy miles southeast of the position shown here.

of Sumerian control of the whole valley belongs rather to prehistory, for by the year 3000 that people held merely the southernmost four of the above-named cities. These four with their adjacent spheres of influence formed the land of Sumer, a confederation united by race consciousness rather than a united kingdom. Roving Semites from Arabia had found the central valley to their liking, established themselves as the ruling class, and united the region in a confederation under the name of the land of Akkad.

Northernmost of the valley's political divisions was the region of Ashur or the land of Assyria. Its racial elements are inadequately known, but the evidence at hand points to a notable mixture. Certain names in the early king lists indicate an invasion or infiltration of Asiatic peoples from beyond the Tigris. Elamites from Awan are known to have controlled Ashur and its environs for a time, so that conceivably a third racial element was thus added to Sumerian and Asiatic. Finally, Ashur was Semitized at about the same time as the land of Akkad.

Thus a map of the early third millennium will divide the valley into three spheres of influence: Ashur or the land of Assyria, with a population consisting of Sumerian, Asiatic, and Semitic strains; Akkad or the land of Akkad, with its blending of Sumerian and Semitic blood; and finally Sumerian Ur, or the land of Sumer. It would be a political anachronism to speak of the three divisions as kingdoms, since the bond of union in each case was not a central government, but race consciousness. Ashur, Akkad, and Ur may be said to have exercised a hegemony among the cities of their respective regions, much as did Athens or Sparta among the city-states of later Greece.

With good cause, however, the peoples of these valley lands directed anxious eyes eastward toward the Zagros Mountains. This range, which paralleled the Tigris through almost its entire length, offered its defiles as a convenient corridor to restless migrants from the north. Beyond the Zagros, on the Asian highland, surged still other tribes of nomadic character. Mountaineers and highlanders found raids on the prosperous region of the two rivers an easy means to relieve their chronic poverty. Our earliest chronicles tell of punitive expeditions sent by exasperated valley dynasts against Guttium, Lullubium, and the territory of the Ellipi. To the east and northeast of the Persian Gulf, in a stretch of country more favorable to a settled population, a powerful kingdom was already coalescing, for there the proto-Elamites were doing their bit in the game of harrying the valley.

To the south stretched an Arabia more habitable than the modern sandy waste in which Colonel Lawrence schemed and fought. Semitic shepherds, who held the great peninsula, were destined to be the founders of the mighty historical dynasties of the Tigris-Euphrates valley. As has been seen, they had already trekked northward in sufficient force to gain control of Akkad and Assyria. About the end of the fourth millennium they began another migration which finally brought them in resistless force upon Akkad and Sumer — a migration which at the outset coveted not the alluvial richness of Babylonia, but the coastal plain and hill country of Palestine.

On the eastern Mediterranean littoral at this time were settled an Armenoid people of short stature, broad head, and dark skin, who had probably migrated from their Armenian home by way of the Lebanon Mountains. Making free with the possessions of the Armenoids, these intruding Semites had settled down contentedly after their wandering. By intermarriage the two racial stocks produced the Chanaanites, so well know from Sacred History. The fusion was a happy one, for it made of the nomads a settled population, while conferring on the indigenes the superior civilization of the Semites.

Many centuries were still to pass before the empire-greedy

tentacles of Assyria and Egypt would reach out to the Jordan, before Ramses III would domicile the rowdy Philistines in their coast cities, before Josue would lead Jahve's host into the Promised Land. Thus Chanaanite national life could develop. A varied agriculture supplanted the haphazard food gathering of the aborigines and stone houses replaced their primitive shacks. Walled towns were built for defense and in them flourished the arts and the amenities of life. In the center of each town rose the "high place" execrated by the Hebrew prophets, a precinct sacred to the rites of the Semitic fertility god or Baal. Modern excavators have unearthed a number of his altars and also of the monoliths which were his cult symbols. Although Baal or "Lord" was his common name, he might have in addition a special title, such as, for instance, the "Dagon of Ashod" worshiped in the Biblical Azotus.

Obviously, now, the Semites were well established in both Akkad and Chanaan, on the opposite horns of the Fertile Crescent, at the opening of the third millennium. Noting how hospitably upper Euphrates bends toward northern Syria, we see that communication between eastern and western Semites was naturally to be expected. Archeological finds are gradually furnishing links in the chain of evidence which establishes the blending of Chanaanite with Babylonian culture in towns along the upper Euphrates and in northeastern Syria.

The infiltration of Chanaanitic Semitism into the Tigris-Euphrates valley progressed steadily as the third millennium wore away, strengthening the hand of Akkadian Semitism against the older indigenous Sumerian culture and affecting the racial purity of Sumer itself. No Sumerian Hitler arose to propagate the poppycock doctrine of race superiority by the enlightened means of civil disabilities and the pogrom. No reinforcements of their own racial stock arrived to counteract the persistent Semitization. Nisin and then Larsa submitted to the rule of Semitic families, while Ur fell a prey to

Elamite raids. Time was ripe for the appearance of a forceful Semitic dynasty to organize racial control of the valley.

Sumu-Abum, of the Chanaanitic stock, was the founder of this dynasty and of Babylon's first period of greatness. He came on the scene about 2230, as Akkad's commander, in repulsing an Assyrian attack. His kingship dates from 2225, the approximate date of his fortification of the city of Babylon. He added to the strength of his position by taking and fortifying Kibalbarru and Dilbat, towns dangerously close to Babylon. With that much accomplished, he next turned his attention to the king of Kish, who seems to have had his own ideas about the control of Akkad. Having reduced this rival to the rank of a vassal, Sumu-Abum made a disciplinary raid on the east bank of the Tigris to remind the tribes there that a strong man had at last arrived in Akkad. The rest of his reign he devoted to his useful hobby of digging canals, while watching jealously the interesting development of events in Sumer. His heir, Sumu-la-ilum, he trained up in his own ideas, so that young man, his successor, became not only an enthusiastic canal digger, but a dynastic ruler devoted to consolidating control in Akkad by strengthening a line of forts along his country's frontier. The Kishites formed a league with the trans-Tigrine tribes in the hope of reversing the old scores of Sumu-Abum's days, but received their second beating from the alert young dynast. By this time the Sumerian plum was ripening and Sumu-la-ilum moved into position to shake it down by occupying Nippur, northernmost of Sumer's cities.[1]

Sumer could do nothing about this act of larceny, because she was already engaged in a losing struggle with another invader. The Elamite Kudur-Mabuk, after freeing Elam from Sumerian control, had seized Larsa for his son Warad-Sin. The latter, and his able brother Rim-Sin who succeeded as king of Larsa, extended Elamite sovereignty to Ur and La-

---

[1] Nippur, in addition to its strategic importance, enjoyed the prestige of a "holy city" of the great gods.

By courtesy of Chicago Oriental Institute Museum

Fig. 2. Sumerians

These stone statuettes were unearthed by the Iraq Expedition of The Oriental Institute of the University of Chicago. The dress is the sculptor's imitation of the rough woolen kirtle worn by the Sumerians. Eyes are inset stones. Adoring the two tall divine figures gash. To Nisin now the patriotic party looked for a last effort in behalf of Sumerian independence.

Two successive Nisin rulers carried on, but their resources, under the alternate harrying of Babylon and Elam, steadily weakened. At last, Rim-Sin executed a clever coup with the aid of his father, Kudur-Mabuk. While the latter distracted the Babylonian Hammurabi by a raid on the eastern front, Rim-Sin smashed through to a conquest of Nisin. Before Hammurabi had recovered from his surprise the Elamite had led his columns into Nippur and established himself as lord of the southland. The Babylonian king evinced the wisdom which has exalted his name in history by accepting the *status quo* and waiting. For nineteen years he maintained a policy of defense and preparedness, till at last, in the thirty and thirty-first year of his reign — approximately in the year 2096 or 2095 — he was strong enough to break Rim-Sin's power and annex the whole southern end of the valley. Elam, after a few growls of protest, relinquished her hard won prey and retired into her own borders.

During the remaining fourteen years of his reign Hammurabi pushed his northern frontier up close to the headwaters of the two rivers. Assyria proved his only serious opponent, but he succeeded in forcing her to be content with the status of a semi-independent vassal state. The complacency of the rest of the northern valley in accepting the Babylonian yoke is to be explained by the blending, in this region, of Babylonian and Chanaanite culture which had been so long in progress. By an administrative genius, far surpassing even his undoubted military talents, Hammurabi welded the valley into a political and economic unit whose form was to be altered but slightly through sixteen hundred years. His successors, it is true, were soon to prove unequal to the task of maintaining the territorial integrity of his empire. Tribes from the Sea-Country that lay along the shores of the Persian Gulf, seized the old cities of Sumer; Assyria declared her independence;

and the day came when the Kassite invader at length ruled in Babylon itself.[2]

But through all these vicissitudes the Hammurabic ideal of the region between the rivers as a great corridor of commerce remained unquestioned. Hammurabic law and administrative policy proved a bond of unity transcending change of overlordship, Babylon's speech and cuneiform writing continued as the *lingua franca,* and Babylonian religious concepts dominated the accepted worship of the land. It was only the Persian conquest of the late sixth century which was to destroy the Hammurabic tradition.

Ashur regained her independence from Hammurabi's immediate successors, though maintaining a close cultural rapport with her southern neighbor. Her historical destiny consisted rather in defending and extending Babylonian civilization than in founding a civilization of her own. In the mixed blood of the Assyrian, combining strains of the Sumerian, Western Semite, and Asiatic nomad, there was a warlike fierceness which qualified him for this office of watchdog and conqueror. Constant pressure of unfriendly tribes on the Assyrian border kept his martial spirit vigorous.

From the experience of successful punitive expeditions during the first half of the second millennium germinated the seeds of Ashur's imperial ambition. A king of this period, Shamshi-Adad, not content with the title of his predecessors, "viceroy of Ashur," modestly appropriated to himself the appellation, "king of the universe," adding to it "builder of the temple of Ashur; who devotes his energies to the land between the Tigris and the Euphrates." On the same stone slab where this inscription occurs he conveys the further personal information: "At that time, the tribute of the kings of Tukrish and of the king of the upper country [Armenia], I received

[2] Kings from the Sea-Country held the old territory of Sumer from 2070 to 746. Assyria's complete independence dates from approximately 2065. The Kassite dynasty endured from 1760 to 1185.

in my city Ashur. My great name and my memorial stele I set up in the country of Laban [northern Syria], on the shore of the great sea [the Mediterranean]."[3] It was customary at this period of history for raided kingdoms to send tribute to the raider as a species of insurance payment, as well as for the raider to set up a monument at the farthest limit of his raid. In consequence we need not interpret the above fine phrases as a proof that Assyria had at this time actually extended her frontier to the interior of Armenia and to the Mediterranean.

The dream of empire cherished by earlier Assyrian kings was finally turned into reality by their descendants. Successively, during the course of more than a century, Ashur-Uballit (c. 1340), Shalmaneser I (c. 1280), Tukulti-Urta (c. 1230), actually won the territory fondly mentioned by Shamshi-Adad, while Tigleth-Pileser I (c. 1100) added northern Syria as well as land to the north and northeast. Babylon, however, remembering jealously the old Hammurabic glories, resented the growth of her former vassal and rose in armed protest. Assyria, having no real quarrel with the southern neighbor and profoundly respecting her culture, was content to administer the necessary discipline of defeat in the field without annexation of territory. Such mildness was remarkably in contrast with the normally atrocious cruelty of Assyrian methods. Prisoners were impaled, beheaded, or burned alive in great numbers; unwanted cities were burned and whole populations herded off to slavery in remote regions. The banner of Ashur, spreading wings and a mail-clad archer, was borne in a series of tireless campaigns deep into Asia, to the shores of the Caspian and Black Seas, through Cilicia and Syria, down to the Second Cataract of the Nile. Under Ashurbanipal, the last of her great kings (669–626), Assyria effectively ruled all this immense region together with Babylon and the Sea-Country.

---

[3] *Ancient Records of Assyria and Babylonia,* D. D. Luckenbill (University of Chicago Press), Vol. I, pp. 16, 17.

What follows can be told briefly, since our subject after all is Assyro-Babylonian religion and not the secular history of these countries. The successors of Ashurbanipal inherited an army weary of conquest and a polyglot empire seething with resentment at Assyrian terrorism. Scythians swept into an easy conquest of the northern provinces. Nabopolassar, of the patriotic Babylonian party, proclaimed the independence of his city. Cyaxares, the Mede, besieged Nineveh, the new Assyrian capital. Necho, the Egyptian, seized Syria. Finally, with the fall of Nineveh, in 606, the mighty empire was dismembered. The Medes occupied all to the east of the Tigris; while Babylon drove Necho back into his Egyptian Delta and established control of the whole Fertile Crescent.

For seventy-five years Babylon now enjoyed a renaissance, rebuilt her temples, "praised her gods of gold, and of silver, of brass, of iron, and of wood, and of stone."[4] But the friendly accord with the Median kingdom was broken when the latter fused with the Persians. Cyrus the Persian, after conquering the Lydian Empire of Croesus, returned from the Hellespont to annex Babylon and accomplished his task with almost no resistance. So, then, the second great empire of Nebuchadnezzar's vision[5] was established, to survive two hundred years (539–331), till the coming of Alexander the Macedonian.

The following outline offers a chronological survey of the field we have covered in this chapter.

Outline of Dynasties

OLDER DYNASTIES

Kish	*Akkad*	*Lagash*	*Ur*	*Nisin*	*Larsa*
2750–2650	2650–2600	2650–2300	2450–2300	2300–2115	2335–2095

[4] Dan. 5:4.

[5] *Ibid.*, 2:39. Contacts of the Hebrews with Assyro-Babylonian and Persian history will be discussed later.

These were Sumerian city-states. The dates given denote, as far as the present state of knowledge permits, periods of greatness, though the foundation of all of these cities must be placed in the fourth millennium.

BABYLON AND ASSYRIA

Again, the origin of the cities of Babylon and Ashur far antedates the following figures.

BABYLON

Dates of Dynasties

1st Dynasty or Hammurabic Age
2225–1926
2nd Dynasty
1926–1760
3rd Dynasty or Kassite Domination
1760–1185
4th to 9th Dynasties
1184–732
10th Dynasty or Assyrian Domination
732–614
11th Dynasty or Babylonian Renaissance
614–539

ASSYRIA

Famous rulers

Ilu-Shuma, c. 2225, opponent of Sumu-Abum
Shamshi-Adad I, 2700 (?) raider and temple builder
Ashur-Uballit, c. 1340, organizer of Empire
Shalmaneser I, c. 1280, conqueror
Tukulti-Urta, c. 1232, conqueror
Tigleth-Pileser, I, c. 1100, conqueror
Shalmaneser III, 860–825, conqueror
Sargon, 724–705, conqueror and builder of great palace of Khorsabad
Sennacherib, 705–681, builder and conqueror
Ashurbanipal, 681–626, founder of library at Nineveh

606 — CAPTURE OF NINEVE BY MEDES
539 — CAPTURE OF BABYLON BY MEDO-PERSIANS

CHAPTER « 2

LORDS OF THE VALLEY

OWING to the wealth of the classics and the relative abundance of monumental survivals, Greek and Roman civilizations have long been known to us. At the same time men have found in the works of classic writers, and still more in the pages of Sacred History frequent and tantalizing hints about the high civilizations of the Tigris-Euphrates valley. Thus Herodotus and Xenophon, writing of Achaemenian times, have furnished information on the older Babylonian and Assyrian empires. In 280 B.C. Berosus, a Greek priest, composed from Babylonian temple records a history of Babylon, but unfortunately we can know his work only by the fragments quoted from it in later writers. Other classical references are even more fragmentary, besides being often a mere rehashing of uncertain traditions. That references to the dwellers in the Tigris-Euphrates valley should be frequent in Sacred History was to be expected from the many contacts of the chosen people with these races, from Abraham's day onward. The body of information thus given us is considerable, though it does not afford anything like a coherent history of Babylonia or Assyria.

Nevertheless the source materials for the composition of an adequate history have not been entirely lost. Neither the Persian nor the Macedonian practised vandalism, and consequently did not destroy the written and monumental records of the older civilizations. What they did do was to establish new capital cities, thus quietly leaving Nineveh and Babylon to sink into neglect and unimportance. As the new divinities, Auramazda and Zeus, with their divine families, claimed state support, it followed relentlessly that the once popular temples of Marduk, Ashur, Ishtar, and the other ancient gods of the valley went without services and so gradually fell into decay. Desert sand and the mud sediment of repeated inundations rose foot by foot, till temples and cities — Ur, Lagash, Nineve, Khorsabad, Babylon, and the rest — slept in forgotten graves with the tops of ruined towers for their headstones. The long rest of centuries was not disturbed as Parthian, Sassanian, and Moslem successively conquered the land.

In the twelfth century of our own Christian era, a pious rabbi, Benjamin of Tudela, was shown by Bagdad Jews the site of Nebuchadnezzar's palace and of the fiery furnace in which the faithful Hebrew children were cast. Four centuries later an English gossip tells what he saw at "the olde mightie citie of Babylon." In the seventeenth century Pietro della Valle set the fashion for modern museum collections by carrying off to Rome some of Nebuchadnezzar's stamped bricks, whose mysterious inscriptions must have puzzled Pietro's compatriots. Such occasional curiosity, however, did nothing to advance knowledge of the buried treasures of history.

About the middle of the past century systematic exploration of the mounds began. Layard and Rassam laid bare at Nineveh six royal palaces, finding in those of Ashurbanipal and Sennacherib real treasure trove in the form of some 17,000 tablets of the royal library. More records, such as the stele of Eharhaddon from northern Syria and the king list from Ashur, together with artistic statues and frescoes have since rewarded the patience of excavators and the generosity of the British Museum and the German Oriental Society which have subsidized the work. Excavation of Sargon's huge palace at Khorsabad, begun eighty years ago but abandoned, has been pushed forward within the past decade by the Oriental Institute of the University of Chicago. In Babylon and the south efforts were slower in securing results, largely because the common building material, bricks, namely, that had been dried or baked, tended to form a homogeneous mass with the overlay of sand and mud. But here, too, notable finds have grown commonplace, as enthusiastic experts of the Louvre, the British Museum, the University of Pennsylvania and the University of Chicago, and of the German Oriental Society have bored in meticulously. To mention a few of the more notable successes: Lagash, Nippur, and Babylon have been almost wholly resurrected; temples have been identified and cult objects recovered; the text of the Code of Hammurabi has been found; royal annals, legal and business documents, religious texts, private and official correspondence for all periods have been brought to light.

Babylonian, Assyrian, and Persian monuments of all kinds are covered with wedge-shaped (cuneiform) marks. The significance of these, if significance really underlay them, long exercised scholars. Theories were advanced that they were nothing more than the work of generations of worms, that they were fanciful and meaningless decorative designs, or that they were cabalistic formulas. Slowly, however, the conviction grew that they were signs of a rational written language and this view finally prevailed. The first step toward translation was the discovery that three distinct alphabets were here involved (Niebuhr, 1790); the second, that in one of these three, namely, the Persian, the signs in question were forty in number (Grotefend, 1802); the third, that these forty signs were true letters (*idem.*, 1802). By such tangible clues the zeal of savants was stimulated to work out the rest of the cuneatic mystery. The method, of course, would be roughly that of code experts deciphering a captured enemy message in war time. Chief honors went to Sir Henry Rawlinson, whose incredible labor finally led, in 1851, to the first translation of a lengthy cuneiform text — Darius Hystaspes' boastful catalogue of the glories of his reign.

With the language difficulty largely surmounted, even

though considerable obscurities still plagued the most competent of linguists, the voices of valley history began to become articulate. Outline histories, indeed, were soon possible, as excavation and decipherment of records supplied material from most periods. However, to quote Fr. Condamin,

> A small part only of the texts buried beneath the sands of the Tigris and Euphrates plains has as yet been discovered; and even of those stored in museums a mere fraction has been published: and of this not all has been seriously studied. This is a motive for prudence and for taking several conclusions as provisory. Alongside of the considerable lacunae in our information, many obscure questions, especially concerning origins, remain even where we possess the evidence.[1]

Especially is such prudence to be commended in a history of religions, in a science still in swaddling clothes, a science whose own first principles cannot be regarded as axiomatic. Hence the student of the present course cannot look for full analysis nor final judgment on the character and provenance of Assyro-Babylonian religious ideas. In particular, what is to be said now about the gods and the Assyro-Babylonian concept of "god" must be considered as, to a degree, speculative and provisional.

The first political picture of the Tigris-Euphrates valley, it will be remembered, shows a number of city-states. Upon the administrative economy of the city-state seems to have been modeled the earliest ascertainable concept of the divine economy. As analogues, that is to say, of the *patesi* (city ruler) and his officials, stood the city "god" proper and his subordinate deities. For the present, we cannot be concerned with the subordinates. The chief gods of the various city-states are listed here:

City-State	*God*	*City-State*	*God*
Eridu	Ea	Cuthah	Nergal
Ur	Sin	Babylon	Marduk

[1] *Studies in Comparative Religion,* Messenger, C.T.S., Vol. II, p. 2.

City-State	*God*	*City-State*	*God*
Larsa	Shamash	Borsippa	Nebo
Erech	Anu	Sippar	Shamash
Lagash	Ningursu	Akkad	Ishtar
Nippur	Enlil	Ashur	Ashur
Kish	Ninib	Nineveh	Ishtar

The nationalizing process by which these local gods passed from the status of protectors of small districts to that of patrons of the whole valley may be reconstructed on the analogy of what we know to have occurred in other lands. The fame of a god's temple and the belief in his power spread. This led first to pilgrimage, then to a separate cult in other centers. His chief attribute — whether an oracle god, a healing god, a god of storm or vegetation — became popularized with the result that elsewhere than in his native city his help was sought in such recurrent crises as the making of important decisions, sickness, or peril of crops. When a forceful ruler won for his state an ascendancy over its neighbors, his god shared in this reputation and power. In brief, a great variety of economic, political, and religious causes conspired toward an interchange of gods by neighboring peoples and toward the growth of a pantheon excessively complex.

From this process, as at work in the Tigris-Euphrates valley, emerged the twelve divinities enumerated above as the great gods, nor did they lose their prestige through the whole period from about the year 3000 to the Persian conquest. Moreover, due seemingly to the systematizing of the influential Babylonian theologians, this Pantheon became a closed circle. The lesser gods — the minor divine figures who had served as officials of the city-state god — were retained in minor roles and appear in litanies and incantations. Further systematizing divided all the gods into celestial, the *Igigi,* and terrestrial, the *Anunnaki.* The system of triads, familiar to us from Egyptian, Greek, and Roman religion, was also employed. The more important triads were:

ANU, god of the sky; ENLIL, god of the earth; EA, god of the waters.

SIN, the moon-god; SHAMASH, the sun-god; ISHTAR, the planet Venus.

ENLIL, the father; NINLIL, the mother; NINIB, the son. (The triad of Nippur.)

SIN, the moon-god; SHAMASH, the sun-god; ADAD, the god of rain.

EA, DAMKINA, and MARDUK. (The triad potent in healing and in exorcisms.)

The *rationale* of these groupings is clear from the brief explanation appended in every case. It is not a little curious to discover in Babylonian religion the same phenomenon as in Roman, Greek, and Egyptian, namely, the association in a unified cult of three distinct divinities.[2] There is evidence that the Roman practice derives from the Greek, but other interdependence cannot be shown.

With the divine family thus summarily introduced, we may proceed to investigate their individual characters, in order to marshal evidence for a judgment on the Babylonian concept of the divine nature.

It is a difficult task to decide which of the great gods should be named as the primate, i.e., which one occupies a position analogous to Persian Ahura Mazda, Greek Zeus, and Roman Jupiter. Were the question merely one of popularity of cult, the choice would lie between Marduk, Ashur, and Ishtar. However, if we apply the theological norm of relative transcendancy of attributes, our opinion is that Anu must be placed at the head of the pantheon. His divine name appears to have been derived from the Sumerian word *ana* meaning "heaven," which probable etymology points to an assimilation of him to the circle of "sky-gods." These in ancient reli-

[2] Explanation of triadic worship will be given in the chapters on Egyptian and Roman religion. Cf. chapter on "Isis, Osiris and Horus" (Egyptian Religion), and on "Divine Newcomers" (Roman Religion).

gions rank as Supreme Beings.[3] Anu's throne was in the heavens, often specifically at their unmoving northern pole. In the astronomical theology of Babylon the other gods were thought to be resident in the stars which perpetually circle about the pole. Though he is not an "originator" or creator of the gods, all the gods at last resort were subject to his will, while the demoniac demigods lay under a like subjection. In the mythological struggle between gods and monsters he was the *de jure* champion, though Marduk was represented in the Babylonian redaction of the story as becoming *de facto* champion, owing to Anu's faintheartedness. Anu ordained human fates and disposed the course of human events. All periods recognized these high attributes in him, though in a theoretic rather than in a practical way, for nationalism gave a preponderance of cult observance to Marduk, the symbol of Babylon's patriotism, and to Ashur, the warrior-god of the Assyrians. We subjoin here several quotations which illustrate the position Anu held in relation to gods and men.

"SHAMSHI-ADAD, whose name Anu and Enlil had named for great deeds." (From an inscription of this king, c. 1800.)

"ANU, king of the Igigi and Anunnaki." (From invocation by Shalmaneser I, 858–824.)

"ANU, mighty and pre-eminent who ordains the decrees of the gods." (From annals of Ashur-Nasiir-Pal, c. 880.)

"ANU, the mighty and primeval, whose word of command no god calls in question." (From annals of Esarhaddon, 680–669.)

"ANU, the mighty and pre-eminent who called me by my name." (From the same.)[4]

From references going back to the second century B.C. we

---

[3] The recognition of the "sky-god" as a central feature of very many religions is the most significant advance in recent history of religions. For explanation of the matter, cf. Fr. W. Schmidt's *Origin and Growth of Religion* (Methuen & Co., 1931).

[4] Translations from Luckenbill's *Ancient Records,* Vol. I, paragraphs 43, 555, 491; Vol. II, paragraphs 574, 667.

learn that in a corner of the ruinous Marduk temple in Babylon worship was still offered to Anna-Bel — a curious survival of the old time when the heaven-god Anu and Babylon's idol Marduk, also named Bel, ruled proudly by the waters of Babylon.

Associated with Anu in a triadic worship were Enlil and Ea. The earth-god's throne was set upon "the great mountain," probably conceived as some peak in the Transtigrine mountains to the northeast of Babylonia. Reference has already been made to the holy city of Nippur, which was Enlil's city wherein the earth-god waited for mortal men to come and beseech his assistance and win his approval for the conduct of affairs. A king, for instance, must needs journey to Nippur to secure approval for his kingship and so might thereafter proudly call himself the "prefect of Enlil."[5] In short, Nippur's god, as god of earth, administered mundane affairs. Since we purpose later to discuss the question of human origins, it will suffice here to note that Enlil is one of those to whom man's "creation" is ascribed. Over the moral conduct of his mortal subjects he exercised censorship, and bestowed reward or punishment. In one of the legends, for instance, it is his influence which especially moves the gods to destroy men for their sins. Of Enlil, as of Anu, we would have much clearer concepts, had not Marduk and Ashur been so exalted by their nationals as to absorb many of the functions of the older gods.

The geographical site of Eridu, the city of Ea, supplies a hint toward the explanation of his outstanding attribute. Eridu lies near, and in antiquity lay much nearer, the head of the Persian Gulf and the embouchure of the two rivers in a region of superabundant water. Here surely was a prime occasion for the exercise of the vain religious speculation con-

---

[5] "Tablet of Ashur-Uballit" (c. 1380), translated, *ibid.*, Vol. I, par. 59. Assyrian and Babylonian kings, if they did not have sovereignty over Nippur, supplied by erecting Enlil temples in their own capitals. Thus Erishum of Assyria built one in Ashur as early as 2300. Cf. *ibid.*, Vol. I, 43.

demned by the Book of Wisdom, for men to "imagine . . . the great water . . . to be the gods that rule the world" (13:2). Ea may with good reason be regarded as a personification of the nature force of water, whose influence for good or ill would obtrude itself on the thought of a population in a region such as Eridu. Moral attributes, however, dignify the Ea-concept, at least as it is revealed in the myths and in the quasi-systematic theology. There he appears as a god of wisdom, as man's helper, and his special pleader in the assembly of the gods. His helping character is developed especially in the literature of the curious medico-magic which has been aptly described as the prehistory of scientific medicine.

To the gods of the triad just considered were assigned as respective spouses the goddesses Antu, Ninlil, Damkina. These female divinities have little importance, being in attribute merely pale reflections of the three male divinities. With the whole triad, however, there was associated in cult a really important goddess, Ishtar.

To historians of religion Ishtar is a familiar figure, for as Astarte, Ashtar, Athtar, and Astar she is found in Canaan, Moab, Arabia, and Abyssinia. She follows the Phoenicians to their far-flung colonies. She invades the Greek and Roman worlds by identification with Aphrodite and with Venus. Etymological and ethnological arguments make it fairly certain that she originated among the ancient Semites in the Arabian peninsula and was carried into the Tigris-Euphrates region on the waves of their migration.[6] Devotion to her in her new home is attested by a king Ititi in the middle third millennium, who "with fervent prayer to Ishtar erects a stele," and by Ilu-Shuma of Ashur in the twenty-third century who "for Ishtar, his lady, built this temple." Erech, Akkad, and Ashur all raised early temples to her, while in later times still more famed were those built at Ninive and Arbela.

[6] For these arguments, cf. Hastings, *Encyclopedia of Religion and Ethics,* articles: "Ashtart," "Ishtar."

Older Sumerian goddesses were absorbed by her and either disappeared altogether or survived in such hyphenated forms as Ishtar-Nana. In historical times, whatever may have been the prehistoric picture, Ishtar stands out as the only important female divine figure in the valley.

Ishtar was originally, it may be confidently conjectured, a divinized personification of the vital principle (*principium vitale*). Philosophically untutored man was incapable of scholastic refinement on that term, but constantly obtruded on his attention were the phenomena of plant growth, of animal and human procreation. To explain them he turned with religious veneration to a mighty earth-mother or mother-goddess fecund of all things and solicitous for all. She became, then, the mistress of the profound mysteries of birth and life. With her, too, was not infrequently connected the equally profound mystery of death, in that she was made out to be a "destroyer" or that she is assigned a male consort doomed to a cruel and untimely death. Isis, Cybele, Mâ, Demeter, and the as yet nameless goddess of the Cretan excavations, are only a few of ancient religion's mother-goddesses.

From the above pregnant naturistic kernel the Ishtar concept developed until her votaries in the valley beheld in her a true "common likeness of gods and goddesses" (*deorum dearumque facies uniformis*). At Eridu she was recognized as Ea's child and dispenser of the fertilizing waters. In the Gilgamesh Epic and the Tammuz Myth she appeared as the divine bureaucrat of crop control. In the same it was she who gave increase to flocks and herds, while Babylonian art symbolized this potency in the cow-horns crown given her. Goddess not only of the love of legitimate wedlock, but of wanton passion, she played the harlot through the myth cycle and numbered among her temple servants the *hierodules*. As mother-goddess in a very precise sense, she was creatress and birth-goddess as well as guardian of man's physical and moral well-being. She revealed future events, as in the famous text from Ashurbanipal's Annals. For the Assyrians especially she became, like their fierce Ashur, the leader of their hosts bearing "quivers on right and left sides, a bow and a sharp sword unsheathed for battle."

To illustrate the universality of Ishtar's functions, we gather here from various periods her divine titulary.[7]

Queen of heaven and earth,
Who goes before my hosts,
Great lady,
My lady,
First among the gods,
Lady of confusion who makes battles terrible,
Who fills full the measure of bravery,
Powerful queen of all the gods,
Whose word is honored,
Bright being who surveys the ends of heaven and earth,
First-born of Anu,
Who stirs up the seas and troubles the hills,
Who causes the heart to attain its desire,
Lover of righteousness,
Bestower of life,
Merciful goddess,
Shining goddess of the stars,
Queen of warfare and battles,
Ishtar of Ninive,
Ishtar of Arbela,
Lady of Erech,
Goddess of all the world,
Who directs the enforcement of laws,
Who directs the divine decrees,
Empress of the goddesses,
Whose word is supreme in the councils of heaven and in the Underworld.

Ishtar, it will readily be seen, had absorbed even the functions

[7] The context may be found in *Ancient Records of Assyria and Babylonia,* Vol. I, nn. 145, 166, 211, 249, 217, 356, 522, 824; Vol. II, nn. 508, 509, 577, 730, 736.

Fig. 3. Shamash the Sun-God

Memorial tablet in the British Museum recording the restoration of the temple at Sippar. Shamash, clothed in Sumerian wool and seated on a throne supported by two monsters, holds the staff and ring as symbols of sovereignty. Twin deities suspend before his tent the sun-disk. A Babylonian king approaches led by a priest and followed by a goddess.

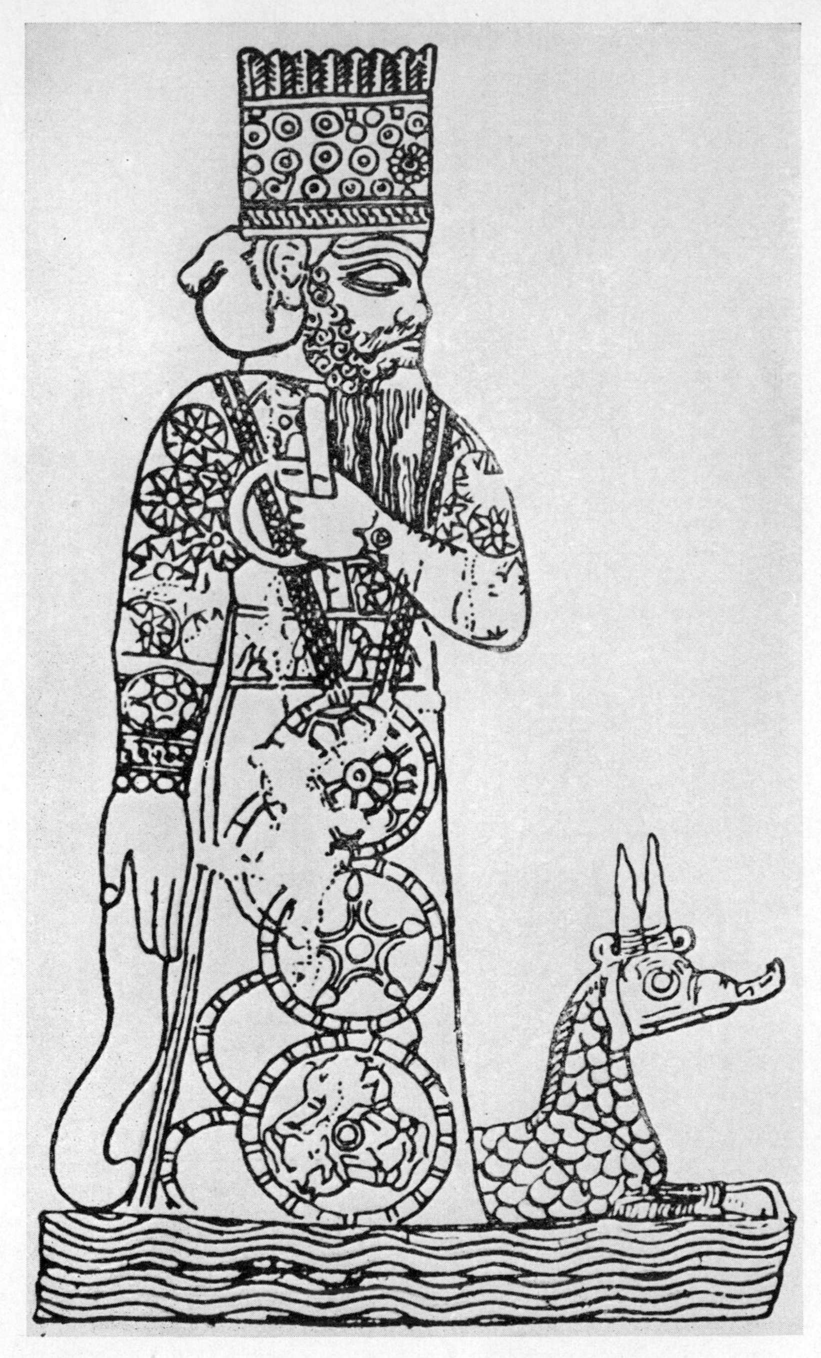

Fig. 4. Marduk of Babylon

Engraving on a cylinder of lapis lazuli from his temple at Babylon. The city's chief god holds the staff and ring symbolic of sovereignty. The watery abyss and dragon recall his victory over Tiamat which won for him the divine hegemony.

of Anu, Enlil, and Ea, into whose august company popular devotion had forced her admission.

With Sin (the moon) and Shamash (the sun), the planet Ishtar (Venus) constituted the great triad of astronomical religion. How ancient this form of cult was in the valley and what racial stock introduced it, are only two of many questions which perplex scholars. A moderate view seems to be that the elements of the cult antedate our earliest sources, but that its organization and propagation are traceable to Hamurrabi. Like many another emperor, he desired unity of religion as a means to unity of government. In outline, Astronomical Religion embraces the following naturistic superstitions. Sun and moon, and to a lesser degree the other heavenly bodies, "are thought to be the gods that rule the world," either in a crudely materialistic sense or in the sense of striking manifestations of divine personalities distinct from the material bodies. In either case, the phases of the heavenly bodies and the accidental changes of them by atmospheric conditions are anxiously watched as revelations of divine will. Especially important in this matter are the waxing and waning of the moon, comets and shooting stars, eclipses. Interpretations of such phenomena are furnished by the priests and soon accumulate into a vast corpus of written or orally preserved lore applicable to the crises of human life. A religious calendar is formed, whose holy seasons and days, lucky and unlucky days, are regulated by the recurrent celestial phases. The number expressing the periodicity of a heavenly body becomes a "sacred number." Mythology contributes its accustomed service of humanizing and popularizing divine beings with its genealogies and its sagas of amours and puissant deeds.

Astral religion reached its highest development during the Neo-Babylonian period, but through all periods was a notable facet of the complex Babylonian religious psychology. However, the theory of Winckler and his school (Pan-Babylonianism), which makes of it a master key in the interpretation of the valley's religious history — and, indeed, of all religious history — can now be classed with Animism, Totemism, and other overenthusiastic totalitarian theses. The Babylonians did identify gods with heavenly bodies, but not to the exclusion of other concepts of the divine being. They did observe changes in the heavens and seek in them guidance. They did, in later days, in their hepatoscopy plot the liver of a sheep on the analogy of heaven's quarters, and seek thence favorable and unfavorable signs. Some of their myths, too, are conveniently interpreted as stories symbolizing the recurrent changes in the firmament. However, it cannot be shown that the Babylonian priests, much less the people, knew astronomy to the extent that Winckler postulates, nor that they thought their humbug astrology to be a universal religious panacea, nor yet that they regarded their mythology as purely astral. Chthonic and elemental concepts of Deity mingled inextricably, even in the priestly mind, with the astral.

Astrology, the offspring of astronomical religion, outlived other features of Babylon's religious culture. The lore of the old priesthood became the property of charlatans, who continued through Persian and Seleucid times to read the heavens and the liver of animals for a credulous clientele. When the center of empire shifted to the west, these pseudo-priests transferred their hoodwinking activities to Tiber's banks, where their popular and lucrative trafficking attracted the amused attention of Rome's Walter Winchell.

> *Chaldaeis sed major erit fiducia: quidquid*
> *Dixerit astrologus, credent a fonte relatum*
> *Hammonis.*[8]

So says Juvenal. The Romans borrowed from the Babylonians the identification of their chief gods with heavenly bodies.

[8] "Still more will they put faith in the Chaldeans; for whatever the astrologer says they accept as though it were an oracle from Jupiter Amon." Juvenal, *Liber Satirarum*, vi, 553 sqq.

Hence the following:

Marduk-Jupiter, the planet Jupiter;
Mercury-Nabu, the planet Mercury;
Nergal-Mars, the planet Mars;
Saturn-Ninib, the planet Saturn;
Ishtar-Venus, the planet Venus.

It is interesting to note that modern astronomy with its 200-inch lenses and its computations in light-years still calls the planets by the divine names given when they were objects of worship.

The last two gods to claim special attention are Marduk and Ashur. To political causes they owe their extraordinary exaltation, not to any legitimate title to primacy in the divine assembly. For they were originally mere city-gods of their respective towns, Babylon and Ashur. Marduk had his happy accident when Hammurabi chose Babylon as the capital of the first valley empire. Hitherto Marduk, a fertility god, had been honored as the divine counterpart of the local *patesi,* but with no pretensions to equality with such great ones as Anu, Enlil, and Ea. Though Hammurabi professed to have received his code of laws through revelation from Shamash — an acknowledgment of the sun-god's traditional position as lawgiver and judge — it was Marduk who profited by the establishment of this code and of Babylon's culture through the Hammurabic empire. How this culture remained the dominant one, even when Babylon was politically eclipsed, has already been noted. Marduk's priests fitted him out with a genealogy and a biography suitable to the god of so important a cultural center. They made him Enlil's beloved son and heir to that god's attributes. They re-edited the Sumerian creation myth, which originally knew nothing of Marduk, so that he and not Anu wins for the gods the heroic conflict with the monsters, receiving as his reward recognition as chief god and proceeding then to form the visible universe. Man was made by him from the body of the slain monster Tiamat.

Marduk kindly relieved his father Enlil of the function of bestowing earthly sovereignty, receiving the aspirant to royalty in his own great temple E-sagila. From Shamash, Nabu, Anu he further borrowed the characteristics of lawgiver and judge, of god of wisdom and oracles, of king of all the Igigi and Anunnaki, the gods of earth and heaven. More and more he came to be named by the appellation *Bel* (i.e., "*the* lord").

Perhaps the most significant testimony to his importance is the honor paid him by the Assyrians, who had their own Ashur to exalt and publicize. In Assyrian records Marduk is not merely given a titulary as flattering as any in Babylonian records, but is explicitly put on a par with Ashur. Assyria's kings built him a temple in their own new capital Ninive and kept it solicitously in repair. Shalmaneser III made a solemn pilgrimage to prostrate himself before E-sagila's cult-statue, to "lavish upon it his splendid sacrifices and pure offerings." After Sennacherib had destroyed Babylon for its treachery and carried off Marduk's statue to Ninive, his successors Esarhaddon and Ashurbanipal invented the fiction that Marduk's wrath against his city had caused this fate and that now he had experienced a change of heart. By the god's command they rebuilt the city and the temple. When all was ready, Ashurbanipal conducted the cult-statue back in a magnificent procession. At Marduk's re-entrance into his homeland "the gods of Sumer and Akkad, like whimpering puppies, comported themselves strangely before him."[9]

Ashur, like Marduk, was the beneficiary of a political build-up. The lord of Eharsagkurkurra — for so his city-temple was called — is an unpretentious figure in the early records. His "viceroys and priests," the successive kings of Ashur, attest their devotion by keeping his third millenial temple in repair, but clearly recognize his local character. Only with the growth

---

[9] References: *Ancient Records of Assyria and Babylon,* Vol. I, pp. 624, 824; Vol. II, pp. 227, 650, 963, 999.

of Assyrian imperialism toward the end of the second millenium does the Ashur-concept show signs of expansion. Then, fired by the experience of successful campaigns under the god's banner, his priests develop the doctrine of his preeminence. Marduk's much earlier aggrandizement is all too obviously the prototype in this process, for in the Assyrian redaction of the myths Ashur usurps in turn the very functions that Marduk had stolen from Sumerian gods. Furthermore, Ashur's fictitious genealogy and catalogue of attributes are rather slavish imitations of Marduk's. Yet the newly fortified Ashur cult remained, so far as we may judge from present sources, an external and official one, never entering deeply into the vital faith of the people as did the cults of Ishtar, Marduk, and the elder Sumerians. In this it would present a strong analogy to the whole genius of Assyrian culture, which, to speak in general terms, was imposed and maintained by force of arms upon reluctant populations. Ashur sank to oblivion beneath the walls of Ninive together with the fiercely brave race with whom he had risen to greatness.

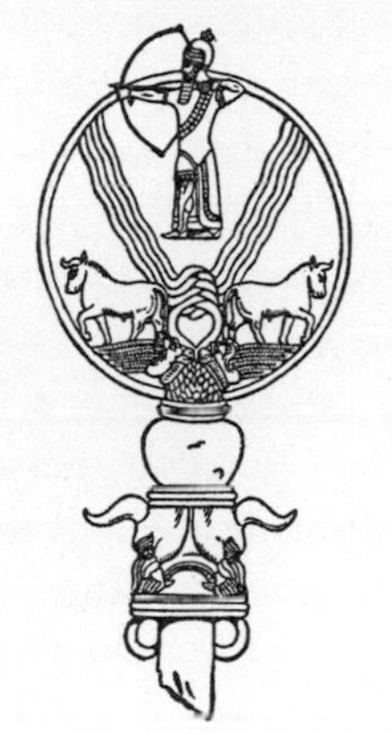

From Olmstead's *Assyria* by permission of Charles Scribner's Sons.

Fig. 5. Assyrian Standard with Image of Ashur
The warlike character of Assyria is indicated by the martial figure of the land's chief god. The lions' heads and bulls denote his invincibility.

The foregoing levee of gods shows that nature worship was the master-idea of Tigris-Euphratean cult. The elements, the heavenly bodies, the principle of earthly life were adored. We have reserved for future discussion the order of demons whose activity was thought to cause man's manifold woes. But, selective though our levee has been, the thoroughly polytheistic character of the Babylonian system is evidenced. The naturistic polytheism was not devoid of moral content, for the gods were definitely the founders of the ethical code and sanctioners of its observance. Some writers would like to read in the evidence an implicit monotheism or, at least a monotheism conceived as an esoteric creed of the educated priesthood. However, an impartial judgment can admit at most an all-tolerant henotheism as Babylon's closest approach to monotheism. That is to say, one of the many gods — for instance, Ishtar, Marduk, or Ashur — magnified by accidental causes, borrowed the apparatus of the other gods' attributes and was accorded the lion's share of cult. But the others remained in the creed real beings and still potent. There is no similarity here to Jahve of Israel, the One True God, before whom the gods of the gentiles were mere nothingness and abomination.

CHAPTER « 3

GODS, MONSTERS, AND HEROES

MYTHOLOGY flourishes on a polytheistic soil. The stories told of the gods are traditions of indefinite age even in the earliest sources available to the historian. As a race advances in culture, its myths may be subjected to beautician treatment at the hands of poets. So worked Homer and his fellows with the immemorial traditions of Greek religion. A priesthood, raised to power by political changes, may re-edit a nation's *depositum mythorum* for the aggrandizement of their local god. Thus did the Theban priests and the Babylonian priests in favor respectively of Amon and Marduk. But, altered or kept intact, the divine fairy tales pass for unquestioned truth and remain a vital part of the polytheistic cult.

Such tenacity of belief cannot be explained by mere omnivorous, untutored credulity. Rather does the myth cycle offer some sort of answer to fundamental questions arising in the religious mind, afford a palliative for urgent religious desires. In default of the light of a rational philosophy, origin myths are taken as explanations of how the gods, the universe, and men came to be. From his sense of intimate dependence upon God (or, for polytheists, upon the gods), flows the desire in man's heart to draw near Him for purposes of praise, impetration, propitiation. Yet this approach implies to the polytheistic and unphilosophical mind a bringing down of the divine beings to the human level. Effectively is the leveling effected in the anthropomorphic myth biography, in which gods speak their minds and reveal their characters and wills in all too humanly understandable action. In addition, the *raison d'être* of much of cult practice — periodic festivals, for instance, and symbolic actions — is found in what the divine overlords have done or enjoined to be done in the myths. One may conclude how closely a heathen joined his preposterously fictitious mythology with the polytheistic "faith" that was in him. His faith being essentially unreasonable, it was but natural in him to seek its justification in the unreason of myths.

Of the original provenance of the myth cycle which goes by the name of Babylonian, scholars speak cautiously. However, a provisional interpretation — subject to modification, but improbably to contradiction, in the light of future discoveries — identifies the basic texture of the stories as of Sumerian weave, with yet a notable interweaving of Semitic thread. To the Semites are to be traced the important roles played by Ishtar and Marduk together with certain changes in the functions of Shamash and in the character of the Underworld.

The Babylonian creation myth, known in part from fragments of Berosus' *History,* was discovered about sixty years ago in a cuneiform document and duly deciphered. Considerable *lacunae* occurred in the original, but it was possible, from the lines preserved and by reasonable conjecture, to reconstruct a coherent whole. The substance of the seven tablets on which the story is inscribed is the following:

1. Two principles, named "the primeval Apsu" and "the chaos Tiamat," conceived as feminine, are described as mingling their waters. The two names mean respectively "Ocean" and "Sea," but this etymology is not particularly enlightening. These two generate the gods, whose activity, however, disturbs the repose of their parent Apsu. He accordingly decides to destroy them, to which end Tiamat produces all manner of serpents and monsters. Ea, the brightest of Tiamat's divine grandchildren, learns of the plot.

2. Ea reports to his papa Ansar, who sends another of his sons, Anu, forth as champion. His precipitate flight at the mere sight of Tiamat and her host gives Marduk his oppor-

tunity. He offers to vanquish Tiamat if the other gods will acknowledge him as their sovereign.

3. The gods, summoned by Ansar, assemble at a great banquet at which they become uproariously drunk.

4. Restored to sobriety, the gods confer omnipotence on Marduk, who manifests the gift by working a magical trick. He then arms for conflict, meets and kills Tiamat, and with half of her body covers the vault of heaven. To check the waters of heaven from pouring down he hurls a lightning bolt aloft and stations a guard there. (All this is insanely incoherent, but so the narrative runs.)

5. Marduk now sets sun, moon, and planets in heaven. (This and the following two tablets are badly mutilated.)

6. Marduk forms men from blood (probably his own or even that of Tiamat, but the fragmentary character of the tablet precludes a more definite statement).

7. Laudation of Marduk, who among other titles is called "creator of grains and of plant life." (His creation of plants probably was narrated in the lost portions of tablets 5 and 6. Since Berosus says that animals were created at the same time as man, we are entitled to draw a similar inference in regard to animal origins.)

Critics, otherwise serious-minded and learned, have pointed to the above grotesque fable as the source of the first two chapters of Genesis. The temperate words of Fr. Condamin are a sufficient comment.

Instead of a crude polytheism, we find in the biblical account the purest monotheism. The One God acts from the start as absolute Master and with genuine omnipotence. He has no hard and doubtful combat against opposing forces, but by His word alone creates and orders all things. Spirituality of conception, dignity of tone, majesty in the whole picture raise the biblical narrative immeasureably above the Babylonian legend and above all the cosmogonies of ancient religions.[1]

---

[1] Art. "Babylon et la Bible" in *Dictionnaire Apologetique de la Foi Catholique,* Vol. I, col. 339.

A tree of knowledge and a tree of life figure in Babylonian mythology, and it is also interesting to note that two of the four rivers which flowed from the Biblical paradise of pleasure were the Tigris and Euphrates. M. Loisy is pleased to see in the Adapa myth a story substantially the same as the narrative of our first parents' fall. The myth may be allowed to speak for itself. Adapa, not the first man but an unusually intelligent man especially created by Ea to be priest at Eridou, goes a-fishing in the Euphrates and finds the boisterous South Wind interfering with his catch. In a rage, he smashes the South Wind's wings with his punting pole, for which act of mayhem he is summoned before the tribunal of Anu. His patron Ea informs him that the celestial judge will offer him a garment, oil, food, and water, but that he must refuse the two latter gifts, as to partake of them will mean death. Adapa repairs to the judgment seat, but there is no judgment, in fact not even a mention of the South Wind's injuries. Adapa, following the tip received from Ea, shows himself discriminating in regard to the four divine gifts. But, alack, someone has blundered, for the rejected food and water are in fact charmed food that would have made him immortal. So Adapa, we may infer, returns to his fishing richer by some oil and a garment, but disillusioned in respect of his divine patron's good judgment. The entire story may be likened in artistry, coherence, moral sublimity to the dramas fed by the U.S.S.R. to the duped peasantry.

Babylon's account of the deluge (found in the twelfth tablet of the Gilgamesh epic) certainly antedates the twenty-second century B.C. For some reason the destruction of the human race is decreed in the assembly of the gods. Ea, however, warns one man, Outanapistim, of the coming flood, at the same time prescribing the measurements of a ship which must be built as his refuge. He is bidden to put on board all species of animals. He obediently builds the ship, caulking its interior with pitch, embarks the animal cargo and with his family enters and closes the door. For seven days the rain falls and the water rises and all other men and animals are engulfed. The ship rests on Mount Nisir. A dove and a sparrow are sent forth, but return to the ship; a crow goes forth and does not return. Outanapistim and the rest leave the ship and a sacrifice is offered. The gods, who themselves have fled to heaven in terror of the deluge, descend and "gather like flies about the sacrifice." Bel (is it Enlil or Marduk?), chief author of the flood, is enraged that some have been saved. Ishtar quarrels with him, because she wanted to destroy men by bloody war. Outanapistim and his wife are then transported to a kind of Elysian fields to live the life of the gods.

Fr. Condamin's words above cited apply with almost equal force to this myth. Nevertheless, it is vain to deny that detailed similarity between the Babylonian story and Genesis, chapters 6 to 9, establishes some sort of interdependence. Of a surety, the Babylonian form of the story antedates Abraham, the founder of the Hebrew race. Can it be said that the Hebrews took over fundamentally true tradition and purified it of its gross features? Perhaps, if this purification was not a mere natural process, but an effect of the supernatural actions of revelation and inspiration. What seems more acceptable as an explanation is that the Babylonians had inherited a corrupt version of the events of the deluge, whereas the Hebrews had inherited through Abraham a version kept incorrupt through a special providence. The philosophy of Old Testament history shows, both for antediluvian and postdiluvian events, the divine providence guarding in the line of the patriarchs, the primitive monotheism, and the whole record of God's mercies to men.

The most elaborate of the myths is concerned with the adventures of Gilgamesh, king of Erech. When he plays the tyrant, his people beseech the gods for a remedy. It is decided to send the bumptious ruler on an indefinite vacation trip, but considerable finesse is necessary to persuade him to go. Eabani, a creature who both in form and in appetites is half man and half beast, is lured into Erech, where a deep friendship springs up between him and the king. Under the monster's influence, Gilgamesh grows tired of his usual amusement of thumb-screwing the Erechites and sets out for Eabani's Transtigrine wonderland in quest of bigger game. Their first bag is the terrible Humbaba, who, it seems, has carried off Lady Ishtar and holds her in duress. When Humbaba has fallen before the onslaught of the two friends, Ishtar tries her courtezan wiles on Gilgamesh, but is reproached with her former amours which have ended in her ruining her victims. Piqued at such plain speech and at added insults from Eabani, the goddess causes the latter to sicken and die, after the two heroes have slain a monstrous ox she has sent against them.

Sorrow and disquietude settle on Gilgamesh and he determines to seek counsel of his ancestor Outanapistim, "the superlatively wise." To reach the deluge hero in his Elysian retreat, Gilgamesh fights his way eastward against more monsters. At long last he arrives, but wearied and aged. Outanapistim calms his mind, but is also at pains to restore him to the vigor of youth. A variety of magical incantations failing, mention is made of a plant named "the gray-beard becomes young." Outanapistim does not have it in stock, but Gilgamesh is lucky enough to find a specimen and starts back to Erech rejoicing. He plans seemingly to impress the Erechites by eating the plant and sloughing off the skin of senility before their eyes. On the way, however, a serpent, possibly seeking a specific to expedite its own skin sloughing, snatches the plant from his nerveless hand and makes off. Back at Erech and resigned to his approaching dissolution, Gilgamesh evokes by necromantic art the spirit of his friend Eabani and learns from him about the realm of the dead.

The "mighty man of old" is familiar to anyone who has dabbled in mythical lore. Cuchullan, Siegfried, Herman—

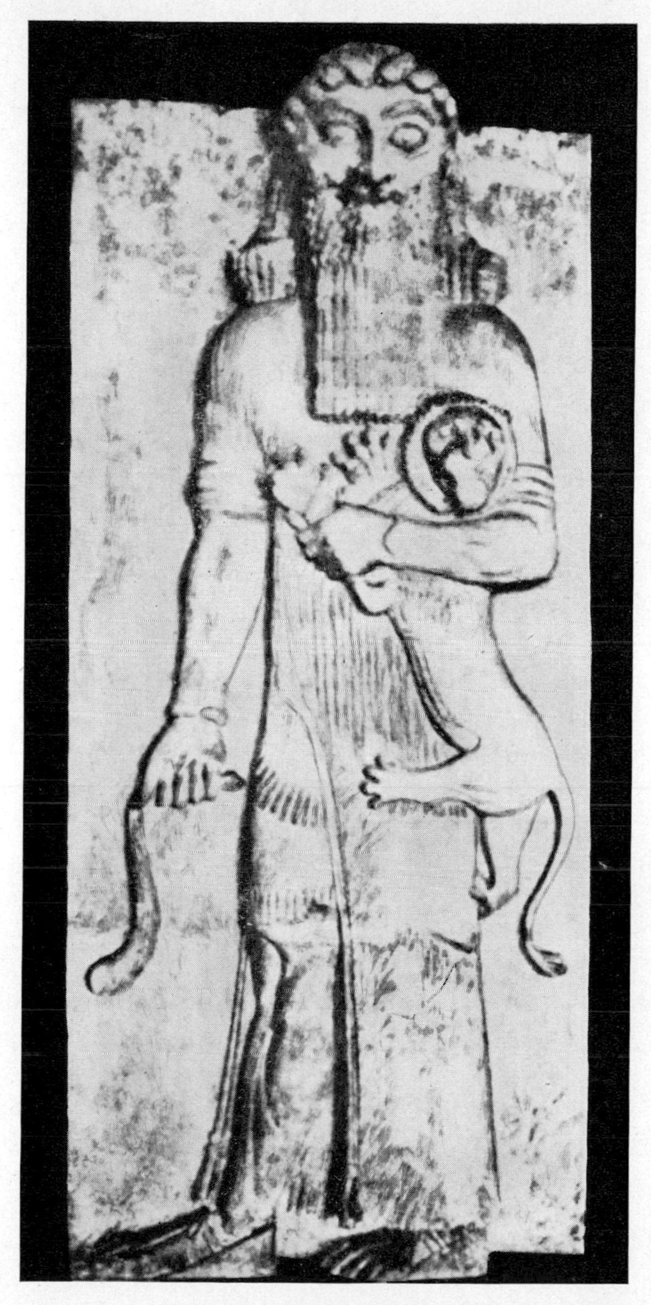

From Olmstead's *Assyria* by permission of Charles Scribners' Sons

Fig. 6. Gilgamesh

The hero of the Babylonian epic here manhandles a lion which opposed his quest of the Elysian abode of the Babylonian Noe.

the factual historian frowns austerely upon the sagas woven about these great names, but modern "debunking" cannot shrink the mighty figures in Celtic, Norse, or Teutonic imagination. The rod of criticism cannot castigate out of the child mind of us all our enthusiastic belief in supermen. For the pagan, hero worship is closely allied to religion, as Carlyle interestingly demonstrates in his first lecture on *Heroes and Hero Worship*. "What I called the perplexed jungle of Paganism sprang, we may say, out of many roots: every admiration, adoration of a star or natural object was a root or fiber of a root; but hero worship is the greatest root of all; the taproot from which in a great degree all the rest were nourished and grown." Surely the *causa exemplaris* (model) of anthropomorphic gods was the hero concept in man's mind, so that the divine beings of developed paganism were practically men of superstrength, superwisdom, superbenevolence. A distinction, often largely theoretic, existed between gods proper and heroes. Not by nature deathless and blessed, the Siegfrieds and the Gilgameshes had to win felicity by their wits and sinews, yet they were likened to the "deathless and blessed gods" in the possession of a *de facto* invincibility. Apotheosis, absolute or relative, was generally the reward of their victories, and explicit cult might even be directed to them.

Whether Gilgamesh was a historical person about whom romantic legends clustered or whether the whole epic is pure romance, cannot be determined. Possibly we should recognize in the Heracles myth certain borrowings from the story of the Babylonian hero, but the similarities are not so striking and numerous as to compel this conclusion. Pan-Babylonians have amused themselves with a fantastic astral interpretation of the "symbolic" epic of Erech's king, but have convinced only their own school. The palm for consistent absurdity must be unanimously awarded to a scholar (P. Jensen in *Das Gilgamesch-Epos in der Weltliteratur*), who undertakes to show through a thousand curious pages that Old and New Testaments are collections of stories based upon the Gilgamesh epic. For instance, Gilgamesh is the prototype of Abraham, Josue, the elder Tobias, St. Peter, and others; Eabani, of Isaac, Sampson, the young Tobias, John the Baptist, and others; Outanapistim, of Lot, David, Elias, Jesus, and others. Of course, if you are unprejudiced, you recognize the identical story in the birth of the monster Eabani and the miraculous circumstances of John the Baptist's conception; in Eabani living in the wild steppes and John's eremetical life!

Before treating the important Ishtar-Tammuz myth, we may profitably outline the minor myths. Two of them are possibly connected with the Babylonian deluge legend — a supposition which, if proved, would lend a higher moral tone to that remarkable narrative. In one Enlil sends plagues and famine on the human race for its sins. Atrakhasis "the superlatively wise" (who seems to be the same person as the Outanapistim of the flood), secures through Ea a cessation of the scourges for his fellow men. In the other myth, a vengeful god Ira sends his "destroying angel" through the world to slaughter men. Since the flood legend, as found in the Gilgamesh epic, makes no mention of the calamity as a punishment, it would surely be interesting if we might understand the chastisements just detailed as admonitory and the flood as the final chastisement for human sin. However, there is no positive proof for this interpretation.

Variants on episodes of the "creation myth" may be recognized in the story of the ravaging monster Labbu and in that of the Zu-bird stealing the tablets of destiny. In each case, the supremacy of the gods being in peril, one of their number goes forth as champion and wins by his victory the hegemony of heaven.

Two other fancies tell respectively of a trip to heaven and a trip to the netherworld. Etana is advised to secure the magical plant which will effect the safe birth of his child, a plant which the birth-goddess Ishtar holds in the high heavens. He mounts an eagle and soars aloft, but loses courage when near his goal and tumbles, eagle and all, to earth. The second fancy tells how Nergal stirs up a feud between the gods of heaven and those of Hades. Recruiting seven fever demons he braves Eresh-kigal, queen of Hades, on her home grounds, but finally falls a victim to her charms and weds her.

Ishtar, we have seen, was reproached by Gilgamesh as a wanton and merciless destroyer of her rejected lovers. The most noted of her affairs was with the youth Tammuz. He originally was a fertility god, but in the poetic embellishment of legend he became a human person. Either Ishtar slays him or he dies from some other cause (the record is not clear). In any case he descends to the dark home of Eresh-kigal. Thither Ishtar journeys and demands admittance. As she passes through the seven doors she is despoiled of her ornaments and attire and at last cast into a dungeon, where Eresh-kigal taunts her. Ishtar is the goddess of all life, so that her imprisonment in the region of death causes all earthly life to wither and pine. But Ea sends a messenger to Eresh-kigal to order Ishtar's release. She will not leave, however, with her purpose unattained, so Tammuz' dead body is brought to her and she breaks forth in a lament which is the model for the great liturgical plaints of the Ishtar-Tammuz cult. Upon his dead form she pours the "water of life" and so resuscitates him. Rejoicing, they seek the upper world, where all life revives. Tammuz dies once more and the plaints are renewed. The myth ends with a tableaux of the gods assembling for Tammuz' funeral rites.

Mediterranean religion offers many parallels of the Ishtar-Tammuz myth. They are all quite clearly chthonic nature myths with an identical theme, the annual death and rebirth of vegetation. The importance for human life of these phenomena made of the principle which controlled them a divinity. Anthropomorphism presented the figure of a mother-goddess. The fresh green of vegetation was poetically conceived as a child or youth beloved of the mother-goddess. When the vegetation in due season withered and died, the child or lover died and the mother-goddess lamented. Her search for him in the region of the dead is poetical imagery for the winter season, her heuresis and return to earth with him is the glad springtime.

In some religious milieus of the old Mediterranean, as in the Eleusinian religion of Greece and the later Osirism of Egypt, the ancient nature myth was transferred by speculative mysticism to human eschatology. In this form, the myth represents the mother-goddess and her companion as prepotent in the matter of human life and death and as conferring on faithful votaries a blessed future lot. Such an evolution of ideas has not been demonstrated for Babylonian religion.

CHAPTER « 4

CULT AND ITS CARICATURES

CARLYLE in *Heroes and Hero Worship* remarks on the difficulty we experience in reconstructing the religious mentality of a vanished paganism. That men like ourselves should turn with aweful reverence to the monstrously fictitious gods of polytheism, should give of their best to them, should regulate the whole conduct of life by the supposed revelation of their wills — all this seems rather a bizarre romance than the sober record of an almost universal pre-Christian history. Deeply pathetic, surely, are the long millennia of cult history in their misdirection of so much good will and effort. Only the thought that pagans were "seeking God, if happily they might feel after Him or find Him," and that "God winked at the times of this ignorance," is able to touch the somber picture with some brighter hues. "The Unknown God" who dwelt not in their temples made with hands could yet read the hearts of His creatures and direct them by His grace. He could appraise the gold of sincerity and never yet has He despised a contrite heart.

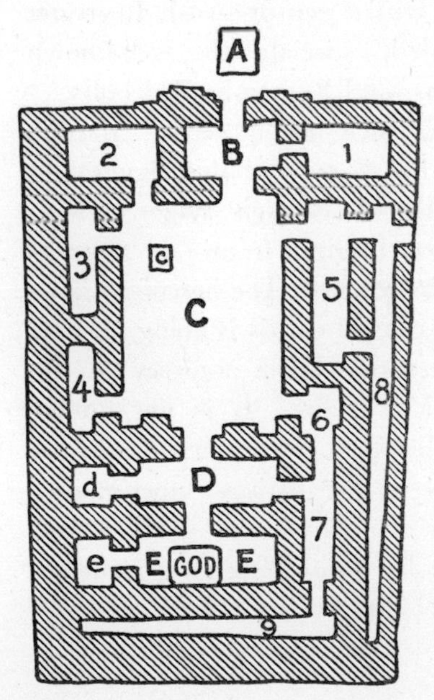

Fig. 7. Ground Plan of a Temple

The temples merit first notice in a discussion of cult

practices. The ground plan (Fig. 7) of one of the simplest of Babylon's temples will be useful. Let the choice be the shrine of the goddess Ninmakh which stood at the southeast corner of the acropolis. It is approximately rectangular, with its sides about 32 and 64 feet. The lettering signifies: A, the altar; B, the vestibule; C, the open courtyard; D, the antechamber of shrine; E, the shrine with cult statue enthroned; c, the well of purification; d and e, small service rooms; 1, the porter's lodge; 2–4, the priests' apartments; 5–7, storerooms; 8 and 9, long narrow passageways.

With the exception of the area designated as A, the whole was roofed over. The purpose of the two blind passageways was probably to accommodate sloping ramps which led up to the roof, though it is possible that the one back of the cult statue served the purposes of pious skulduggery. A priest, that is to say, might conceal himself back of the idol and make it speak or move its head or arm. The building material was sun-dried bricks colored white with a gypsum wash. In greater temples decorations were added, especially the well-known conventionalized lions, dragons, and human-headed bulls.

Adjoining greater temples, such as those of Marduk in Babylon and of Nabu at Borsippa, rose the Ziggurat or temple tower. Herodotus speaks of the eight stages of Marduk's tower, and of the steps leading from one stage to another till the altar on top was reached. The herculean labor of clearing away thousands of tons of debris is going forward at Babylon and will doubtless reveal the accuracy of this description of the ancient globe trotter. It is not known whether the ziggurat was a solid mass of masonry or whether there were interior chambers in the various superimposed rectangles. Traditions, which Fr. Condamin in the work already cited proves to be wholly groundless, have identified both Marduk's ziggurat and Nabu's as the Biblical Tower of Babel.

Tithes collected by the king's officials furnished the ordinary revenue for the expenses of the cult, but in addition the temples possessed lands and herds in their own right. Royal piety underwrote the bills for repair or reconstruction and enriched the temple corbona with rich spoils after successful campaigns. The mites of the humbler votaries — contributed for private sacrifices, healing incantations, oracular utterances — flowed in steadily. Altogether, the numerous priests attached to temple service do not seem to have wanted for their hire. There is evidence, though still incomplete and confused, of a hierarchical order and a specialization of function among the priests. The king, according to widespread oriental theory, was chief priest, but in practice he lived in multiple subjection to the professional holy men. The terms "great priest," "mighty priest," "supreme priest" are applied to certain members of the sacerdotal caste, but it is hard to say whether any real primacy is meant. Again, the records are too fragmentary to decide whether priestly consecration was to a universality of function or merely to a specialty, such as liver reading. A few of these specialties may be noted in the following priestly titles: anointer, singer, seer, healer, master of incantations, reader of omens.

Sacrifice was the central act of worship. Oxen and sheep principally, but also other domesticated and wild animals as well as fowl and fish, were slain on the altar, the god's portions burned, and the rest given to the priests of the temple. Bloodless oblations to the divine beings took the form of the most desirable foods the people knew — butter, milk, honey, wine, bread, and fruit. Incense made from various aromatic substances, such as cedar and cypress wood, was burned in honor of the gods in vast quantities.

A quotation is here in order from the *Annals of Ashurbanipal:* "Marduk entered and took up his abode [in the restored temple of E-sagila]. Great bulls, fat sheep I sacrificed.

The abundance of the waters [fish sacrifices, no doubt] I brought near him. Oil I poured out like a pouring rain. Rich gifts I brought before him as presents. Priests for his ritual I appointed before his face."[1]

All the glamor of liturgy was requisitioned to appeal to popular feeling on New Year's Day. Back of the external celebration was the doctrine that on this day the gods met in council to determine the fates of men for the coming year. At Nineveh Ashur, at Babylon Marduk appeared as the central figure in the celebration. At both cities there stood special temples "of the New Year's Feast," which, so far as we know, were used only at the annual solemnity.

On the spring equinox, then (for that was the New Year of their calendar), Marduk's priests dressed the golden cult statue in glittering raiment and jewels. A car built in the shape of a ship waited at the gate of the E-sagila temple. Marduk was carried out to the car, and the oxen began to plod with liturgical slowness along the Sacred Way. Still other cars bearing the idols of the other city temples and the idols of neighboring towns, all dressed in their holiday best, fell in line behind Babylon's darling. Files of priests marched beside the sacred images, swinging censers, sounding musical instruments, singing hymns in praise of Marduk's attributes and mythical deeds. The people, who thronged every coign of vantage, loved it: it was their Mardi Gras, Aksarben, and Veiled Prophet, yet much more, for their deepest religious beliefs were bound up with the pageantry. Arrived at the Temple of the New Year's Feast, the gods (with assistance, of course) descended, to proceed to the "chamber of destiny." There, reclining on couches or seated, they settled in advance (at least, the people thought they did) the fortunes of the state and of individuals for the year just opening.

The powwow satisfactorily concluded, they were returned

---

[1] *Ancient Records of Assyria and Babylonia,* Vol. II, par. 989.

in solemn procession to their homes and pedestals. Back at E-sagila, Marduk gave audience to the king, grasped his hand, and received the renewal of his royal vows. On this day, too, was proclaimed the name by which the new year would be known in the records—the name of a favorite official, of a recent victory, of the cutting of an important canal, as occasion warranted. Throughout the day, but especially in the hours of the night, the townspeople sought solace in secular recreations which were a fair prototype of the "New Year whoopee" with which we are familiar.

The naturistic interpretation of the Ishtar-Tammuz myth was given in the preceding chapter. Beloved of the nature-goddess, the godling flourishes, dies, and is brought back to life, thus typifying the seasonal changes of vegetation. The period of Ishtar's search for him in the lower world is the winter. Mediterranean lands, where this myth theme was known and popular, delighted in ritualistic commemorations of the divine love story. Its episodes might be dramatized in a "mystery play" or the ritual might consist merely of threnodies and canticles of joy. Of a Babylonian or Assyrian sacred drama on the theme no clear records have been discovered, but the valley did re-echo with plaint and canticle at the Tammuz holydays. A few brief samples may be given, interesting both religiously and as the earliest contributions to the long history of Adonic poetry.

Go, then, lord Tammuz, on the road of no return!
Alas! he goeth to the bosom of the earth.
To the land of the dead will he give abundance.
Bewail the day, bewail the unblest season of his fall.

* * *

Oh, weep with your sweet tears and mourning chant
O'er this dread loss of Heaven's queen.
With her, O mortals, join your sweetest plaint
O'er our dear Tammuz, Tammuz slain.

* * *

The queen of love comes to his arms.
Her faithful eyes have sought him out,
His love comes to him with her charms.
Let all the world now happy be;
His love has come again.[2]

In the Babylonian calendar the fourth of the twelve months was named Tammuz. This would correspond partly to our June, partly to our July. Seasonally, the month Tammuz marked the end of summer, and during Tammuz quite naturally the threnodies of the dying vegetation-god were sung. In the month next following, namely in Ab, there was a holyday commemorating the descent of Ishtar into Hades. Beyond these jejune facts — the existence of Tammuz hymns, the two annual holydays — we know nothing definite about the Tammuz liturgy of the valley. To transfer to Babylonian soil what we know of the observances of analogous cults in Syria and elsewhere, would be a temerarious *saltus logicus*.[3] Future discovery and decipherment of Babylonian and Assyrian documents will doubtless justify a more satisfying reconstruction.

When man senses deeply his sinfulness and manifold needs, and so turns his mind to prayer, his ideas of God are clarified. Hence, in pagan prayer the miasmic fogs of polytheism are

---

[2] The translations, slightly modified for the sake of coherence, are by T. G. Pinces from a Sumerian text and by L. L. C. Hamilton from an Assyrian text.

[3] Jeremias and Ezechiel tell of the abominations of Tammuz cult among the Hebrews. "Seeth thou not what they do in the cities of Juda and in the streets of Jerusalem? The children gather wood, and the fathers kindle the fire, and the women knead the dough, to make cakes to the queen of heaven (Ishtar), and to offer libations to strange gods" (Jer. 7:17, 18). "And he brought me in by the door of the Lord's house which looked to the north; and behold women sat there mourning for Adonis (Tammuz in the Hebrew text)" (Ezech. 8:14). Among the Greeks the Adonic Laments are clothed in the fairest poetic garb by Theocritus, Bion, and Moschus. The laments for Osiris, the Egyptian form of Tammuz, and the whole Egyptian ritual celebrating his death and resuscitation will be described in chapters to follow that deal with the Egyption Religion. Similarly, in the chapters on Roman Religion the ritual of the Cybele and Attis cult will be studied.

not infrequently pierced by a ray from "the light that illumines every man who cometh into this world." A partial demonstration of this truth has already been given in the "Ishtar litany" which was compiled in a previous chapter. From a mass of other hymns and prayers the following selections furnish further proof.

Oh, Enlil, councillor, doth anyone comprehend thy form? . . . As the air, thou art all-pervading. . . . The proud and haughty thou dost humiliate. . . . The wrath of thy heart, can anyone appease it? (From an ancient hymn.)

Ashur, immense lord, omniscient, who fixes destinies. . . . His spirit is like the mountains whose foundations are not seen, like the stars whose number is limitless. . . . Thy counsels, Ashur, no god has learned: they are beyond understanding. (From an Assyrian hymn.)

Where thou [Ishtar] lookest in pity, the dead man lives again, the sick man is healed. The afflicted is saved from his affliction when he beholdeth thy face. I, thy servant, sorrowful, sighing and in distress, cry unto thee. Cry unto me "It is enough" and let thy spirit be appeased. How long shall my body lament, which is full of restlessness and confusion? (From a Babylonian prayer.)

The god, my creator, may he stand by my side. Keep thou the door of my lips! guard thou my hands, O lord of light! (A private prayer.)

O lord, do not abandon thy servant. In the waters of the great storm, seize his hand. The sins which he has committed, turn thou to righteousness. (Assyrian penitential prayer.)

O my god, my sins are seven times seven. (Assyrian penitential prayer.)

Like a bird, may it fly to a lofty place! To the holy hands of its god may it ascend! (Prayer for a departing soul.)

The gods here addressed are nominally the gods of the temples — the obscene Ishtar, the grotesque Marduk, and the cruel Ashur — but the human suppliant has found in his sore need a means of transcending the absurdities of the mythonaturistic creed upon which he has been nurtured. We can agree with Professor Jastrow that the devotion here manifested does not, in general, rise higher than a selfish love (*amor concupiscentiae*). The god is sought not for himself, but for his favors. Yet, in these direct pleadings of the heart appear the best elements of Babylonian religion, a keen sense of divine omnipotence and mercy. Correlative with that sense appear, on man's part, an appreciation of his own weakness and defilement joined with hope of support and cleansing by the divine grace. Nowhere, of course, do Babylonian hymnody and prayer attain to the sublimity or the selflessness of Old Testament Psalms and prayers.

For devotion to one of religion's unlovely caricatures, Babylonia must be conceded the palm. Beyond all nations of antiquity, Babylonians practiced the magical art. In the lines of Juvenal's *Sixth Satire* we see the Chaldeans still at their hoary deceptions in the streets of imperial Rome, while we hear in the Inspired Pages the thunders of Isaias against "the daughter of the Chaldeans." "Stand now with thy enchanters and with the multitude of thy sorceries, in which thou hast labored from thy youth, if so be it may profit thee anything, or if thou mayest become stronger. Thou hast failed in the multitude of thy counsels: let now thy astrologers stand and save thee, they that gazed at the stars and counted the months, that from them they might tell thee the things that shall come to thee."[4]

"Magic is the despair of religion" is an aphorism neatly expressive of the genesis of magical art. Man feels himself dependent upon God (or the gods), and so by religious and moral practice seeks to maintain right relations with Him (or them). He expects that his "praise, reverence, and service" will keep open the channel through which flow the good gifts necessary for his well-being. But divine providence sends and permits manifold evils seemingly to frustrate such sanguine expectation. It is hard for man to say with Job: "If we receive good things from the hand of God, why not also evil things?" Especially where ideas of the divine nature are confused, as in polytheistic religion, misfortune speedily under-

---

[4] Isa. 47:12, 13.

By courtesy of Chicago Oriental Institute Museum

Fig. 8. Temple Tower of E-sagila at Babylon

Tentative reconstruction by Professor Unger. A curious, but groundless, legend long identified this "ziggurat" with the Biblical Tower of Babel. At the top of the structure was a mines confidence in the legitimate practices of cult. In drought, sickness, every present or threatened disaster, the gods are hysterically canvassed for remedy and enlightenment. Failing prompt succor, man turns to occultism, much as a sick person who despairs of the slow methods of reputable physicians and puts his faith in the "home remedy" and the quack.

This occultism will be either purely magic or magico-dynamic. Here we cannot improve upon the analysis of Andrew Lang:

> Magic or witchcraft falls into two main classes. The former is magic of the sort used by people who think that things accidentally like each other influence each other. You find a stone shaped like a yam, and you sow it in the yam plot. You find a stone like a duck, and expect to have good duck-shooting while you carry the stone around in a bag. In the same way the part influences the whole; you burn some of a man's hair, and so he catches a fever. The second sort of magic acts by spells, which constrain spirits or gods to do the will of the magician. This magic involves itself in religion when the magical ceremonies are, so to speak, only symbolic prayers expressed in a kind of sign language. But if the idea is to put constraint by spells on a god or spirit, then the intention is magical and rebellious.[5]

Occultism's illusion, then, is that man, through the inherent efficacy of "stone ducks," the action of "familiars," bends nature to his will. Occultism further claims that its magico-dynamic formulas can secure knowledge of past, present, and future events. How flattering to human vanity is this twofold illusion, hardly needs demonstration. Possession of the right formulas and paraphernalia puts man very much on his own, dispensing him from the labor of praying the gods for what he needs, coercing even the gods to the fulfillment of his desires. Hence the popularity of magic and hence the picketing of antiquity's temples by professional magicians with their claims to "strong medicine."

Fr. W. Schmidt, in *The Origin and Growth of Religion,*

---

[5] *Magic and Religion,* Longmans & Co., 1901, pp. 46 sq.

interestingly sketches the diffusion of magical art among pagan peoples. The truly primitive, whose God is the one Supreme Being, knows nothing of the tricks of the shaman, though he gives evidence of magic's allure by a little inexpert dabbling in the art. Pastoral people, more diffident in the Supreme Being because of the intrusion of nature worship and more confident in themselves because of the partial sway of their intelligence over animate and inanimate creatures, employ much magic with the hope of extending this sway still further. Agricultural folk, who recognize the dependence of their crops on mysterious *numina* of weather and soil, seek to learn by omens and signs what these *numina* have in store for them. In a culture blended of the agricultural and the pastoral, a body of magical laws is crystalized, professional magicians flourish, the *numina* have developed into familiars subject to the skilled practitioner. "The further development of magic [in middle and high civilizations] is due chiefly to continually increasing specialization in magical materials and practices; to the forming of a hierarchy among those persons who engage in them, in accordance with their degree of activity and the size of their clientele; and to the establishment by inheritance of an equipment of magical knowledge and elements."[6] Both the savant here quoted and Andrew Lang note that the amount of magical practice will not vary precisely according to these sharp ethnological classifications. The racial penchant of certain peoples, as well as accidental causes, greatly affect the intensity of devotion to this caricature of religion.

From the vast pseudoliturgy left us by Babylonia may be detached the two key superstitions of apotropaism and omen reading. It is suggestive to view them as the respective grotesques of our physical and intellectual miracle. In the matter of apotropaism, prophylactic charms against every possible physical evil were first necessary. On doors, on household

[6] *Origin and Growth of Religion,* p. 160.

furniture, on the person, amulets and "words of power" were hung. Against the demoness Labartu children wore a stone charm inscribed with the words: "By the great gods mayest thou be exorcised; with the bird of heaven mayest thou fly away." Pregnant women girded themselves with bands on which was written: "I am N., the servant of Adad, the favorite of Marduk."

But much more important was the procedure to be followed once the pyxies had actually done their nefarious work. Then an exorcist had to be hired to cast out the evil one. The mighty man would come to the sick man's house with a porter or two carrying his ritual. (A ritual of clay tablets could not conveniently be slipped into one's sleeve or cincture.) If he found that prophylaxis had been neglected, he supplied: "Place the guardian statues of Ea and Marduk at the door, on the right hand and on the left. Right and left of the threshold of the door, spread out holy texts and sentences. Place on the statues texts bound around them. In the night bind around the sick man's head a sentence taken from a good book."

Now the exorcist began his direct attack on the demon of disease. Let us suppose that a modern diagnosis of our sick Babylonian would read: streptococcic infection of throat, bladder disturbance, heart complications. The magic physician chose the proper tablets (clay, not medicated), and droned out:

> The burning spirit of the neck which seizes a man, the spirit of the neck which works evil, the creation of an evil spirit. Spirit of heaven remember: spirit of earth remember. . . . Sickness of the entrails, sickness of the heart, sickness of the bile, noxious illness, lingering sickness. Spirit of heaven remember: spirit of earth remember.

Perhaps some enemy had "hexed" the poor fellow: the careful doctor overlooks no possibilities, so another tablet was read:

If an image of this man has been made and pierced in the belly, the neck and the heart; spirit of heaven and spirit of earth, remove the spell.

Now water was brought to lave and sprinkle the patient, while the fitting incantation was said:

All that is evil in the body of N., may it be carried off with this water, and may the river carry it away downstream.

He was rubbed with oil to the tune of:

The oil of Marduk's incantation I pour over thee; with healing oil of Ea I rub thee; oil of life, I give thee.

For the final stage of the cure, the wizard had something special. From his magical kit he took out small wax images of the demons of disease. With a lighted torch he melted them, chanting meantime:

I raise the torch, their images I burn,
Of the Utukku, the Shedu, the Rabisu, the Ekimmu
The Labartu, the Labasi, the Akhkhazu,
Of Lilu and Lilitu and Ardat Lili,
And every evil one that seizes hold of man.
Tremble, melt away and disappear!
May your smoke rise to heaven,
May Shamash destroy your limbs,
May Ea's son Marduk, the fire-god,
The great magician, restrain you.

If the demons had resisted all this, a suckling pig or kid might be slain and laid beside the sick man, so that the magician might conjure his disease into the carcass. The wretched patient did not remain passive through the appalling rigmarole, but had to chant, to twist himself into symbolic attitudes, to swallow substances of varying degrees of palatableness (such as onions, flour, dung).

Omens were read from the flight of birds, the behavior of animals, from unusual natural occurrences of all sorts. However, in the phases of the heavenly bodies and the appearance of the liver of sacrificed sheep the Babylonians especially sought enlightenment. In general, certain heavenly bodies stood for certain important persons and the quarters of the heaven for certain important nations. Similar charting of the parts of a sheep's liver was made. But the system of interpretation amounted to a vast pseudoscience, covering casuistically all conceivable findings in the sky or the liver. Thus the soothsayer's textbook would explain the conjunction of two stars or the discoloration of a sheep's liver in terms of a promise of success or a threat of failure: the soothsayer, then, would apply this to the particular matter about which his advice was sought.

Closely connected with the soothsayer's art was that of oneiromancy. Dreams were believed in, and were even sought, as revelations from the gods. The believer might sleep in the temple, in the hope of hearing from the divinity during slumber. What the dream meant, was learned from the dream priest who had his own body of traditional lore upon which to base his interpretations. Examples are Esarhaddon's dream vouchsafed by Ishtar, and Nebuchadnezzar's dream of the colossal statue smashed by the stone falling from the mountain. Both kings believed the dreams to be divine messages, though objectively only Nebuchadnezzar's came from God.

CHAPTER « 5

MORALITY AND THE FUTURE LIFE

DURING the early part of the twelfth century Babylonia shook off the humbling rule of the foreign Kassites. Two Elamite kings, Shutruck-Nakhkhunte and his son Kutir-Nakhkhunte, had raided the central valley at will and were checked only when the patriotic Babylonian party set up a native dynasty in Marduk-shapik-zerim and his great successor Nebuchadnezzar I. To the raiding Elamites historians are grateful for preserving in their capital city, Susa, several important items of booty. One of these was a copy, in cuneiform on black stone, of the Code of Hammurabi. French archeologists, delving in the mound that once was Susa, unearthed the stone toward the end of the year 1901, and in the following year the linguist Scheil published a translation. At the top of the stone the figures of Babylon's first emperor and of the sun-god Shamash are cut in bas-relief, the former with left hand on breast and right raised in an attitude of adoration, the latter enthroned with right hand extended graciously toward the suppliant. The king, in brief, is receiving by revelation the laws which are inscribed below in a number of narrow columns.[1]

Hammurabi's Code, it will be remembered, was promulgated about the year 2000, continuing to serve through the rest of Babylonian and Assyrian history as the foundation of civil and criminal law. It must be regarded, moreover, not as an original composition, but rather as a codification of immemor-

[1] There is also a Prologue enumerating the twenty-four chief cities of Hammurabi's empire with their respective gods, praising the king and asserting his divine commission to formulate the laws.

ial Sumerian and Semitic laws—itself a work of genius. It is clear, then, that the Code is a primary source for the study of Babylonian standards of right and wrong. We shall select some detailed legislative enactments and point out leading characteristics of Hammurabi's masterpiece, in an endeavor to throw in focus the moral facet of the Babylonian religious mind.

1. Contracts, of which the Babylonian was very fond, must be drawn in form, duly witnessed, sealed by both parties before a notary. The obligations mutually embraced bound strictly and there were judges to award damages for breach.

2. Oaths, usually by the local god, were commonplace. For instance, they confirmed more important contracts; they cleared men of certain criminal charges; they attested the amount of damage one had suffered from a thief or a cheat.

3. Marriage was a special form of contract, arranged between the prospective bride's father and the prospective groom. The latter regularly paid a sum of money to his father-in-law, but this need not lead to the conclusion that a system of marriage by purchase existed. Monogamy remained the ideal, but certain customs rendered the ideal more or less inoperative. For instance, the Code permitted a wife to deliver her handmaid to the husband; established sterility and misconduct as grounds on which the husband might repudiate his wife, neglect as grounds for the wife so doing.

4. Adulterers were drowned. Temple prostitution was officially recognized.

5. A thief had to repay double or, failing means, he was executed. "The highway" was punished by death.

6. Slaves might be treated in any way that pleased a master's caprice. If a fugitive slave were harbored by a citizen, the citizen was executed.

7. The *lex talionis* (an eye for an eye, etc.) was applied to an almost unbelievable extent. For instance, if a citizen

killed another citizen's daughter, his own daughter was executed.

The above selections, though few and fragmentary, sufficiently demonstrate Babylonian recognition of certain important standards of natural morality. Rights of property owners, the matrimonial bond, inviolability of the plighted word, sanctity of oaths are safeguarded by explicit legal enactment. Perversion of moral ideas is, of course, evident in points 3, 4, 6, 7. The harshness of pagan legalism — mercy tempering justice came into the world with the rest of Christianity's "folly" — is illustrated in the Code's attitude to slaves and in the application of the *lex talionis*. Hammurabi, moreover, imposes the death penalty for no less than thirty-five different crimes. Finally, in the admirably utilitarian laws which he gave his valley empire, he makes no appeal to religious or moral motives, is wholly silent about the principle of love of one's neighbor, legislates for the external act with an almost total abstraction from the thought or desire back of it. In these last-named points, were one minded to develop a too obvious contrast, it would be easy to indicate how the Law of Exodus and Deuteronomy transcends Hammurabi's Code.

The material-minded Babylonian rejoiced in physical well-being as a pledge that the gods were pleased with his conduct, while regarding physical evil, especially sickness, as punishment for sin. He was usually not clear as to what that sin might have been, still less clear as to the identity of the offended god who was scourging him. With his conscience once stimulated, much as a small boy's conscience is first stimulated by the hairbrush, he might have recourse to the following incantation:

I invoke you, great gods, lords of deliverance,
I who am sad, ill, anxious and afflicted.
Have I injured my grandfather, hated my elder brother?
Have I weighed with false weights, used false money?

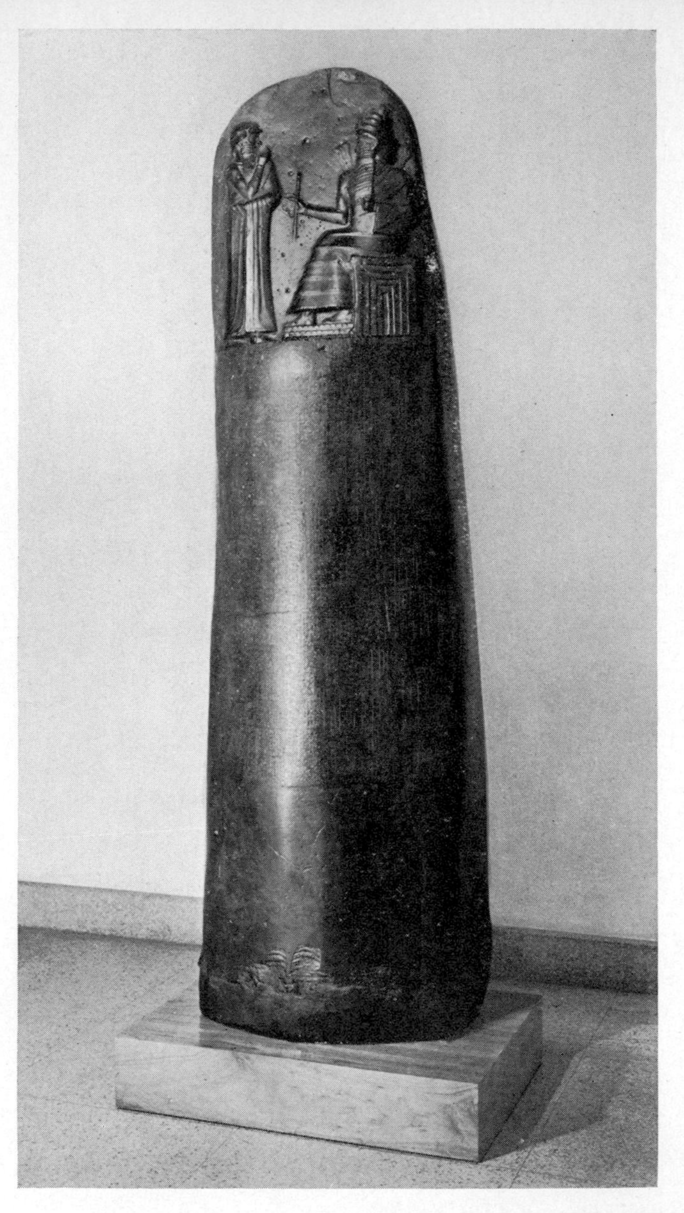

By courtesy of Chicago Oriental Institute Museum

Fig. 9. The Code of Hammurabi

The first Emperor of Babylonia had his code of laws cut on a stele of diorite. When the King of Susa carried off the monument to his own capital, he chiseled off a portion of the inscription with a view to substituting something of his own. The lines so lost have been found on other fragmentary monuments, so that the laws under which Babylonians of 2000 B.C. lived are wholly known.

Have I entered my neighbor's house, spilt his blood?
Have I had frankness in my mouth and falseness in my heart?
Have I withheld what I consecrated to the gods?
Is it a grave sin which I have committed?

From this and other texts of the Babylonian "penitential" literature a very fair sin catalogue might be composed, which would supplement the principles of right and wrong recognized in Hammurabi's Code. The subjective attitude toward sin, however, is most disappointing. The "penitent" regretted his fault, too often admitted only vaguely and hypothetically, not because it offended the divinity, but because he himself was suffering physical pain. Relief from the physical pain, not atonement to the offended divinity, was the boon for which he prayed. In vain, too, do we search the overpraised Babylonian "penitentials" for promise of amendment, for promise of satisfactory works, for petition for divine help to avoid future lapse. For the want of such essential elements of true repentance, the dominant impression left by the oft-praised "penitentials" is one of dejected scruples, intense and complex. The Babylonian penitent was far from the sentiments of King David:

Wash me yet more from my iniquity and cleanse me from my sin.
For I know my iniquity and my sin is ever before me.
To Thee only have I sinned and have done evil before Thee. . . .
Thou shalt sprinkle me with hyssop and I shall be cleansed; Thou shalt wash me and I shall be made whiter than snow. . . .
Create a clean heart in me, O God, and renew a right spirit within my bowels. . . .
I will teach the unjust Thy ways and the wicked shall be converted to Thee.
A sacrifice to God is an afflicted spirit: a contrite and humbled heart Thou shalt not despise.[2]

[2] Psalm 50.

What awaited man after death? This is a question to which our sources give a most unsatisfactory answer. Two lands are indicated in the myths—the far eastern region of joy to which Outanapistim was translated, and the gloomy subterranean kingdom to which Ishtar descended in her search for Tammuz. In the former immortality, peace and philosophic calm are the portion of the deluge hero and his wife, but we have no positive proof of a belief that other mortals might pass thither. Kigallu, on the other hand, is described as a country peopled by the shades of the dead. For them it is "the land of no return," in which they are cloistered by a sevenfold barrier. They flit about in thick darkness like vampires, feeding upon dust and mire, drinking nauseous draughts. It would seem that proper burial of their mortal remains secured for the shades a less unlovely lot. Death in honorable battle, also, gave a title to better treatment at the hands of Nergal and Eresh-kigal, the sovereigns of the Babylonian Hades. The character of this better fate, however, is described merely in terms of beds to rest on and fresh water to drink. Was Babylonian materialism so thoroughgoing that the people never envisaged the future state more clearly, never understood better the connection between earthly conduct and future retribution? Perhaps; but the analogy of other ancient religions justifies the expectation that future exploration of the buried records of the Tigris-Euphrates valley will discover documents attesting a more developed eschatological belief.

PART TWO

RELIGION OF THE PERSIANS

CHAPTER « 6

MEN FROM IRAN

DURING sixty-five years after the fall of Nineveh (606 B.C.), four powers shared territory which we nowadays call the Near East. Freed from the terrorism of Assyrian overlordship, Egypt under the Saitite Pharaohs relived some of her ancient glories, while neo-Babylonian dynasts ruled the Fertile Crescent from the Egyptian frontier to the Persian Gulf. To the north the kings of Lydia held most of Asia Minor together with the Ionian Islands. Media, after engorging Assyria, lay vast and mighty to the east and north of Babylonia, tolerant for the present of the empire pretentions of her neighbors.

The *entente,* more or less *cordiale,* was shattered by the Persian Cyrus, who in 550, when Prince of Anzan, had seized the Median kingship by overthrowing Astyages. His first act of kingship was to initiate a more vigorous foreign policy. Catching Croesus unprepared he won the Lydian domain of that fabulous plutocrat by victories at Thymbra and Sardis. Into the Tigris-Euphrates valley he then dispatched his general Gobryas against the Babylonian crown prince Belshazzar. The captive Hebrews now saw the beginning of the woe denounced by the Prophets against their oppressors. At the field of Opis Babylon's grand army under Belshazzar was badly beaten and its scattered fragments never effectively reunited. Sippar, a kind of Thermopylae by reason of its situation just where Tigris and Euphrates bent inward almost to a confluence, could have held back the invader, but treachery opened its gates. The city of Babylon thereupon deemed its case hopeless and readily welcomed Cyrus to the throne of

Hammurabi. Efficient Gobryas speedily mopped up the outlying districts, to bring to an end a kingdom which had endured for seventeen centuries. Cambyses, Cyrus' successor, conquered Egypt and Cyprus; Darius Hystapes, next in order of the Great Kings, extended his empire beyond the rivers Oxus and Indus, to the Caucasus Mountains, into Thrace.

The remote ancestors of the Persians had formed part of an early second millennial migration of Aryan peoples. The wave had flowed through the Caucasus Mountains into the steppes which lay to the east of the Zagros range. Further progress of the migration was fourfold and gave origin to four historic peoples—Medes, Hindus, Mitanni, and Persians. The main body of the migrant horde gradually became dominant on the steppes, to appear in Assyrian annals of the early first millennium as the Madai. Southward the migration found its term only in India, where the Hindu culture grew as a close parallel to the Medo-Persian. Aryan penetration of the Zagros appears to have been relatively late, save for one spearhead thrust through the range at least as early as the sixteenth century, for the chiefs of the Mitanni, whom Thutmose III fought at the great northern bend of the Euphrates and whose daughters his successors espoused, were steppe Aryans who ruled the upper curve of the Fertile Crescent. Later by several centuries, Aryans took over the region of Parsua in the northernmost Zagros, but by 815 this group was driven by the Assyrian southward into Parsumash. Finally, with the decay of Elam, they were able to establish control over Anzan and Parsa. These Parsans, or Persians, remained in nominal vassalage to the Medes till Cyrus II, Prince of Anzan, made himself Medo-Persian king by overthrowing Astyages.

Darius I, called Hystaspes, built a gorgeous palace in his capital, Persepolis, about five hundred miles southeast of Babylon and a hundred from the Persian Gulf. In the foundation stone he placed gold and silver tablets (excavated and deciphered in 1933) cataloguing the provinces he ruled, while on the stairway (excavated 1931–1935) which led to the audience chamber he carved figures of provincials bearing him tribute on the New Year. The provinces, whose total area approximated that of the United States and its territories, he governed through satraps responsible to himself alone. The satrap's job was secure, and his head remained where nature had placed it, so long as he dispatched his province taxes to Persepolis, levied his quota of troops for the huge imperial army, and kept his provincials at least passively loyal to their Persian overlord. The structure of the empire was essentially brittle, for it was made up of such heterogeneous elements as Greeks, Egyptians, Babylonians, and semi-savages from the far steppes. Unable to depend on any imperial *esprit de corps* in their subjects, the Great Kings contrived to eke out two centuries of rule through dread of their name, through political and religious tolerance, and through a generally equitable administration of justice.

Herodotus and Xenophon give details of Persian appearance and customs. The Persian was tall with aquiline nose, brownish hair, brown or blue eyes. Tonsorially he affected bobbed and carefully combed hair, together with a moderate beard. Loose trousers—the variegated "bags" which amused Greek Aeschylus—a vest and an ornamented cloak were the garments of your Persepolitan. Soft leather shoes and a cloth cap, frequently conical, completed his costume. Herodotus tells us that Persians were temperate in their diet, but addicted to wine-bibbing, adding the improbable assertion that they made it a point to discuss and decide all important affairs on two occasions, once when intoxicated and once when sober. Pure Persian blood was a man's chief honor, though foreign customs were readily embraced, among these being, according to the same Herodotus, "the Greek vice." Indeed, it would seem that their sudden rise to empire control, with the consequent contacts with more effete civilizations, contributed much to weaken the fiber of a people originally trained in a simple and hardy life. Among Persian virtues those most in repute were truthfulness, bravery, and filial piety.

The Achaemenian dynasty which Cyrus had founded fell at the battle of Arbela in 331, and a decade later the empire's territory was divided among Alexander's generals. Iran — to use the modern name for the eastern steppe land — together with the Tigris-Euphrates valley, was one of the divisions, remaining a Hellenistic state till 250 B.C. Then a patriotic uprising was successful in north-central Iran, which swept the storied Parthians into power in the room of the Seleucid Greeks. The Parthians were true Iranians, though less cultured than their Persian cousins. After causing imperial Rome many a headache, the valorous Parthian dynasty yielded in A.D. 216 to another Iranian family, the Sassanids.

Under Parthian tolerance, Christianity had progressed miraculously and was striding through the open door of Iran to the conquest of the far Orient. But the Sassanids were under the thumb of the Zoroastrian Magi, and besides jealously identified Christianity's aspirations with those of Rome and Byzantium. The chapter of Christian Martyrdom which followed was a glorious one, though its sequel was less happy than the sequel in the Western Church. For the cloud of Nestorianism settled upon Babylonia and Iran. Then came Timur Leng and his Tatars to destroy even Nestorian Christianity on the Asian steppes. The bright prospects for the Christianization of the Orient vanished. As for the Sassanids, they made their four centuries of rule the greatest period of Zoroastrian religion and of Iranian culture in general. In 651 Islam engulfed Iran. Conversion to the pleasant illusions of the Koran was as rapid as was decay of Iranian political importance. Today, Persia as a national unit survives in small Mohammedan Iran; Persian religion, in the Parsi community of India and in the Gabar communities of Iran.

From a handbook of the Chicago Oriental Museum

Fig. 10. Stairway of the Palace at Persepolis

On one side the palace guards stand at attention. On the other subject peoples bring the Great King gifts on the occasion of the New Year. The sculptor skillfully distinguishes the various races by dress and features.

CHAPTER « 7

THE SACRED BOOKS OF IRAN

THE Parsis of India and the Gabars (scattered Zoroastrian communities still resident in modern Iran), are living sources of our knowledge of Persian religion. Of written sources there exists a fair abundance; for Greek and Roman classics speak of matters Iranian, while present-day linguistic scholars have made available the text of the Sacred Books of ancient Iran. Archeologists constantly add fresh information in the shape of monuments and inscriptions from the ruins of Achaemenian cities.

The Sacred Books have had a romantic history. Under the Achaemenians, when the Magi were highly influential, copies were multiplied for use in the established religion of the vast empire. To the same period, probably, the fixing of the Canon must be ascribed. When "the accursed Iskander" shattered the Persian power, the Magi and their sacred lore sank into eclipse. Neither Alexander nor his Seleucid successors were persecutors, but they had Zeus-worship to exalt as a part of their policy of Hellenization. Eighty years as political "outs" weakened the Magi, while their Sacred Books, being no longer the rule of the empire's faith, began to disappear and to suffer time's ravages. The Parthians were nominal, though unzealous, Zoroastrians, so that their five centuries of rule effected little for the advancement of old Persian religion. The text of the Books was partly lost as manuscripts faded out and passages had to be reconstructed from the Magi's oral tradition or liturgical extracts.

The Sassanids, proud of their pure Persian ancestry, committed themselves to a policy of renaissance of the old order, specifically to a Zoroastrian revival. By command of the first Sassanid, Artakhshir, a priest named Tansar began the work of re-editing the *Avesta*—a work completed toward the middle of the fourth century under Sepor II, when the latter's prime minister brought out a final revision in twenty-one Nasks or books. For the glory of the *Koran,* persecuting Islam, which in the seventh century overran the new Iran, made bonfires of the Zoroastrian religious literature. What fragments escaped were concealed by a few faithful who resisted Islamic proselytism or carried by the Parsis in their flight to India. Oldest Parsi manuscripts of the *Avesta* are dated in the thirteenth century; oldest Gabar manuscripts of the same, in the seventeenth.

All that remained of the *Avesta* after the Islamic cataclysm, was salvaged and submitted to a new recension by the distressed descendants of the Magian priests. This recension consists of seven divisions or books, and is the form in which the old manuscripts just mentioned and others present the *Avesta.* The western world's acquaintance with the *Avesta* may be said to have begun in 1723, when the Englishman George Boucher brought a manuscript of the *Vendidad* (one of the seven aforesaid books, containing the liturgy for dealing with demons), to the Bodleian Library at Oxford. The challenge of the unknown script of the Bodleian curiosity was taken up by the Frenchman Anquetil du Perron, who went out to India as a *poilu* on a troop ship. There, during seven years he learned from Parsi priests the language of the *Avesta* and secured from them several manuscripts. Back in Europe, he spent ten years in preparing a translation that appeared in 1771. Interest being thus aroused, other scholars—Rask, Burnouf, Westergaard, etc.—worked out a more perfect knowledge of Avestan language through comparison with the closely related Sanskrit and with "middle" and modern Persian. At present we are in possession of the fruits of their labors in the form of satisfactory translations of the canonical holy books of the Zoroastrians.

By the "middle" Persian just referred to, is meant the language of Sassanid times and of the first few centuries of Mohammedan occupation. Religious literature in this tongue comprises the doctrines, customs, and traditions of Zoroastrianism, as well as translations and commentaries of the *Avesta*. In modern Persian we have, of course, what Parsis and Gabars have written about their beliefs, but the chief work is by the eleventh-century poet Firdausi. His *Shahnamah* (Book of the Kings) is an epic poem lauding the exploits of the mighty men of Persia's prehistory, full of myth and marvel, yet a valuable witness to ancient beliefs and customs.

The best critical opinion assigns the composition of the various parts of the *Avesta* to the period between 560 B.C. and A.D. 375. Obscurity still prevails as to the precise provenance of its contents. Iranian provenance is patent, but a finer discrimination of diverse intra-Iranian sources is desired. A working hypothesis quite favorably received, names three such — Iranian nature-worship, Zoroaster, the Magi. The cosmogonic and cosmologic framework of Avestan doctrine together with the (god) pantheon are taken as traditions from the ancient days when the men of Iran bowed before the mighty forces of nature. To "the prophet" are commonly ascribed spiritualization of the gods and the finer elements of the moral code. Dualism with its (evil) pantheon, much of ritual and of magical practice, seem to have been the contribution of the Magi to the blended religious draught which we call the *Avesta*. The Magi, of course, were the official priesthood from at least the middle fifth century B.C., but they were wise and willing enough to combine with their own peculiar tenets the other elements just mentioned.

The historicity of Zoroaster himself, and the claim made for him of divine revelation, are questions to be discussed later. For the present, it is manifest that the books upon which the orthodox Parsi or Gabar must found his act of faith: (*a*) are of diverse and frequently anonymous authorship; (*b*) cannot claim substantial identity with the originals; (*c*) must be rejected as serious history because of obvious myth spinning and romancing. The term "Sacred Books," then, is applied to the Persian religious literature merely to connote the subjective reverence of Persian votaries. Objectively, these ancient documents contain neither a historical record of the establishment of a divine dispensation nor doctrines supernaturally revealed.

It is helpful to consider the totality of Iranian religion as an elaboration of a theory on the problem of evil. The theory, already charged tentatively to the Magi, was Dualism. It became, presumably through Magian theologic interpolation, the master idea in cosmology and cosmogony as well as the leaven of Zoroastrian teaching. The root and reason for Dualism derived from the nature of the gods themselves, who were eternally divided into two divine courts, the one wholly good in attribute and purposes, the other wholly malignant and maleficent. The lords of good and of evil together with the peers of their respective realms may be introduced in the following table:

TABLE OF PERSIAN DUALISM

The Lords of Good:	*The Lords of Evil:*
AHURA MAZDA	ANGRA MAINYU
or Ormuzd, the shining one, transcending all others, wise creator of all good beings.	or Ahriman, often called Druj or Deception, creator of darkness, sin, and suffering, tempter to lying and impurity.
AMESHA SPENTAS	DAEVAS OR DEMONS
or Immortal Holy Ones, who were:	Aeshima or Wrath and Violence;
Asha or Righteousness, the Spirit of Fire;	Aka Manah or Evil Mind; Bushyasta or Sloth;

AMESHA SPENTAS	DAEVAS OR DEMONS
Vohu Manah or Good Mind, protector of herds; Khshathra Vairya or Desirable Kingdom, patron of metals; Spenta Armaiti or Wise Conduct, presiding over earth; Hauravatat or Happiness, presiding over water; Ameretat or Immortality, patron of plants. (Through these Ahura Mazda rules world, sanctifies men.)	Apaosha or Drought; Nasu, who makes bodies corrupt. (Through these Ahriman afflicts earth, defiles men.)
YAZATAS	**YATUS**
or Venerable Ones, old Iranian divinities reduced to rank of "good angels," auxiliary to Ahura Mazda and the Amesha Spentas, such spirits are: Atar the Spirit of Fire; Anahita the Spirit of Water; Mithras the Spirit of Truthfulness; Rashnu the Spirit of Justice; Sraosha the Spirit of Discipline.	or sorcerers.
FRAVASHIS	**PAIRIKAS**
originally perhaps the Manes of dead ancestors, but in historical Iranian religion spiritual doubles of individuals, akin to Egyptian *kas* and Roman *genii.*	or fairies, spirits of seduction.

Men by their free actions, and indeed all creatures by their useful or noxious natures, play parts in this universal drama of Good and Evil. The various chapters of Persian religion, still to be considered, will reveal the drama's plot. It is a drama whose denouement is preordained in favor of Ahura Mazda and his forces, for finally an ordeal by a flood of molten metal will purify all men and destroy all the forces of evil.

CHAPTER « 8

CREATION AND COUNTERCREATION

MODERN Parsis indignantly reject dualism. They keep within their own rights in so doing, if there be merely question of a choice of beliefs, but it is another matter to explain away the manifest dualism of Persian religious documents. The *Avesta* and the other written vehicles of legitimate tradition do not present a picture of creatures rebellious against their Creator and working evil, which He permits but regulates by His providence. On the contrary, coeval with the good god and independent of him there exists a malignant divinity who creates beings in his own evil image.[1]

Eight episodes of creation are balanced against eight of countercreation in the "middle" Persian Bundahisn. Ahura Mazda, dwelling in infinite light, produces his creatures as spiritual entities. It might be better to describe the beings thus produced as the order of *absolute futura,* i.e., beings that are destined to be created, for they are unthinking, unmoving, and intangible. Precise definition is, however, impossible when we are handling myth-fabric. Aroused in his abyss of endless darkness, Angra Mainyu rushes up into the region of infinite light, only to retire affrighted. He countercreates, seemingly again as *absolute futura,* demons and noxious

[1] Several theories have been advanced in exegesis of the *Avesta's* unsavory dualism. Both Ahura Mazda and Ahriman are described as produced by a primordial being, Zervan Akarana (Endless Time). Or Ahriman is said to have sprung from an impure thought of Ahura Mazda or of some good spirit. Or, finally, Ahura Mazda and Ahriman are understood to be, respectively, good and evil inclinations in man himself.

beings of all sorts to aid him in his war against light and goodness.

Negotiations ensue. An alliance is offered Ahriman. "Forego your dire purposes. Help my creatures, and for reward you and yours will receive immortality." But the lord of misrule will have none of this, vowing to win the affection of the good creation and destroy it. "Agree, at least, to an ordered struggle. Let our warfare endure for thrice three millennia." Ahura Mazda foreknows that in the first of these periods his will must prevail, that the second will witness a mixture of right and wrong, that in the third evil will be overthrown. Ahriman, who is as ignorant as he is vicious, accepts the proposed ground rules, and the first of the trimillennial chukkers gets under way. Ahura Mazda then recites a prayer-formula of such potency that his adversary is confounded and lies prostrate and despairing for three thousand years.

As yet, all creatures remain *absolute futura*. At the commencement of the second of the fated thrice three millennia, the Amesha Spentas and the Yazatas are actuated by the good divinity. He also sets the stars, sun, and moon like a warlike army in the firmament. Countercreated by Ahriman are Aka Manah and the host of other demons. Roused to action by the she-devil Iahi, the father of ill invades the firmament, whose order he confuses by making the planets with their eccentric movements. The heavenly militia is called out and for ninety days battles in the heights against the invading demons. Ahriman and "his'n" are at last forced back into the abyss of endless darkness, while against their further aggression the regions of light are encircled with ramparts.

Midway between the regions of light and darkness, the earth appears in obedience to Ahura Mazda's creative will. To prepare it for living beings, he causes a heavenly reservoir to overflow and supply rain, while he leads water from the same source through golden conduits into the terrestrial seas. The naïve myth goes on to narrate Ahriman's vengeful sabotage: how he lunges against earth's underside and dents its symmetry with the excrescences called mountains; how he creates the demon of drought Apaosha. Since to Tishtrya (Sirius, the Dog Star) has been committed the regulation of moisture upon the earth, Apaosha tries to destroy him, but is overcome in epic combat. This episode of creation closes with the springing up on one of the mountains of the Haoma-tree, whose fruit is destined to be used in compounding the Iranian sacrificial drink-offering.

Ameretat, the Persian Demeter, renders the earth fruitful by mixing the germs of all plants with the raindrops. Still marring what he cannot wholly destroy, Ahriman instills poison into the sap of many growing plants, coats others with rough bark, furnishes still others with thorns. During this same period of plant-creation, Ahura Mazda produces the useful and (to the Iranian religious mind) divine element of fire. Upon that, too, Ahriman puts his mark, for he mars its clarity with dusky smoke.

Fated to be progenitor of all animal forms, the Primeval Ox appears on the earth. But he pines and dies, probably from poisoned herbage above mentioned. Returning to Ahura Mazda, the soul of the Ox complains of frustrated destiny and of the might of the evil god. By way of consolation, the Ox-soul is introduced to the soul of Zoroaster, the prophet and saint who in the destined cycle of time will smite the forces of evil. From the dead limbs of the Ox, nevertheless, spring two other oxen, and from this pair spring all the species of animals.

The first man whom Ahura Mazda saw fit to make was an Aryan, for of Gaya Maretana (Human Life) we read in *Yasht,* 13:87:

> Who first of Ahura Mazda
> Heard the mind and heard the teachings;
> From whom, too, Ahura Mazda
> Formed the Aryan country's household
> And the seed of Aryan countries.

This proto-Nazi was formed from Ahura Mazda's sweat as an adolescent of fifteen years. Real Teutonic *Weltschmertz* engulfs him, for the world is full of darkness, poison, and demons. After he has moaned through thirty years, the demoness Iahi, who no doubt was a proto-Semite, brews a poisoned cup too potent for even his Aryan constitution and he dies. Of his members are formed the various metals, while his seed is preserved in the ground by Spenta Armaiti.

After forty years there springs from the seed an anthropodendron, whose two forks have respectively the semblance of a man and a woman. Ten species of monster-men are the tree's fruit. The two forks grow into the perfect semblance of human bodies, are given human souls by Ahura Mazda, commanded to be good and sent forth into the world. Named Mashya and Mashyoi, they at first praise their creator and offer sacrifice, but fall into the error of attributing the works of creation to Ahriman. They clothe their nakedness with leaves and animal pelts, and soon discover the arts of life: weaving cloth, fashioning metal tools, and building a house. But more and more they fall under the sway of the evil spirit, till at last they offer sacrifice to him. After this act of impiety they quarrel with each other, their altercations ending in an effective hair-pulling and scratching contest. The aftermath of this first recorded domestic squabble is a half century of despair and sickness, but they finally return in penitence to the worship of Ahura Mazda. Of them are born Siyakmak and Nashak; of the latter pair, Fravak and Fravakain, who are the progenitors of the fifteen races of men. The Iranian plateau, where all this fairy tale is enacted, becomes so overcrowded that nine races migrate to other regions. The stay-at-homes propagate the holy Aryan people. All this is interesting ethnology with the same claim to scientific accuracy as the noisy blasts that are blown through the trumpet of Hitler's ministry of propaganda.

A variant of the creation-myth, probably of later date, presents Mithras slaying the Ox, so that plants and animals may be born of its blood. In general, the theology of creation believed by the Iranians was as dualistic as, let us say, the theology of the United States "Bible-Belt" Christians on the question of intoxicants. Were the remaining points in the myth's exegesis as simple as this one of a dualistic motif, Iranian scholars would be spared many a headache. We cannot neglect to pose the problems involved nor to notice the more reasonable solutions hitherto advanced.

The first anomaly is the cross weaving of reflex philosophic ideas upon a naïvely primitive naturism. In Ahura Mazda—unproduced, holy, knowing, potent creator and author of morality—is recognizable the imposing figure of the primitive Supreme Being. Yet he produces the demiurgal Amesha Spentas and Yazatas, who resemble nothing so much as the demiurges of Neoplatonic, Philonic, and Gnostic speculation. These "divine" beings are, in turn, both naturistic numina and philosophic Deified Abstracts. The table at the end of the last chapter may be consulted, but, to recall a single example, Vohu Manah personifies the desirable quality of right intention while serving as the tutelary spirit of the flocks.

One solution offered suggests that Iranian religion somehow got off with merely a light infection of the deadly virus of polytheism; that Ahura Mazda's uniqueness remained unclouded through long centuries; that Amesha Spentas and Yazatas were pale hypostatizations of the Supreme Being's attributes, hardly acknowledged as distinct from him and certainly not comparable to him. In appraising this solution, one is first struck by the improbability that any ancient people of the higher culture bracket kept primitive religion so incorrupt. Secondly, the Amesha Spentas and Yazatas were, as has been partly demonstrated and will later be more fully shown, definitely the nature-gods of typical ancient polytheism. Finally, the mental process which makes a divine hypostasis of "Righteousness" or "Wise Conduct" is so highly philosophical that one hesitates to admit it in the dim prehistory of human thought.

The other solution of our anomaly, and the preferable one, leans heavily on the purifying and systematizing activity of a reform party. Whether we identify this reform party with a historical Zoroaster or with a group of Magian zealots, its work would have been the following. Ahura Mazda had to be restored to a position of uniqueness. The discords of naturistic polytheism had to be muted, yet without offending ears tuned to catch the immemorial rhythms of nature-worship. Reason had to be soothed by a spiritualization of the concept of divinity and a plausible cosmogony. Such a work of recasting we believe, in default of certain proofs, to have been responsible for the systematic creation-myth which has been detailed.[2]

The process itself of creation is no less marked by curious anomalies. When creatures are made in a "spiritual" state, the mind yaws about uncertainly in quest of an intelligible sense. Can it be that the "original ideas and archetypes"[3] of neo-Platonic and Philonic speculation have been interpolated into Iranian mythology? Not an impossible solution, but one which presupposes a very late redaction of the myth. When creatures are to be given actual existence, Ahura Mazda seemingly by an act of omnipotence poises the material earth and spreads the firmament above it, but the rest of the drama falls short of this sublime beginning. Demiurges fantastically take over the action, as Ameretat mixes the powdered germs of plant-life with the fertilizing rain supplied by still another demiurge (Ardvi Sura Anahita); as from the members of the poisoned Ox all animal forms derive. Savagely grotesque are the episodes of Gaya Maretana, produced by the sweat of Ahura Mazda; of the anthropodendron with its monstrous fruit. Mark Connolly missed a trick when he neglected to "pass" a few of these Iranian creation miracles in "Green

[2] The interpretation here follows Fr. Lagrange in his "Iran" in *Dict. Apol.*
[3] Philo Judaeus in *De Mundi Opificio,* par. 23.

Pastures." No doubt, our Iranian grotesques originated in a semicivilized religious mentality akin to that of certain colored strata of the "deep South."

An imprint of ancient savage mythology is found in the tale of the "protoparents" Mashya and Mashyoi, in that they are said to devour their first pair of offspring. Apart from this casual cannibalism, the tale is reasonable enough and its moral tone elevated. Their sin may be classified as devil-worship, the form of sin which Dualism, of course, constrained the mythographer to describe as primal. Both their biography and that of their quasiparent, Gaya Maretana, are so evidently poured into the dualistic mold that we must recognize a tendentious recasting of whatever elements of primitive religious tradition the stories contain. This first human trio are dropped into a world already committed to the eternal struggle between Ormuzd and Ahriman, already pixilated by the latter's lurking agents. They do not induct evil into an unspoiled creation by willful original sin, for evil is antecedently present in the very essence of creation. Nor is there the least suggestion that their sin of devil-worship passes by way of inherited taint into the natures of their descendants. Here we are very far from the concepts of original justice and original sin.

As for the rest, there seems to be no difficulty in admitting a connection between the Iranian story of protoparents and first sin, and the Genesis history of Adam and Eve. A like connection may be admitted for the Iranian creation legend and the inspired narrative of Genesis. Resemblances — six stages of creation in each case and the same order, human protoparents, and a first sin — are not so striking as to dictate such admissions, but the Persians may well have preserved elements of the primitive tradition which God kept wholly incorrupt among the Jews. Or, as Fr. Lagrange is inclined to believe, Zoroastrian reformers, who knew something of Jewish religion, may have retouched their own mythical grotesques with Genesis as a model. The famed scholar would assign the work of retouching to Parthian days, its canonization through royal edict to the early Sassanids.

Picking up the thread of Iranian origin-legends, we are next led to Vivanghvant, who first offered the Haoma sacrifice, and to his more illustrious son Yima, the Brilliant. As King of the Iranians, Yima receives from Ahura Mazda a golden arrow and a golden scourge. His wars with Ahriman's daevas are so successful that they are all enslaved to the holy Aryan people. After three hundred years the earth is overcrowded, so Yima strikes its western edge with his arrow and strokes it with his scourge. Whereat the earth expands its area by a third, a proceeding which is repeated after two similar periods of three hundred years each. At the end of these nine hundred years of Golden Age — for Yima has taught men all the arts of life — Ahura Mazda reveals the proximate coming of a winter baneful to all forms of life. By divine command, Yima encloses a great area, puts in it nine hundred and fifty men and nine hundred and fifty women all of the best — no Semites, we presume, being eligible — as well as the best animals and plants. Ahura Mazda supplies a lighting system, for the luminaries of heaven are to be seen but once a year. Within the enclosure the elect lead a prosperous life, sheltered from the rigors of the winter which has gripped the rest of creation. At intervals of forty years every enclosed pair, whether of human or animal kind, procreate a male and a female of their species.

The duration and outcome of the dispensation of the enclosure are not explained in the myth. Some Zoroastrian theologians hold that in the final millennium of the world a demon will destroy all life by the rigors of winter, and that then Yima's enclosure, which they locate in the interior of the globe, will be opened to repopulate the earth. Yima's personal fate is clearer in the myth, for by sinning he loses the *Hraov-ena* (the divine effulgence that clothed an Iranian king and rendered him invincible) and is sawed in twain by the demon Azhi Dahaka.

India's mythology has its Yama, son of Vivasvant, whose career and character parallel those of Iranian Yima. Probably, then, the Yima myth derives from the ancient times before the Aryans trekked to the southern shores of the Indus. Avestan Yima is both a religious and material culture-hero, but the Zoroastrians, who reserve the prophet's mantle for Zoroaster, acknowledge Yima as merely a material civilizer. In the *Shahnamah,* Firdausi names him Jamshid and places him fifth in the royal line of Iran. Mohammedan tradition identifies him with the wise Solomon and with Noe, the preserver of the seed of all life and the discoverer of wine. That his enclosure is a variant of Noe's ark can hardly be seriously maintained, yet there are critics who have toyed with this theory. An explanation on purely naturistic basis suffices, for the whole tale is rather clearly a medley of naturistic myths: sun-myth (Yima the Brilliant); storm-myth (Azha Dahaka is a storm-demon); seasonal myth (baneful winter and reflorescence of life in spring); first-sin myth (Yima's transgression and punishment); eschatological-myth (reopening of the enclosure at end of the world).

CHAPTER « 9

ZOROASTER, PROPHET OF IRAN

THE Iranians shared with other Indo-Europeans — Indians, Greeks, Teutons, and the rest — in a common deposit of primordial conflict-myths. Of these, some narrate fancifully how the gods struggled for their overlordship against hostile powers; others, how a hero fought to win benefits for men from jealous overlords. For instance, the Greek gods' tenure of Olympus is disputed by the Titans, Trita of the Indian Veda wins the gift of fire by smiting the dragon Visvarupa. In Iranian myth-cookery the inevitable seasoning of dualism is added to the common Indo-European ingredients, in that the adversaries of gods and heroes are consistently presented as Ahriman's daevas. Speculative Zoroastrianism synthesizes the conquerors of the ancient nature-myths in the form of a genius of victory, Verethraghna (Victory against adverse attacks).

The traditions which have carried down the history of ancient Iran are quite the despair of scientific historians. Persons and events that seem to belong to factual chronicle are made the actors and the scenes of a dualistic drama. The preternatural is not the occasional and plausible embellishment noted, let us say, in Shakespearean historical drama, but is rather a constant obtrusion of demonology and magic thaumaturgy. Religious myth and sober record interweave almost inextricably. How, for example, will the critic separate fact from fancy in the story of King Faridun? A demon-king Dahak has fed Faridun's father to a dragon and imprisoned two Iranian princesses. Faridun, after storming Dahak's stronghold, chains him in a mountain gorge and converts the princesses from the idolatry into which they have fallen. Iran is then divided among Faridun's three sons, but fratricide liquidates one of them. The murdered man's son Minuchir ousts his uncles from the throne by the aid of the Iranian Heracles, Keresaspa. Keresaspa's Omphale, the witch Knathaiti, seduces him into demonolatry, for which sin he is afflicted with a lethargy. At the end of time he will be aroused, to lead Ahura Mazda's forces in the final conflict against Ahriman.

Throughout Firdausi's *Shahnamah,* which is by far the most complete written record of Iranian tradition, the medley of fact and myth is maintained. This is especially worthy of note, for here amid the Bluebeards and Jacks the Giant Killers of Persian lore rises the figure of the Prophet of Iran. A brief abstract of the epic's action will illlustrate the "historical" setting in which he appears. The period treated extends from the mythical first king, Kaiumers, to the conquest by Alexander of Macedon. The central theme of Iran against her enemies is embellished in epic fashion with amours, intrigues, and heroic deeds. For Iran there contend with preternatural strength and magic art the heroes Minuchir, Isfendyar, and Rustam. Opposed are first the Arabs under their king, Zohak, who has sold his soul to Ahriman for a thousand years of rule, then the Turanians (probably a term embracing a number of hostile tribes of the Iranian plateau) led by the demon-magician Afrasiyab. In Arab and Turanian hosts are always battalions of Daevas and Pairikas obligingly levied by Ahriman. A curious bit of patriotic romancing is introduced to prevent the overthrow of the Persian power by Alexander from being an anticlimax. For the youthful conqueror himself is made out to be of the Persian royal line, having been born of the union of the last king but one with the daughter of Philip of Macedon.

Zoroaster enters the action of the *Shahnamah* when

> Later times produced idolatry
> And Pagan faith; when Ormuzd's name was lost
> In adoration of created things.

He is a member of a fire-worshiping sect called Gubers. To Iran's king, Gushtasp (uncertainly identified with Hystaspes, father of Darius the Great), he introduces himself as the recipient of a divine revelation written down in the book *Avesta.* He has ascended to heaven and gone down into hell, to either of which regions he can commit whom he will by his mere prayer. All heavenly secrets are made known to him by his attendant angel. The miracles he offers as credentials for his divine ambassadorship are the cure of Gushtasp's ailing sire and the springing up before the palace of a tree whose fruit makes men wise, holy, and instructed in the mysteries of the future life. The king accepts the new faith and sends his son on a crusade to propagate it. The choice given to the countries invaded by the youthful hero seems to have been: "Believe, or else — " From this point on Firdausi refers on occasion to Zoroastrianism, most notably at the end of his fine poem, when the dying king Darius (the Third or Codomanus) entreats Alexander:

> . . . I have a daughter
> Dearer to me than life, her name is Roshung;
> Espouse her, I beseech thee, and if Heaven
> Should bless thee with a boy, Oh! let his name be
> Isfendiyar, that he may propagate
> With zeal the sacred doctrines of Zerdusht,
> The Zendavesta; then my soul will be
> Happy in Heaven; and he, at Nau-Ruz tide,
> Will also hold the festival I love,
> And at the altar light the Holy Fire.
> Nor will he cease his labor till the faith
> Of Lohurasp be everywhere accepted
> And everywhere believed the true religion.[1]

The *Shahnamah,* then, is not helpful in the matter of Zoroaster's biography, but does furnish a good example of the myths which in later Gaber and Parsi tradition clustered about

[1] Translation by James Atkinson. In the *Shahnamah* Zerdusht is the form of Zoroaster's name, *Zendavesta* is used for *Avesta.* Lohurasp is the old king whom Zoroaster cured, as told above.

the prophet's figure. Searching for further light, scholars turn in vain to the inscriptions of Achaemenian times, which present neither reference to the man himself nor any distinctly Zoroastrian religious doctrines. However, such inscriptions are as yet few in number, nor are those available religious in theme. Two other sources of information are the *Avesta* itself and classical, i.e., Greek and Latin writers.

The testimony of the *Avesta* is twofold. In the Gathas, which scholars regard as the oldest and least corrupt portions of the work, Zoroaster speaks in his own person, instructing the people in his doctrine and claiming that it is a revelation from Ahura Mazda and the good spirits. He personally gives vent to expressions of hope and of despair in the face of success or of persecution. He appears convinced that the end of the world is near at hand. On intrinsic evidence, the Gathas can perhaps be accepted as utterances of a historical person, but they furnish no specific biographical details.

On the contrary, the rest of the *Avesta* is profuse in explanation of the who, when, and what of the prophet's life. His father, the fourth priest of the Haoma sacrifice, was named Pourushaspa. Ahura Mazda places the procreated soul of Zoroaster in a fruit of the holy Haoma-tree, and this fruit Pourushaspa eats. Pourushaspa weds Dughdhava, who had received the *Hraovena* (the Divine Glory once possessed by Iranian kings, but taken away from them for their sins) and she bears Zoroaster in northwestern Media, despite an earnest obstructionist policy on the part of Ahriman's daevas. All nature rejoices at the child's birth. He grows up famous in the old Iranian sport of demon-hunting. At last, he receives his revelation and begins his preaching. It is slow work, what with Ahrimanic temptations to diffidence in his mission, demoniacal trickery, the harrying of priests of the old religion. With the conversion of King Vishtaspa, the prophet's fortunes start on the upgrade. However, during the religious wars in which the royal convert engages, Zoroaster himself is slain by an idolatrous priest. Three germs which the dead reformer leaves upon earth are deposited by the fire-god Agni in the Hamun Swamp in Seistan. It is fated that at intervals of a thousand years a maiden, bathing in the waters there, will become pregnant and bear a prophet. These three prophets will all be named Saoshyant. The last will be the greatest and at the end of the world will destroy by his preaching the principle of evil.

Turning to classical writers for light on Zoroaster's historical or mythical character, we find that Herodotus does not mention the prophet nor his book even in a fairly detailed account of Persian religion. The religion he describes is not characteristically that of the *Avesta.* This testimony is remarkable, for Herodotus could not have written later than 425 B.C. Plato, in the First Alcibiades, composed not later than 350 B.C., speaks of Persian princes being "instructed in the magianism of Zoroaster the son of Ormuzd, which is the worship of the gods." Plutarch in his *Numa Pompilius,* which appeared at about the year 100 of our era says: "Why should we judge it incongruous that a spirit of the gods should visit Zaleucus, Minos, Zoroaster, Lycurgus, and Numa, the controllers of kingdoms and the legislators for commonwealths?" Pliny the Younger in his *Historia Naturalis* narrates curiously of Zoroaster that he is the one human being who laughed on the very day that he was born and that his baby head pulsated violently by way of presage of his future intellectual gifts.[2]

Perhaps Zoroaster's infantile mirth was inspired by a foreknowledge of the future labors of scholars on the complex question of his personality and work. Did he exist? How much did he contribute to the so-called Zoroastrian religion, even if he did exist? The evidence presented in this and in preceding chapters leaves the answers to both the questions unclear.

---

[2] *"Risisse eodem die, quo genitus esset, unum hominem accepimus Zoroastrem. Eidem cerebrum ita palpitasse ut impositam repelleret manum, futurae praesagio scientiae."*

CHAPTER • 10

CULT AND MAGIC

THE teeming magic of the Tigris-Euphrates valley has inspired a previous chapter on this unlovely caricature of religion. All that was there explained in regard to the relation of magic art to legitimate cult, will serve as theoretic background for the present discussion.

Herodotus gives a description of Persian practices which may be taken as our text:

> The Persians, according to my own knowledge, observe the following customs. It is not their practice to erect statues or temples or altars, but they charge those with folly who do so; because, as I conjecture, they do not think the gods have human form, as the Greeks do. They are accustomed to ascend the highest parts of the mountains and offer sacrifice to Jupiter, and they call the whole circle of the heavens by the name of Jupiter. They sacrifice to the sun and moon, to the earth, fire, water and the winds. To these alone have they sacrificed from the earliest times; but they have since learned from the Arabians and Assyrians to sacrifice to Venus Urania, whom the Assyrians call Venus Mylitta, the Arabians Alitta, and the Persians Mitra. The following is the established mode of sacrifice to the above mentioned deities. They do not erect altars nor kindle fires when about to sacrifice. They do not use libations or flutes or fillets or cakes. When one wishes to offer sacrifice to any one of these deities, he leads the victim to a clean spot, and invokes the god, usually having his tiara decked with myrtle. He that sacrifices, is not permitted to pray for blessings for himself alone; but he is obliged to offer prayers for the prosperity of all the Persians and for the king, for he is himself included in the Persians. When he has cut the victim into small pieces and boiled the flesh, he strews under it a bed of tender grass, generally trefoil, and then lays all the flesh upon it. When he has put everything in order,

one of the Magi standing by sings an ode concerning the origin of the gods, which they say is the incantation; and without one of the Magi it is not lawful for them to sacrifice. After waiting a short time, he who has sacrificed carries away the flesh and disposes of it as he thinks fit.[1]

There is some evidence that the Iranians in very remote times did worship idols. Figurines of terra cotta and bronze, though no large cult-statues, have been excavated from old Iranian sites and are evidently images of gods. Moreover, Avestan and later tradition constantly mentions the abolition of idol-worship as one of Zoroaster's reforms. The worship of the *Avesta,* however, and of later Persian religion was definitely aniconic. In all the written fonts of Persian tradition those who adore images are upbraided and classed among Ahriman's followers, while the faithful are repeatedly exhorted to shun idolatry. Archeological investigation confirms the argument, for the statues of gods, so abundant in other excavations, do not appear in Persian diggings. The most that the spade has turned up in the latter are conventionalized demi-figures of Ahura Mazda hovering over a king's head and one representation of the same god conferring sovereignty on the first Sassanid. In these bas-reliefs, whose theme is the exaltation of the king, Ahura Mazda cannot fairly be called an idolic figure, i.e., one set up for adoration.

Herodotus, in saying that "it is not their practice to erect altars," is thinking of the stone *bomos* familiar to him in Greece. "The highest parts of the mountains" may well have been regarded by the Persians as natural altars for their sacrifice to the lord of the heavens, while the Greek historian's account of the sacrificial ritual implies still another form of altar. The "bed of tender grass" which is prepared for the reception of the sacrificial flesh-offering cannot be other than a primitive altar. It is odd that Herodotus does not mention the "fire-altar," so frequently pictured on Achaemenian, Par-

[1] Bk. I, Chs. 131–132.

thian, and Sassanid coins and mentioned in Xenophon's *Cyropedia.* The typical "fire-altar" consisted of a plinth of masonry, a pedestal, and an urn to contain the sacred fire. The one seen by Xenophon, since it figured in a religious procession, must have been of the portable variety which the coins occasionally depict (Cf. diagrams). For a time, under Hellenic and Babylonian influence, the *bomos* was adopted and on it animal sacrifices were offered to the Persian divinities. But from Sassanid days onward altars for animal sacrifice are unknown. This may be taken as only one more fact pointing to a late reformation of the religion, such as was proposed in a preceding chapter. In present-day Parsi cult the "fire-altar" is central, though supplementary altars for certain ritualistic functions may be placed around it.

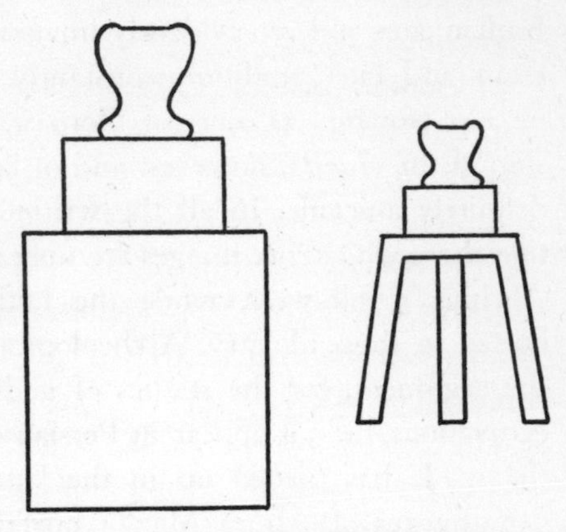

Fig. 11. Reconstruction of Persian Fire-Altars

We have evidence for an early date for the "fire-temples" on the above-mentioned coins, though again Herodotus is silent. Arguing *a priori,* we may say that a fire, whose sacredness demanded that it never be extinguished, must certainly have been housed against the inclemency of the weather. Such a house might not have rejoiced in the technical name of temple, but would have been such, since it sheltered a divine element and was the scene of religious exercises. For the Sassanids and for subsequent times the "fire-temple" is definitely the holy house in which the business of cult is conducted. There are world-famous fire-temples supported today by wealthy Parsis of India.

In earliest Iran fire was regarded, no doubt, as a divinity. In the systematized Zoroastrianism, it became confusingly a divine person, a symbol of divinity, the most valuable of creatures. Atar (Fire) of the myths was the son of Ahura Mazda, while Avestan ritual contains prayers addressed directly to Fire. In the Fourth Episode of creation, we find Ahura Mazda actuating five kinds:

1. Spenishta or Most Holy, burning before the creator in Paradise;

2. Vazishta or Best Carrying, the lightning;

3. Bahram or Very Useful, the sacrificial flame on earthly altars;

4. Vohu Fryana or Good Friend, warmth in human and animal bodies;

5. Urva Zishta or Most Delightful, the life-force of plants, from which man primitively secured fire through friction of wood on wood.

The sanctity of fire, and *a fortiori* of the fire on the altar, is clear for all periods. One might not spit in the fire, nor place a corpse nor any unclean object in it. Frankincense and sandalwood were, and are, put in the altar-fire as tokens of religious reverence, while to allow the sacred fire to be extinguished has always been a grave sin. Modern Parsis are referred to as fire-worshipers, but their regard for the element is rather akin to that paid to statues (*cultus relativus*). For them, namely, it is not divine, but the chief symbol of divinity.

Inseparable from Parsi religious rites is the Barsom, a bundle of twigs, or of lengths of thin wire, bound round with a string of leaves from the date palm. Its cultual use dates back to the earliest of our sources, for it has always been employed in religious and magical ceremonies and has rated a place with Fire and Haoma in a triad of sacrosanct objects. It has been protected by the same taboos as Fire against contact with the unclean. Its concept has been partly that of a sacramental, akin to holy water and blessed salt; partly that of a magic spell to avert the malice of Daevas. Most plausible explanation of its origin is that the twigs and leaves represent the boughs which were laid on the ground to form the primitive altar of sacrifice.

The myths tell us prettily of the origin of the Haoma and of the Haoma "sacrament." In the Third Episode of Creation Ahura Mazda draws good out of evil by making the Haoma-plant spring up on one of Ahriman's mountains. Another myth tells how a proto-Zoroaster, named Haoma, was meditating on Mount Elburz when he found the plant, whose juice he found healthful and exhilirating. Whereon, the holy man composed a ritual for extracting the juice and drinking the same. The *Avesta* is lavish in its praise of Haoma-bibbing. The drink confers wisdom, courage, health; heaven, power over demons, prescience of danger; husbands on old maids, fecundity on the barren; in fact, what you will. Conditions for drinking profitably are the Iranian moral triad: good thoughts, good words, good deeds. Lacking these, the drinker will find the draught a curse.

Parsi ritual of the "sacrament" is extremely elaborate, and is, of course, a development of simpler forms derived from tradition. The stalks of Haoma are kept for thirteen months and thirteen days after gathering. When the ritual is to begin, either at midnight or in the morning hours, the following paraphernalia are at hand; the aged stalks of Haoma, blessed bread, holy water, mortar and pestle, frankincense, sandalwood, a cup, a strainer. The officiating Parsi priest seats himself on a stone near the "fire-altar" with all these materials ready for use. It would be wearisome to detail the ceremony, which is as long, though not as reasonable nor sublime as the ceremonies in a parochial church on Holy Saturday. Central act is the pounding of the twigs in the strainer to extract the Haoma juice. When the extract is ready, a second priest receives the cup of juice, which he carries three times around the fire-altar to the accompaniment of Avestan praises of Haoma.

Returning to the first priest, he says: "May the Haoma be to thee of twofold, threefold, ninefold efficacy," presenting the cup. The first priest takes three sips and the rite concludes.

In India's *Veda* and among the Hindus, the soma plant and drink are reverenced just as the Haoma. Botanically, Haoma belongs to the Ephedra group of the genus Gnetaceae. It is a shrub growing in semiarid regions of Iran and Afghanistan, with jointed stalks and almost leafless.

PART THREE

RELIGION OF THE EGYPTIANS

CHAPTER « 11

THE LAND AND THE PEOPLE

TO IDEAS and aspirations current in the old Mediterranean world, criticism hostile to supernatural religion turns for a natural explanation of Christian origins. In this soil, it is asserted, lay seed which awaited only the warmth of a new emotion to spring up as Gospel message and flower into Pauline theology. No new claim surely, but today insistently voiced as a necessary conclusion from modern archeological finds. Were our goal apologetic, it could be shown that this conclusion rests upon irrelevant parallels between old natural religions and the Christian miracle. However, a sufficient apologetic will be evident even in the purely historical treatment of the facts. Honest gazing into the old Mediterranean kaleidoscope will not discover elements capable of being pieced together into a mosaic resembling Apostolic teaching.

To particularize for the present subject of investigation, it will appear from a simple study of cultual facts that Christianity did not come out of the land of Egypt. Divine triads, for instance, are not genuine analogues of the Trinity. In the Osirian myth-cycle, which is adduced as a source of much New Testament teaching, a fair observer fails to see the prototypes of Divine Maternity and Resurrection so patent to the singular intuition of a Frazer and a Reinach. Remarkable document though *The Book of the Dead* be, no unbiased judgment deems the eschatology presented in this tissue of myth and speculation the inspiration of Christ's doctrine on the future life.

Egypt's contacts with Sacred History in Old Testament times are too well known to need detailing. Modern research is slowly unearthing on the lower Nile and in Palestine evidence confirmatory of the narratives of the Hebrew chroniclers. In fact, Egyptology has become one of the newest fronts in the war for and against revealed religion. Professor Breasted, for example, stated as his conclusion from a lifetime of Egyptian studies that: "Had the western world never lost all knowledge of the origins and development of civilization, it would never have occurred to any one to place Hebrew history anywhere else than as the culmination of a long preceding development of morals and religion."[1] Three or four crucial distinctions must be made upon this thesis of the eminent Egyptologist, but they will be reserved for future pages. One must first hear the evidence at hand before pronouncing historical judgment upon this and similar statements of antisupernaturalism, and we have yet to learn from monuments and documents what the true facts are. It must be noted, however, that the reconciliation of the Hebrew Scriptures with Egyptian records can be but a secondary and incidental feature of our study, which is not of an apologetic nature.

Historians of religions employ what is known as the comparative method in correlating and interpreting the facts with which their science deals, a method both fruitful and fundamentally sound.[2] Its application to the beliefs and rites of the people of the Nile valley reveals interrelation between this religious culture and other parallel or lower cultures of Africa and Asia. Libya to the northwest and Somaliland to the southeast are recognized as most probably the homeland of important members of the Egyptian pantheon. Burial customs, ideas on the human soul, and a strange theriolatry connect Egypt with the retarded cultures of central Africa. From the Euphrates valley seem to have come with the invaders who established the first dynasty of Pharaohs the doc-

---

[1] *The Dawn of Conscience*, by James H. Breasted (Scribners, 1933), p. 385.

[2] An outline of this method may be found in the last chapter of this book.

trine of divine kingship as well as the sun-worship which was to dominate the creed and ritual of historic times. These connections, it must be admitted, are rather conjectured than absolutely demonstrated, but are gratefully acknowledged by scholars as suggestive contributions to the reconstruction of early Mediterranean history. In particular, every finding that links together the early religions of the "cradle lands" of man's history brings closer to realization a scientific synthesis of the religious knowledge possessed by our race in origin days.

"The tawny Tiber" and "the waters of Babylon" are phrases naturally rising to the mind at thought of two of the great empires of antiquity, but neither Tiber nor Euphrates had the vital connection with Roman or Babylonian history that the Nile had with Egyptian. The Nile runs a course of some four thousand miles from a point at three degrees south latitude to the Mediterranean delta at thirty-one degrees north latitude. At Khartoum, in Anglo-Egyptian Sudan, it enters upon a series of six cataracts effected by a hard sandstone formation that stubbornly resists erosion and renders navigation impracticable. The course is twisted by this obstacle into a great double horseshoe shape and straightens out only when the northernmost cataract is passed near the island of Elephantine. From this cataract the Nile flows on sleepily at a rate of only three miles per hour, to debouche through two (anciently seven) mouths into the Mediterranean, seven hundred miles to the north.

This last seven hundred miles' course marks the length of the land of Egypt: its width was no more than the ten to thirty miles between the cliffs which parallel the Nile's course (and which in the hoary past of which geology tells were the river's proper banks). Behind the cliffs to east and west were desert lands, beyond Elephantine to the south rose the natural barrier of the cataracts. Egypt, hence, was accessible only from the north, practically speaking, and that only by narrow coastal strips. The geographical stage was thus set for development of a civilization distinctly nationalistic, inasfar as the infiltration of foreign culture elements was difficult, while conquest by foreigners was hampered by splendid natural defenses. Her geographical isolation secured for Egypt long periods of peaceful economic development, progress in the arts and learning, and preservation through whole millennia of earliest beliefs and cult practices.

One of the reasons for England's altruistic attempt to rescue Haille Selassie's sheep from a Fascist shearing was undoubtedly the torrent of the Blue Nile. Rising in Lake Sana to the north of Addis Ababa, the stream twists through Ethiopia's mountain gorges and the plain of the Sudan, joining the White Nile at Khartoum. England had prudently acquired the right to dam this Ethiopian torrent at discretion, to insure fertility for the land of Kipling's "Fuzzy Wuzzies" and of Lord Kitchener's storied conquest. Downing Street considered it just possible that Mussolini's benevolent plan of bringing civilization's light to the otherwise contented Ethiopians might include the diversion of the Blue Nile's waters into the romantic desert regions of Ethiopia. For the torrent's volume is very great and its waters are charged with rich loam from the highlands. With the aid of another highland stream, the Atbara which enters near the fifth cataract, the Blue Nile raises the Nile's water as much as fifty feet when Ethiopia's snows melt and her summer rains fall.

The Pharaohs early turned to practical use the fluid treasure from the Ethiopian mountains. Rainfall in Egypt proper is so extraordinary in occurrence, sunshine so constant and the atmosphere so dry that the only land naturally arable can be the immediate riverbank. To widen this fertile ribbon, a system of reservoirs was constructed to retain the flood waters, and of canals to release them at need into the grain fields, a system extending from the first cataract at Elephantine to the Delta and securing a tillable area ten miles on the average in

By courtesy of the Chicago Oriental Institute Museum

Fig. 12. Model Nile Boats

Since Egypt's prevailing wind was from the north, the boat with sails set must be understood to serve for trips up river. These boats, found in a Pharaoh's tomb, were meant to serve him in the business and pleasure of the Afterlife. The boatmen are dressed with the simplicity which marked all periods of the people's history.

By courtesy of the Chicago Oriental Institute Museum

Fig. 13. A Pharaoh

The statue of red quartzite bears the names of the Pharaoh's Eye and Harmhab, but is a likeness of that Tutenkhamen the wonders of whose tomb have been recently unearthed. He wears the double crown of Upper and Lower Egypt.

width. At flood times the water was allowed, under careful control, to inundate the fields and deposit rich loam to replenish the soil. When the level in the canals grew lower, primitive water wheels were employed laboriously to dip up the water and to pour it into the fields. The Pharaoh, who was in control of this vast public utility, kept through his officials a vigilant eye on the moods of the Nile. His people's prosperity and his own taxes depended directly upon the amount of water available annually and upon its proper distribution through the irrigation system. On the rocks at the second cataract may still be read the annual records of the Nile's maximum level. It was Amenemhet III in the nineteenth century B.C. who first ordered these records kept as a means of predicting the volume of water that would pass the first cataract and the consequent good or bad crop year.[3]

Paradoxical though it may seem, our knowledge of Egyptian daily life is derived largely from the tomb. Eschatological beliefs are the explanation of this, for the Egyptian thought that his *ka*, or spiritual double, would inhabit the mortuary chamber after death and would need for his solace all the creatures that had made life pleasant for the living man. Great solicitude, therefore, was lavished by him who could afford it upon the "house of his eternity," much time and treasure being spent on its embellishment and endowments left for its maintenance.[4] There had to be pictures of the owner's illustrious deeds, if any, sculptured on the walls of the sepulchral chamber and narrated in appropriate hieroglyphic text. *Ka* would thus have material for an eternity of complacent gloating. More important still was it for *ka* to be assured proper sustenance and the means for enjoying the

---

[3] High water in these remote times averaged twenty-five to thirty feet above present-day highs.

[4] The common people being, in general, too poor to afford such large outlays, evidence here must be drawn from the tombs of Pharaonic, noble, and priestly families. What known of the groves of the lowly will be treated later on.

otium cum dignitate, the dignified leisure befittting a man of station. An application of a law of magic (to be analyzed later on) was invoked to secure these services for the deceased. Magic held that the statue or picture might take the place of the reality. On the walls of the vault, then, and even on the wooden mummy-coffin appeared pictures of delectable viands and beer together with representations of the business occupations and diverting avocations of the well-to-do Egyptian. The floor of the vault was strewn with miniature furnished houses, with model boats and oarsmen, with statuettes of servants engaged in a variety of work for their lord's comfort. From papyrus rolls, finally, stored away in the tombs we gain a further insight into Egyptian daily life, for on them not infrequently are painted scenes of the occupations of the departed in the future life, a life imagined on the analogy of earthly life.

The sources just noticed and others picture the typical Nile-dweller as a man of average height, erect in his carriage and physically well developed by an industrious outdoor life. His face was oval with chin firm but small, lips rather broad, large and expressive eyes, nose slender and small, forehead moderate and slightly receding. Artists make the most of their compatriots' rather graceful physique and fine features by contrasting them with the oddities (exaggerated, to be sure) of Negroid and Semite types. Egyptian dress was sketchy, as befitted an equable and rather warm climate — a kirtle of about the dimensions of the Scotsman's plaid for men, a single garment close-fitting and reaching from neck to ankle for women. Sandals and headdress were not unknown, but were not *de rigeur.*

Houses of the ordinary folk were of ephemeral character, stone and good hardwood being in the class of expensive imports and consequently reserved for the temples and the dwellings of the upper classes. The Nile's bounty supplied, except in the rare years when the inundation failed, an abundance of fruit, vegetables, and grain. The last-named produce was, likewise, the base of the beer of which the Egyptian was inordinately fond, if one may judge from the frequency of this motif on the pictured monuments. Herds of sheep, cattle, and domesticated antelopes furnished the meat supply, while fish and water fowl seem to have been plentiful at all times in the Nile. One of the finest features of Egyptian social life is the constant solicitude of the Pharaohs and their officials that the people might not suffer want. Pharaoh and his nobles held, practically speaking, title to all the land, but their demands upon their tenantry were tempered by due regard to the poor man's right to a decent living.

Egyptian life, though predominantly agricultural in all periods, exhibited other features. The building arts, and the hard manual labor incidental to them, occupied a considerable part of the population, while great building projects consumed much of the nation's wealth even in the remote age of the pyramids and of the early temples. In the Middle Kingdom and Empire days artisans and scribes must have numbered tens of thousands, to estimate from surviving jewelry, statues, wall carvings, papyri documents, and the like. The official family of the Pharaoh was always large and branched out into every corner of the country. Trading and merchandising stepped into the ranks of "big business" when foreign conquest effected contacts with other nations. Soldiering was a career which did not appeal to the placid Egyptian, so that warlike Pharaohs soon found that they must hire mercenaries to carry out their plans of bringing Egyptian civilization to benighted neighbors. Egypt's decline may be traced to her conquests, which led to the evils incidental to the maintenance of a great mercenary army, to costless slave labor which impoverished the native population, and finally to the luxury of the rich and ruling classes.

CHAPTER « 12

THE COMING OF HORUS AND HIS ARMORERS

GEOLOGISTS have been at work in the Nile valley for only a few years, so that their results thus far are admittedly no more than a preliminary survey. The river's prehistory they have traced from present depth and width to a period when the waters were held in by the western and eastern cliffs and reached a depth of several hundred feet. Prehistoric man followed the receding banks, leaving the usual fragmentary records of his earthly sojourn to tantalize the archeologist. Our concern is with the latest stages of prehistory, when, at least by conjectural comparison with earliest historical facts, the religious ideas of the Nile dwellers may be partially understood.

Sir W. Flinders Petrie, who has lived with two generations of Egyptologists and within the past few years has gone, Nestorlike, on expeditions with yet the third generation, offers a theory both on the religious character of this late prehistoric time and on the chronology of the same period. Though admittedly only a theory, his explanation commends itself because based upon exhaustive examination of thirteen hundred and fifty prehistoric graves, and because advanced by a scientist of Petrie's eminence.[1] He chooses, then, to divide the Late Prehistoric Age into three periods, which are to be understood as three cultures that entered the Nile valley at dates not rigidly determinable but fused one with another.

[1] In account for 1920 of British School of Archeology. Petrie further develops his views in *Religious Life in Ancient Egypt* (London: Constable & Co., 1924).

From the theater of the Italo-Ethiopian war, tribes akin to the Galla and Somali followed the rivers or perhaps the Red Sea and desert route into the land north of Elephantine. They were totemists and worshipers of a great phallic god named Min. Petrie, on certain sepulchral evidence, would indite them as cannibals. With this southeastern and scarcely amiable immigration stream there came in contact a culture of what seems a higher order from coastal tribes of Libya. Since they were worshipers of the fertility god Osiris, it is not unreasonable to attribute to them the first impulse to that settled, agricultural mode of life which became characteristic of the Nile dwellers. Petrie interestingly surmises that it was the Libyan immigrants who originated the theriocephalous divine form, as a compromise with the animal venerated by the totemic southeastern Africans. The third culture element was not African, but Asiatic. Semites, entering the Delta probably by way of the Isthmus of Suez, brought about important modifications both in the language and in the religion of the land. They worshiped gods of earth, air and sky, but especially a sun-god, whose Egyptian name was Ra (or Re), and further believed in a solar mythology which even in prehistoric days began to weave into its complex pattern all the gods of Egypt.

To sum up, the prehistoric picture presents the divine figures of Osiris and of Ra — figures destined to loom large through all subsequent developments — and of Min, who in historic times was to lose importance. Others there were, but these at present do not call for discussion. Focal points of religious belief were totemism, worship of the principles of vegetation and of generation, sun-worship. All that can be added to this picture is belief in magic, attested by a variety of amulets; and in a future life, attested by the food and utensils buried with the corpse.

Arguing chiefly from ceramic grave-findings, Professor Petrie computes the beginnings of the period just sketched.

His conclusion dates the starting point at 11,000 B.C. Geologists, on the basis of the yet very imperfect evidence at their disposal, give a date somewhere between 10,000 and 20,000. Anthropologists incline to a date rather before 8,000. These surmises, of course, are advanced in every case as contributions to a working hypothesis, and experience has shown that in the obscure field of prehistoric dating constant revision of opinions is the rule. Let us be satisfied, then, with the concept that for several millennia before the earliest accurately assignable date in Egyptian history the religious elements detailed in the preceding paragraphs were slowly entering into a species of syncretic compound, under the influence of a developing consciousness of national unity.

To reconstruct the next period of history and religion—the period, namely, just preceding the time when definite dating and documentary sources become available—recourse must be had to a method of serving up a few meager, though significant, bones of information in a generous sauce of interpretation. Our facts are as follows: First, at the opening of authentic history, about 3500 B.C. a company of great gods, irreducible to the gods already noted is enthroned in the land. Second, the Pharaohs who first move across the historic stage claim for themselves definite divinity. Third, the ruling class in Old Kingdom days boast of the title "followers of Horus." Fourth, a myth fairly bristling with euhemeristic elements indicates the main political and religious developments of the period immediately before the emergence of this Old Kingdom.[2]

The new company of gods just mentioned had, it would seem, the common characteristic of being personifications of abstract principles. Ptah was the creative force. Thoth was a personification of intellect. Maat stood for truth. In Hathor was deified the female principle of procreation. Nor do these

[2] An euhemeristic myth is one which magnifies and divinizes the person and deeds of some great historical figure.

worthies exhaust the list of the new gods, but let them serve as illustrations of a rather evident importation into the stock of prehistoric religious ideas in Egypt. Speculating on the homeland from whence the newcomers migrated, historians of religion fix attention on the region about ancient Babylon as the most likely, for there analogies of this sort of divine concept are numerous.

Further indications that the lower Tigris-Euphrates valley did its bit toward the complication of the Nile valley's religious culture are seen in the matter of the divine kingship. The king was a god to the peoples — Sumerian, Babylonian, Assyrian — who succeeded one another as lords of the fertile region that lies between the Tigris and the Euphrates. The Pharaoh, too, at the very beginning of dated Egyptian history stands out as a divine figure, not merely realized as such in a vague and inchoative sense, but saluted and worshiped as kin and compeer of the land's great gods. Now, have we here a case of independent development of the same religious idea or a case of borrowing? And if of borrowing, who borrowed from whom? Detailed similarity between the Sumero-Babylonian concept and the Egyptian argues against, though it does not wholly disprove, the theory of independent development. Some light on the question of borrowing is furnished by the fact that migratory waves in prehistory seem to have moved from the Tigris-Euphrates valley to the Mediterranean rather than in the reverse direction. Moreover, the whole genius of early Egypt was that of a land-locked people satisfied to stay at home and develop their own culture rather than to fare forth as conquerors or culture missionaries.

Though in the immediately predynastic stage of which we are treating the north and the south were ruled by two independent kings, both sovereigns, together with their respective nobles, boasted of the titles "Worshipers of Horus," "Followers of Horus." Through north and south, too, we find in early historical times literally hundreds of individual centers of Horus-cult. But, Horus, though a sun-god, was certainly not identical with the old sun-god Ra. Briefly, then, what had happened in the transitional period between the prehistoric and historical days was that a new god had taken over the divine hegemony. To what causes the change was due, we may only conjecture; however, there is sufficient weight of critical opinion to incline one to the theory of a Babylonian origin for Horus. His coming this same critical opinion would attribute to importation by tribes from the lower Euphrates region.

The progress of the "followers of Horus" toward winning control of the land may be conjectured from the details of the Ra-Horus myth. Ra the sun-god and giver of all good is represented as at war with Set, the principle of evil, the latter having allied to himself all evil influences such as darkness, storm, and rain as well as malignant animals, such as the alligator and the hippopotamus. It would have gone ill with Ra, whose sacred boat is sorely beleaguered by his foes, were it not for a rescue effected by Horus and his followers, who appear in the myth as "blacksmiths" or "men who work with iron." The hero meets Set in a series of fantastic encounters and breaks his power; he leads his followers in great swamp-hunts against the hippo and the alligator and these, too, are vanquished. For his reward, Horus is received permanently into the sun-boat and becomes the prototype of Pharaonic royalty by his adoption as son of Ra.

Of this myth we make bold to offer the following interpretation. Its purpose is to legitimize Horus, a newcomer, by bringing him into the family of Ra. Incidentally, the legitimation will propagate the doctrine of divine kingship, for the new rulers of North and South will claim, in accordance with the old Tigris-Euphrates usage, identification with their god Horus. Further we may read into the myth a record of a real military conquest of Egypt by the "followers of Horus," for the motif of Horus' victories is thus best explained. The chief factor in deciding this conquest seems hinted at in the term "men who worked in iron"; that is to say, the "blacksmiths" or armorers who by their use of iron armor and weapons prevailed over a population that still depended upon stone and wood.

Theory, of course, is not established fact, and it is only as theory that one may sanely assert an early Babylonian element in Egyptian life. What future excavation and study will contribute toward the confirmation or the discrediting of the theory, one would need the prophet's mantle to be able to say. But it is time to leave origin speculations and to conclude the present chapter with a sketch of the Nile valley just before the unification of government under Menes the first Pharaoh.

Pottery finds of the period show a marked advance in artistic workmanship, the ware being beautifully incised and decorated, while the shape approaches at times the gracefulness of Greek art. There begins that wealth of pictorial representation which in historical days reveals the ordinary life of the people. Hunting scenes on the vases tell of the presence in the Nile valley of lions, elephants, hippopotami, antelopes, and of a queer extinct species called the okapi which might best be described as a Darwinian progenitor of the Missouri mule. Commerce on the river is indicated by barges of rather pretentious design. These barges, driven by many oars and by sails, carry standards with designs suggestive of the distinguishing emblems of the later Egyptian nomes or administrative districts. The agricultural motif does not appear as prominently as might be expected, but perhaps the primitive artists were not duly awakened to the poetry of rural life.

There were two kings, the Red and the White. At Sais in the Western Delta reigned the former, the king of the north. Red was his distinctive color, his house and his treasury both being denominated by this color. His royal brow was surmounted by an odd crown, difficult to describe save by using the rather unroyal comparison of a coal miner's cap, the lamp's position being occupied by the erected uraeus serpent of the goddess Buto. Neit, too, was a protecting goddess of the North, her emblem of crossed arrows being as characteristic a symbol of that kingdom as was the tuft of papyrus plant. Just how far south the Red King's domain extended cannot be definitely said. The record of the deeds of these shadowy Red Kings, if any exists, lies buried beneath the hundreds of feet of alluvial soil that the Nile has deposited on the Delta cities. Of their names, though later romancers drew up long king lists, scholars admit that seven alone are surely authentic. To their kingdom belongs the renown of establishing the first reliable calendar, so far as is known, and of giving us the year 4241 B.C. as the earliest fixed date in history.

Nearly six hundred miles up the Nile on the river's right bank was established Nekheb, the "White House" and capital city of the "White King" of the South. From the menace of invasion from Nubia he was protected by the natural barrier of the first cataract, while to the north some peaceful agreement on frontiers seems to have been made with the Red King. Across the river from Nekheb stood Edfu, one of the greatest centers of Horus cult, and the White King boasted of close identification with this god (though it must be remembered that the Red King was likewise a "follower of Horus"). Nekhbet, vulture goddess of the South, also had special care for the southern king and his city. On the royal head was worn a tall, white, sugar-loaf-shaped crown; a cluster of water lilies was a common symbol of him and his kingdom.

The shadowy White and Red Kings were regarded in later mythology as the offspring of the great gods who in early days had ruled Egypt before ascending to the heavenly regions. At Sais and at Nekheb the worship of the old rulers of North and of South continued far down into historic days.

CHAPTER « 13

NAIVE ORIGIN MYTHS

ANCIENT scientists of the Red Kingdom established a system of dating admirably practical. They observed that the beginning of Nile's inundation about coincided with the appearance of Sothis (Sirius or The Dog Star), as morning star, and that these two events seemed to recur at intervals of 365 solar days. The number 365¼ represents, of course, the accurate figure, but this divergence was not appreciated. They established a year, then, of twelve thirty-day months and five intercalary days, initiating their calendar in 4241 B.C. Now, it is obvious that the Sothic Festival (a religious solemnity commemorating Sothis' appearance and the beginning of the inundation) was destined to creep forward on the artificially constructed calendar, until after a little matter of 1,460 years it would reach the position of a true New Year Day. Sothic New Year Days, thus, occurred in 2780 and 1320 of the old era and 140 of the new.

Just an example or two to illustrate how from the above data it is possible to fix events in Egyptian history in terms of B.C. In the tenth year of Sesostris II, a contemporary record informs us, the Sothic Festival occurred on the fifteenth day of the eighth month; that is to say, on the 225th day of the calendar year. Now the reader will recall that, because of the ¼ inaccuracy in the calendar, a constant astronomical phenomenon such as the rising of Sothis must be a full day later every fourth calendar year. The 225, then, of the Sesostrian record must be multiplied by 4 to bring us back to the date when the Sothic Festival was a true New Year Day. Now 225 × 4 gives 900. It follows then that the last Sothic New

Year, namely 2780, minus these 900 years, brings us onward to 1880 B.C. as the tenth year of Sesostris II. He was the fourth Pharaoh of the Twelfth Dynasty and other records establish that the combined reigns of his three predecessors lasted 110 years. To authentic Egyptian history is thus added 2000 B.C. as the date of the beginning of the Twelfth Dynasty. Similarly, a computation based upon a record of a Sothic date in the reign of Amenhotep I proves the accession of the Eighteenth Dynasty to have occurred in 1580, while a third Sothic date determines that the Egyptian Napoleon, Thutmose III, ruled from 1501 to 1447.[1]

Many other calculations have contributed (or rather are contributing, for the work is by no means completed) to the settling of Egyptian chronology. A date from which we can reckon backwards is furnished by Cambyces' conquest in 525 B.C. A tolerably complete list of the Pharaohs has been compiled from the history of the Ptolemaic priest Manetho (283–246 B.C.) as corrected by tomb records unearthed in modern times. From carved or written panegyrics of dead rulers of the Nile valley precise information has been derived as to the length of individual reigns and as to the relative dates of important events. When conquest and trade brought contacts with Palestinian and Babylonian civilizations, comparative chronology entered as a factor in the dating of Egypt's history. Where records almost disappear, as for instance in the Dark Age following on the fall of the Sixth Dynasty, recourse must be had to meager references in later writings to estimate the probable duration of the obscure period.

Scholarly research upon all the above sources of information may be said to have established a skeleton chronology, though one fundamentally reliable, of the Pharaonic reigns as far back

---

[1] On chronology cf. Breasted's *History of Egypt*, pp. 13–25, and his *Ancient Records of Egypt*, Vol. I, pp. 38–57. Also Weigall's *Tutankhamen and Other Essays*, pp. 158–170. Also *Dictionnaire Apologetique de la Foi Catholique*, s. v. "Egypte."

as 2160. Back of this date, the reckoning is subject to a variation error of about a hundred years on either side of any assigned date. In addition to the Pharaonic dates, a fair number of dates of outstanding events in the country's history have also been determined. We present on the two following pages the briefest of synopses, referring the reader to approved sources for a more comprehensive table.[2]

The outline here introduced may serve as a ready reference table for the coming chapters. Since we deal with the religion of the Egyptians, their history does not call for detailed treatment except when secular events had religious repercussions. Hence, the reader will readily see that neither carelessness nor lack of interest motivates the sketchiness which here and later characterizes the treatment of purely historical topics.

To Old Kingdom days belong our oldest written sources, namely, the inscriptions deciphered from the walls of pyramidal and other tombs, which go by the name of the *Pyramid Texts*. Their subject matter, while not exclusively religious, is largely so. They furnish, with the clearness peculiar to written sources, the first relatively adequate outline of the official faith of Egypt.[3] Beliefs in regard to the origin of the gods and of the world, man's nature and his afterlife, the efficacy of ritualistic and magical practices — such are the central doctrines of the "creed" presented by the *Pyramid Texts*. For the remainder of the present chapter we shall confine ourselves to the cosmogonic and theogonic notions, leaving the other points to be studied in the light thrown on them by the later developed theology.

Since this mythopoetic age of religious thought in Egypt ex-

[2] In our synopsis, the term "Period" is borrowed from modern Egyptologists to signify a span of years dominated by a distinctive political organization. "Dynasty" is Manetho's term for "ruling family."

[3] The theology taught by the powerful priesthoods — Heliopolitan, Memphite, Theban — and closely allied to the political power of the divine Pharaoh was the official and national religion. Together with it there flourished among the people the cult of local gods and a great body of superstitious practice.

Chronological Table of Egyptian History in Outline

Period	*Dynasty*	*Names*	*High Lights of History*	*Religious Development*
Old Kingdom	I–VI 3400–2475	Menes the unifier. Khufu builder of Great Pyramid.	Egypt unified under Menes of Thinis. Extension of system of irrigation. Copper mining in Sinaitic peninsula. Military expeditions in Nubia. Beginnings of commerce with Punt, Syria, the Mediterranean islands. Age of Great Pyramids.	Ra of Heliopolis, Ptah of Memphis, Horus and Osiris the greatest of the gods. Cosmogonic and Osirian myths. Imposing temple structures. Evidence of ritualistic and theologizing priesthood. Imhotep the Wise Man.
Dark Age	VII–X, 2475–2160		Disunion, struggle between Heracleopolis and Thebes, the latter finally triumphing.	
Middle Kingdom	XI–XII, 2160–1788	Intef I, reorganizer. Amenemhet III, promoter of public works.	Feudal state under Theban Pharaoh. Organization for justice, taxation, defense. A noteworthy literature. Class consciousness evinced by nobles, artisans, scribes. Irrigation marvels. Foreign commerce. Nubia conquered.	Amon, god of Thebes, syncretized into Amon-Ra and made sun-god. People exalt Osiris. Dramatic representations of his myth. Development of Osirian eschatology and mortuary customs. Important doctrinal and moral writings.
Hyksos	XIII–XVII, 1788–1580		Pretenders to power rapidly succeed, till Hyksos (Semitic raiders?) overrun and subdue land.	Destruction of many of finest religious monuments. Probable period of Joseph's viziership.
Thutmosid	XVIII,	Thutmose III, empire builder.	Military dictatorship from 3rd cataract to Euphrates. Wealth from	Theban priests of Amon dictates to crown, extorts revenue.

Empire	1580–1350	Iknaton, monotheist.	abroad, order at home. International politics. Graceful naturalism in art succeeds formalism of older schools. Through Ikhnaton's neglect internal and foreign affairs get in sad state.	Growth of magic. Temple of Karnak. Cliff tombs of unexampled grandeur. Ikhnaton defies Theban priests and propagates monotheism with Aton as sole god.
Ramsid Empire	XIX–XX, 1350–1090	Ramses II	Harmhab restores internal order, Ramses II reconquers foreign vassals. Mercenaries. Golden Age of art, literature.	Theban priests again dominate. Ramesseum, mortuary temple, and other structures at Karnak. Sublime religious hymns. Hebrew exodus.
Libyan Kingdom	XXI–XXIII, 1090–718	Sheshonk I	Virtually foreigners holding loose control of land.	Reign of Solomon in Jerusalem probably coincides with early part of Libyan period.
Nubian Kingdom	XXIV–XXV, 718–663		A decadent period, ending with Egypt an Assyrian fief.	Hebrew Prophets make Egypt's humiliation a theme.
Saitic Kingdom	XXVI, 663–525	Necho	Renaissance of Old Kingdom ideas in art and government.	Isis worship popular. Formalism. Crass theriolatry.

The Persian Cambyces conquered Egypt in 525. Thereafter, except for the ephemeral periods called the XXVIII–XXX Dynasties, the country remained a province of the Great King till 332. The Persians were the XXVII Dynasty.

Alexander the Great seized Egypt in 332. With his death begins the long line of Ptolemaic rulers and the Hellenization of Egypt. The Ptolemies were the XXXI Dynasty.

Egypt became a Roman province in 30 B.C.

pressed its divine concepts not in philosophic form, but clothed in the garb of mythical story, precisely as was the case in the other countries already considered, we may here take occasion for offering some further remarks on the significance of mythology in a people's religion. All ancient races, with the possible exception of the strictly primitive, believed in myths which had come down to them from an immemorial antiquity. When the stories originated and who first told them, the people did not know. They were content to accept them with an acceptance that was fideistic and literal. For their minds these strange fairy tales of divine, cosmic, and human geneses, these biographies of gods and demigods served the purpose of apologetics. The myth caricatured the philosophic truths and historical facts which found genuine assent of faith. That is, it possessed a paregoric efficacy to quiet the intellect's craving to know the reason for faith.

The more accurately we can determine the origin and sense of a people's religious myths, the more adequate will be our understanding of their beliefs. The determination, however, presents many problems, nor is there at hand any one master key serviceable in their solution. A Catholic apologetic tendency — more zealous than wise and happily losing ground nowadays — once sought to read into all myths a survival of God's primitive revelation. On the other hand, consigned to the junk heap of wrecked totalitarian theories, now lies the Nature-myth theory, so ingeniously constructed by German scholars of the latter nineteenth and early present centuries, which interpreted all myths as stories symbolizing the operations of nature's great forces.[4] Both theories, while still useful as partial explanations, are now known to enunciate principles too restricted to cover the whole field of mythological fact.

---

[4] Of the Catholic tendency one striking example may be cited in the book entitled *Prehistoric Religion* by P. L. Mills whose orderly and laborious treatise is marred by too earnest an apologetic penchant. The name of Max Mueller is prominent among the Nature-myth promoters.

By courtesy of the Chicago Oriental Institute Museum

Fig. 14. Horus Falcon

The Egyptians associated the falcon with Horus and gave even his human figure a falcon head. The bird pictured above may have been used for oracular responses, since a hollow tube from beak to tail could have been used by the priests as a speaking tube, or else for moving the beak by means of strings.

As working rules for the interpretation of religious mythology, one might propose: first, the notion already stated that religious mythology is a species of naïve apologetic; second, that myth is distinguished from fiction in that the former embodies a kernel of fact. Thus a myth may be either embellished history (the euhemeristic-myth), or a story spun to justify an actual belief or practice (the aetiological-myth). An euhemeristic-myth has been analyzed in the preceding chapter. Aetiological-myths are as manifold as the desire of man for explanations is insatiable. To answer the question of origins, mythology tells of the hatching of the primeval egg, of the fashioning of beings on a potter's wheel, and so on. The tale of Demeter, Persephone, and Dis is an old Greek justification of the worship of the changing seasons. Almost every natural religion sought to make concrete its faith in an afterlife by apocalyptic myths describing that undiscovered country. Shrines, cult practices, sacred objects all secured a *raison d'être* for the veneration in which they were held through being woven into the myth history of the gods.

Of Egypt's myths the one meriting first attention is the origin story taught by the priests of Heliopolis, the ancient On in the eastern Delta. It told how in the beginning the god Atum dwelt in a chaos called Nu, from which he rose as Ra the sun. Atum is pictured as a human figure, Ra as a beetle-headed man or a hawk-headed man. The generations of Ra are Qeb (Earth) and Nut (Sky), Shu (Atmosphere) and Taphnut, the last named probably merely a pale double of Shu, introduced to fill out the parallel. These are all pictured as human figures. Now Shu, standing upon Qeb's midsection, raises Nut aloft so that her fingertips and toes alone touch Qeb's head and feet respectively. Of Qeb and Nut are born Osiris (the life-giving waters of Nile) and Isis (the fruitful earth); Set (the deadly desert) and Nephthys, another pale parallel. With the exception of Set, who has an opaki head, the last named four are pictured as human figures. The whole myth is an explanation of the origin of the material world, not of men; however, men were later introduced into it as the offspring either of Ra or of Nut and Qeb.

Still another naïve cosmological fancy showed Hathor, the Heavenly Cow, bestriding the earth. Her belly was studded with the stars, while Ra in his sun-boat made his daily journey along her length, just as in the preceding cosmological economy he traveled in his boat along the length of Nut.

Since the details of Horus' battles in behalf of Ra have been dwelt upon in a former chapter, we here merely recall from that legend how Ra struggled against enemies who disputed his rule. This struggle between good and evil appears in other early myths in variant forms. There is the cycle, for instance, in which the serpent Apophis figures, instead of Set, as the chief adversary. There is a story suggestive of the Prometheus myth which tells of Ra's eye being stolen and given to men, among whom it works cultural wonders. A retribution myth pictures the sun-god Ra as growing old. Men lose their respect for him and try to throw off his authority. In punishment he sends the goddess Hathor to slaughter them. She undertakes her task so zealously that the Nile valley is inundated with human blood and Ra repents of the severity of his judgment, resolving to save a few of the rebels. He, therefore, has beer brewed and mixed with the blood. Hathor, drinking of the mixture, becomes so intoxicated that she cannot see to finish the job.

There is a savagery of concept about these early myths that allies them to the myths of races properly called savage, such as, for instance, many American Indian tribes; African tribes except the primitives; Australian tribes, with a like exception. We here have instances of what the ethnologists call the *Fortgeschrittene Kulturen*. What is strange, is that the Egyptians with a rigid conservatism carried over the crude concepts of the savage days of their prehistory into periods when they are definitely one of the loftiest civilizations of antiquity. No

Egyptian Homer arose to beautify and soften these nightmare fancies. Even when, in Empire days priestly religious speculation arrived at relatively sublime appreciation of the divine attributes, the harshness of the orthodox mythology was but slightly tempered.

Egypt's origin myths return a disappointingly negative answer to the eager searcher for vestiges of the primitive revelation. Creation certainly cannot be read into the "organization" myth narrated in the preceding pages. (Later on, we shall find what is perhaps a nearer approach to this great concept in studying the Memphite god Ptah.) The enthusiasm of a Doctor Mills alone will see in the dualism of Ra and his adversaries, in man's rebellion against the senescent sun-god, a garbled version of the history of our first parents' defection. The Nile valley inundated with blood, together with Ra's purpose of rescuing a few from Hathor's vengeance, is too faintly reminiscent of the Biblical narrative of the deluge to be seriously interpreted as a survival.

CHAPTER • 14

GREAT GODS OF THE EARLY TIME

REMARK has been made on the conservatism of the Egyptian religious mind. A miserly unwillingness to part with any element ever held sacred in the Nile valley soon led to a body of belief vast and intricate. Especially is this the case with the pantheon. To quote Professor E. A. W. Budge: "The denizens of heaven consisted of the Great and the Little Companies of the gods; and of a large number of beings who may for convenience be called the inferior gods [e.g., the Assessors in the Tuat, the region of the dead]; and of several orders of beings who possessed some characteristic which caused the Egyptians to assume that they were divine [e.g., the Swallower in the same Tuat]; and of the shadows, doubles, spiritual bodies, souls, powers, hearts, and spirits of those who had lived upon this earth [for the accepted psychology held a manifold composition in the human being]."[1]

With a view to orderly treatment of this complex subject, we shall confine our present attention to the great gods of the first eleven dynasties, whose rule extended approximately from the year 3400 to 2120.

Since nothing further need be added in explanation of Nut, Qeb, and Shu to what was said in the last chapter, and since the important Osiric-Isiac theology may more conveniently be treated in later pages, only Ra of the eleven cosmological divinities demands further analysis. His emergence from primeval chaos under a new name and as a sun-god seems to indicate a bit of syncretic theology thought

---

[1] *The Gods of the Egyptians* (London: Methuen & Co., 1904), Ch. V. The bracketed phrases are not the author's, but illustrate his classifications.

up to justify his substitution for Atum, the old god of Heliopolis. As sun-god, a personal being undoubtedly, he begets of his own substance other personal beings who are the elements of the material universe. If we recall that it required centuries of Greek philosophy to disentangle the personality of the divine being from its identification with material nature, the clumsy savagery of the Egyptian god-concepts will seem less strange.

After all, there is something better here than crass materialism. Ra moves through the universe by day in his royal sun-barge attended by other gods, passing at evening beneath the western horizon into the region of the Tuat or of the dead. Just as the myth, narrated in former pages, shows him as lord of living men, so the dead beheld him as avenger and rewarder, who received the just into the fellowship of his sun-barge during the night and who directed avenging spirits in their torments of the wraiths of the wicked. He takes the living Pharaoh for his son and establishes his rule against all his enemies; the dead Pharaoh he raises to his own level of divinity. In pictorial representation, the body of Ra is anthropomorphic, while his head is either the sun-disk surmounted by the uraeus serpent gardant, or a beetle representing him as the rising sun, or a hawk head. In the latter instance he is identified with the hawk-god Horus and regarded as flying over the vault of the heavens. He carries the crooked scepter characteristic of Egyptian royalty and the odd hooked symbol of life.

Principal feminine counterpart of Ra was Hathor, though she entered Egypt on a different stream of religious ideas than the solar theology. Somaliland, probably, was the soil of her origin and her attributes were those of a mother-goddess and principle of fecundity. How the Heliopolitan priests wove her into the myth of their sun-god has been already noted, while a similar syncretism with the Osiric religion was effected by identifying her with Isis. Pictorially, she is the Celestial

Cow holding the sun-disk between her horns, if her role in the Ra legend is to be symbolized; or she is a woman crowned with horns, disk, and erected serpent, and rattling the joyful sistrum, if her identification with Isis is meant.

The entanglements of Horus with the various skeins of mythology was inevitable, for he was the great god of the early dynasts and his name the talisman of their power. Perhaps no better illustration of the apologetic aspect of mythology is at hand than the assignment to Horus of such diverse mythological rules, that so his worship might stand justified before every scruple of belief. Hathor was made out to be his mother as well as Isis. Osiris was variantly his father or his brother. Ra was rescued by him in the primeval battle and received the hero as coregent of the heavens. Horus was equally with Ra the tutelary of the reigning Pharaoh. For Horus both the orthodox eschatologies make room, so that we find him sailing through the Tuat in the sun-boat as well as performing important functions in the Osiric hereafter. He is pictured as a man, a child, a hawk-headed man or a hawk. He bears as attributes, with readily understood symbolism, the double crown of Egypt, the horns-disk-serpent crown, the papyrus sheaf, the lotus flower, the symbol of life.

When Ra's eye has been stolen and given to men, the ibis-headed god of Hermopolis searched for it and brought it back. This was Thoth, originally a supreme god in his own right, but subordinated like many another to the great god of the Heliopolitan system. Reminiscences of his original importance are recognizable in such attributes as "heart of Ra," i.e., his reason or understanding. Being thus associated with the thoughts of the supreme god, Thoth through anthropomorphic fancy became his inseparable physical companion and scribe. Close to the sun-god he stands in the daily and nightly journeys through the heavens and the Tuat, his ibis head cocked attentively and his stylus poised, as beseems a good secretary. This close association could not but lead to a development of Thoth's functions, so that in later explanations he stood as inventor of the hieroglyphs, as the teacher of all cultural arts to man, as the Egyptian counterpart of the Greek Hermes and inspirer of the Hermetic Writings. A very early adaptation of him to the solar theology made him out to be the moon. In all periods he had for familiar the ape, though he never appears, as one might expect, as an ape-headed god, but always ibis-headed. He and Isis were, beyond all others, the patron divinities of Egyptian magicians and many a myth tells of the tricks and spells these two employed to hoodwink both the celestial and the terrestrial citizenry.

Balancing Thoth among the goddesses was placed Maat. She personified physical and moral law, order and truth. Essentially she was in earliest times, and remained, a divinity closely akin to the Deified Abstracts (Fides, Spes, Pax, etc.), which appear in Roman religion. What mythology attached to her appears to be mere symbolism, as when in the afterworld judgment the soul is weighed in the balance against the Maat-plume. This plume is an ostrich plume and when Maat is represented in the monuments she is a woman holding the symbol of life and crowned with the ostrich plume.

Ptah entered into power with the Memphite family which founded the Third Dynasty. Although he did not replace Ra as head of the solar theology, his own proper attributes were publicized and magnified by the Memphite priests and for a time he stood at the head of a rival theological system and never lost rank as one of the greater of Egyptian divinities. He is the god who fashioned all living and inanimate beings. The concept of "fashioning," in its cruder form, is that of molding from clay primeval; in its elaborated form it knocks at the door of the concept of creation. To illustrate, we quote from a work attributed by Breasted to a date between 3400 and 3000.[2]

---

[2] Breasted's dating is disputed by others, such as Weideman in *Hastings Encyclopedia,* and can only be taken as the more probable dating. The oldest extant copy is of the eighth century B.C.

The Memphite gods are in the mouth of Ptah, which pronounces the names of all things. . . . Ptah made Atum and caused the gods to be. He fashioned the gods: everything has come forth from him. . . . Thus it was found that Ptah's strength was greater than all gods, and thus was Ptah satisfied after he had made all things and every divine word. He fashioned the gods, he equipped their shrines. Thus the gods and their functions gathered to him, the Peaceful, the Reconciler.

From our roster of great gods of the early time are omitted Amon, who grew great only in the Middle Kingdom, and the Osirian family, which can be studied conveniently in the light of later developments. What circumstances led to the making of a great god cannot, for the most part, be accurately determined. A certain universality of functions seems to have been required as a condition, but the real cause seems rather to have been the rise to political importance of a particular district, sweeping a local god along to a position of eminence. Once arrived, the great god was tolerant of all others, but one probably would err in taking this as an indication of commendable broadmindedness in the votaries. What is indicated, is a superstitious fear lest the other gods might retain "potent medicine," and so low a valuation of divine attributes as to be content with giving the great god the station of "primacy of honor."

Besides employing the device of syncretic polyonomy, as in the case of Amon-Ra, and besides casting all possible gods for roles in the composite mythological fancies, theologizers had recourse to the ennead and the triad to emphasize the relation of the great god with others. The ancient Ra ennead has been noted above, and is typical. With the chief god are associated, by a loose bond of similarity or complementariness of function and often by the fiction of generation, four pairs of divinities, a male and a female in each case. In cult observances they are treated as a group. Of divine triads Mediterranean religions are prolific, as witness Zeus-Hera-Athene and Demeter-Persephone-Dis, with their Roman counterparts.

Cast in the Chicago Oriental Institute Museum from original in British Museum

Fig. 15. The Rosetta Stone

The subject of this highly important monument is the praises of Ptolemy Epiphanes on the occasion of his coronation as Pharaoh in 196 B.C. Since three scripts — Greek, Hieroglyphic, and Demotic — were here employed for an identical inscription, the stone afforded linguists their chief clue in deciphering the Egyptian language.

Egypt knew, among others, Ptah-Sokhmit-Nefertum and Amon-Mut-Khonsu. The fictitious bond in the triad is commonly that of father, mother, and child and the three are made a group in worship. The construction of the Egyptian triad, then, is artificial, as is that of the ennead. It is at best, a grouping for cult convenience of distinct gods on the scheme of the magical numbers three and nine. In Egyptian triads—need we remark?—there is no obumbration of Christian Trinitarian doctrine.

To smelt out the Egyptian concept of divinity from the ore of myth, laudation, and prayer-formula is a task apposite to the purposes of our present inquiry, but one which does not promise wholly satisfying results. It does not appear that any known record, even of later times, contains a definition of the word "god." Its ideogram is an ax,[3] while its hieratic equivalent is *neter*. Two root meanings, both tantalizingly suggestive, are assigned to *neter* (*a*) to strike, knock down or throw; (*b*) to grow, thrive, be young. May one find in this etymology a proof that the fundamental Egyptian concept of divinity was "irresistible power, immortal life"? It is wiser to be contented with the "not proven" answer, though tomes have been written in support of a categorical affirmative answer.

Certainly, an eclectic synthesis of the nobler attributes of the divine worthies already studied constitutes a reasonably sublime concept. Both Ra and Ptah rate as organizers of all material nature, as givers of all life. Hathor is considered to be the principle of renewal of life. Thoth personifies reason and understanding; Maat, law and truth. In the Tuat Ra rewards or punishes human conduct. In the worship of nature-gods, in general, there is a fumbling, though partial, apprehension of the power of the real God.[4] These were glimmers of light in the "night of the gods" that engulfed Egypt, but how insufficient they were to guide man to the truth amid the

---

[3] Usually single-bladed, though the double-bladed form is found. The ax was a symbol of divinity in ancient Crete, in Babylon, in Cappadocia.

[4] Cf. *Book of Wisdom*, Ch. 13.

jungle of superstition and magic and the monstrous shapes which haunted the darkness!

In Egyptian belief there was an order of superbeings, a godkind as real as is mankind. It was of crucial importance for the latter to acknowledge the former's suzerainty which extended to all the conditions which made human life comfortable here and blissful hereafter. Praise, thanksgiving, and sacrificial devoir were obvious corollaries. The complaisance of the gods was read in abundant crops, successful wars, and the like; their displeasure in the contrary occurrences. Their will in doubtful matters might be learned by oracles; their power might be constrained to the line of human desires by magical formulas. They had a concern for decent, just, and merciful conduct, and they duly sanctioned these in the afterlife.

There prevailed a crude anthropomorphism. Ra grows old and decrepit; he treads on a serpent, the poison of whose bite courses agonizingly through the divine arteries till the magician Isis cures him for a fee of part of his sovereignty. Osiris is hacked into fourteen parts, while his son Horus suffers headaches and "the gripes." How Hathor drank herself stone blind has already been told. Temple offerings of food were understood to be the furnishing forth of a hungry god's table. A stereotyped sepulchral incantation purported to secure godhead for the deceased by naming every one of his members a corresponding member of a divine body: "thy eye is the eye of Ra, thy right hand is the hand of Horus, etc." The Unas Papyrus tells how that cannibalistic shade would attain godhead by the digestive process, devouring all the gods he met in the nether world. But the point needs no further illustration, so clear is it that the gods physiologically and psychologically were conceived on the human model.

The question of monotheistic tendencies among the Egyptians will come up for discussion in connection with the Pharaoh Ikhnaton's reforms.

CHAPTER « 15

THE HOUSE OF MAN'S ETERNITY

OF NONE of Egypt's beliefs have we such adequate information as of her belief in the hereafter. Findings from thousands of prehistoric pit-burials have been studied, while for historic times mastabas, pyramids, and cliff tombs have told their stories to the relentless archeologist. So greatly, in fact, does the mass of mortuary survivals overshadow other records that Professor Petrie warns against a misconception of the Egyptian as a man far more interested in the future than in the present life. The permanent nature of the material used in tomb construction, and the custom of entombment in the dry western desert, well explain why more sepulchral evidence has survived than evidence of the busy secular life of the irrigated strip along the Nile.

For the present chapter a sketch will be attempted of the three historic tomb forms just mentioned — mastaba, pyramid, and cliff tomb. There will follow an inventory of tomb findings. Finally, the tenant of this house of eternity will come up for examination.

Shaped like the bench upon which the Egyptian *fellah* lounges before his hut, the first tomb form has received the name of *mastaba.* A rectangle with sides sloping at about a 75-degree angle, it is a solid mass of brick and mortar, except for two openings: a shaft piercing the top toward the southwest corner and a door cut in the eastern front. The shaft descended to the native rock below the mastaba structure proper, and in this native rock was cut the burial chamber. Down the shaft, after being duly mummified, the dead man was lowered, to rest in wooden coffin and stone sarcophagus. Now the

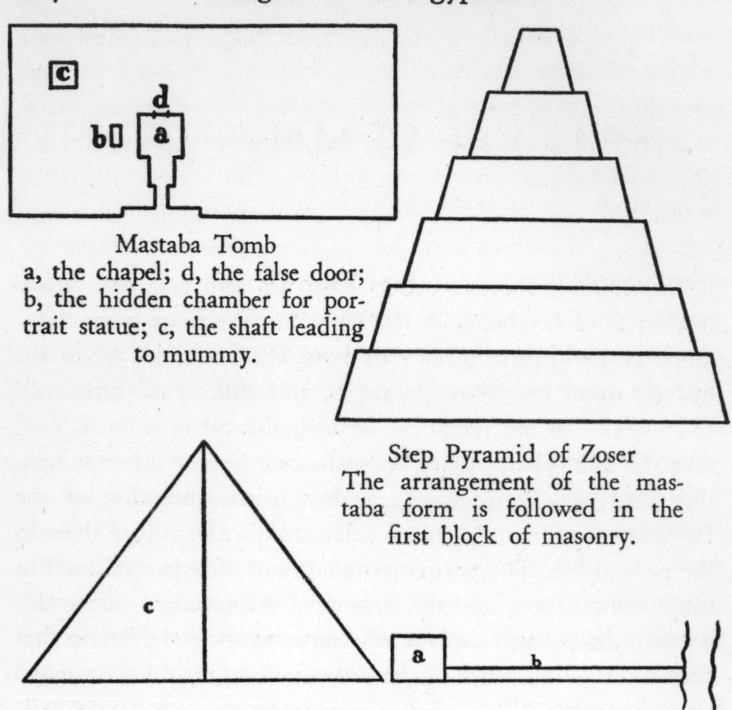

Mastaba Tomb
a, the chapel; d, the false door; b, the hidden chamber for portrait statue; c, the shaft leading to mummy.

Step Pyramid of Zoser
The arrangement of the mastaba form is followed in the first block of masonry.

Pyramid of Cheops
Length of side at base 755 ft.; height by plumb line from top to center of base 481 ft.; a, the mortuary temple; b, the causeway leading up from Nile; c, the concealed opening in eighteenth tier of stones leading through labyrinth of passageways to tomb chamber.

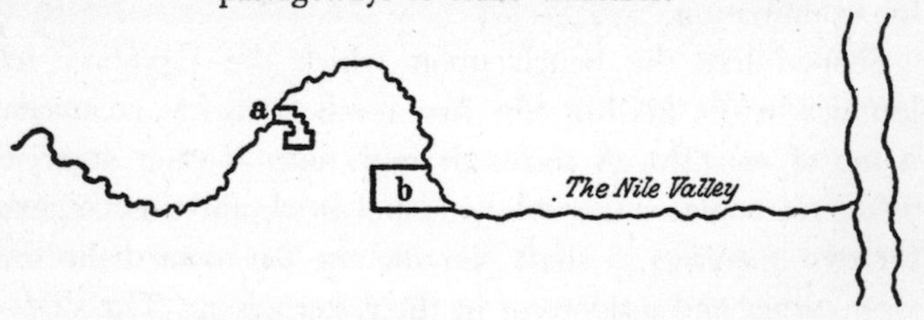

Valley of Tombs of Kings
a, the tomb opening leading through passages to tomb; b, the mortuary temple.

Fig. 16. Diagrams of Tomb Forms

chamber was sealed up and the shaft filled with sand and rubble. Entering the door on the eastern front, one walked through a narrow passage to the mortuary chapel, whose walls were covered with scenes depicting the dead man's servants busy with occupations tending to his comfort. It is from these scenes that most of our knowledge of daily life in Old Kingdom days is derived—of herding of cattle and tilling of fields, of bailiffs dragging delinquent taxpayers to the scribes for a reckoning, of artisans squatting cross-legged in the shops, of shipbuilding, of the recreations of the master in the hunting field or on the river. As has been remarked in a previous chapter, the painted and sculptured scenes were meant to afford the dead man the same satisfaction that he had derived from the realities during life. However, more material means were also taken to solace him. Provision of food and drink was maintained fresh in the mortuary chapel together with toilet accessories, such as eye paint, so essential to the well-groomed Egyptian. To enjoy these comforts the spirit of the dead entered the mortuary chapel either through a false door pictured at its western side or from the *serdab*. This latter was a secret chamber to the south of the chapel and contained the portrait-statue. The Pharaoh or wealthy noble constructed his mastaba tomb during life, at great expense, and willed permanent endowment for its upkeep, for the offerings, and for the sustenance of the priests who conducted services in the mortuary chapel.

With the Memphites and the Third Dynasty the mastaba developed into the step-pyramid and the pyramid. Zoser, the first of the line, imposed on his mastaba five successively smaller rectangles, to effect a transition form and to fire Professor Mills with the fancy that here was an Egyptian reminiscence of the Tower of Babel. Snefru added another rectangle to his own construction, but seemed to have been dissatisfied with the result and leveled off the sides by filling in the steps. He also built another and true pyramid, the first in all probability. From his time on all three forms appear — mastaba, step-pyramid, and pyramid — until the Thebans of the Middle Kingdom introduce the cliff-tomb idea. On page 124 we present a series of sketches of the various tomb forms.

With the pyramid form entered a change in mortuary arrangements. Now the mummy, whose inviolability had been secured by the deep shaft piercing the mastaba, was concealed deep in the interior masonry of the pyramid. From his vault a series of passages, often very intricate and after the burial blocked off one from another, led to a door somewhere on the sloping side of the pyramid. Yet even this door was carefully concealed by being surfaced over, for the fear of ghouls haunted the mind of the Egyptian. The fear was not so much of the theft of costly ornaments, but of the pain the dead man would experience in the hereafter through the disturbance of his mummy. The mortuary chapel was now a separate building, close to the pyramid and to its east. The Egyptians, it must be noted for clarity's sake, were sun-worshipers, and from this cult-idea had evolved elaborate superstitions in regard to east and west. Cemeteries were regularly on the west bank of Nile, for the west was the land of the setting sun, of Osiris, of the dead. In all tomb forms the mummy lay to the west of the chapel. This latter was the link between him and the land of the living, for into the chapel there entered from the east his friends to bring him gifts, while he himself came through the false door from the land of the west to refresh himself and to look out upon the scenes he had cherished and upon Ra rising in splendor beyond the Nile.

The dimensions of the Cheops pyramid (each side 755 feet at the base, with a height of 481 feet), afford some idea of the labor and expense of such a tomb. The wonder grows with our knowledge of the 2,300,000 finely dressed stones that it is estimated to contain, each one averaging a ton and a half. Nor were the quarries close at hand, but lay on the east bank of the Nile. Thus it was necessary to float the blocks over the stream before placing them. No less than 100,000 men labored for 20 years on Cheops' pyramid, narrates Herodotus, nor do his figures sound improbable in view of the magnitude of the task and the primitive character of the mechanism available.

The troublous times that marked the decay of Old Kingdom civilization, absorbing the Pharaohs' whole attention in holding together their imperiled country, probably account for the passing of the art of pyramid building. The structures steadily become more meager, are often of brick and of evidently hasty workmanship, till finally the form is abandoned in the Dark Age.

Theban princes restored order and one of them, Intef, established a new dynasty of Pharaohs. Thebes now being the capital city, it was natural that Abydos, located just opposite to it across the Nile and an ancient mortuary site, should be adopted as the royal cemetery. The dead Pharaoh had, of course, to see his capital when he gazed out across the river. Pyramid succeeded pyramid, but all were unpretentious as befitted feudal kings who had no power to commandeer unlimited revenues. But the problem of tomb robbery grew so acute that some other tomb form was sought than the conspicuous pyramid. (Ahmose I even went to the extreme of building a dummy pyramid filled with rubble, while constructing a secret tomb elsewhere.) A barren valley cut in prehistoric times by a vanished river behind the western cliffs offered an ingenious solution. Here, in the land of the west, the mummy could be secretly buried, while the temple could be erected with all the pomp of publicity on the eastern slope of the cliff. Thus, in the delusive hope of hoodwinking the ghouls, the Theban Pharaohs began to commission trusted officials with the task of piercing unobtrusively the western slope and cutting there tomb chambers for their overlords. This was the beginning of the Valley of the Tombs of the Kings, so highly publicized in Sunday pictorials since the day sixteen years ago when Mr. Howard Carter disturbed Tutankhamen's long sleep.

The mummy is naturally the first sepulchral object to be noticed. Effective means of preserving the dead body were known in Egypt in the fourth millennium and for all periods from this remote date down to the first centuries of Christianity there have been mummy finds. Technique and perfection of work varied, but the following description embraces essential details. The brain was removed through the nose, eye cavity, or an incision. After the removal of the viscera and heart and the washing of the abdominal cavity, a stone or metal scarab replaced the heart, and bundles of aromatic substances, the viscera. All incisions were now sewed up and the body immersed for several days in natron, apparently a solution of sodium chloride, sodium sulphate, potassium nitrate. Brain, heart, and viscera were separately treated before being placed in canopic jars, which were named from the heads that surmounted them the Four Sons of Horus. Reams of resin-treated cloth awaited the body as it came out of its natron bath, to swathe it in hundreds of tight folds. The swathed figure was received by a wooden coffin of a shape corresponding to the figure itself, then by a second but larger one, finally by a stone sarcophagus. The innermost coffin was painted to represent the mummy figure, but the hands were shown bearing Osiric symbols as also was a conventionalized face with the Osiric beard. The Underworld and its gods furnished the motif for the decoration of the second coffin and sometimes for carvings on the sarcophagus.

Enough mummies have been unwrapped to satisfy archeological curiosity as to the state of preservation. Flesh, teeth, and hair are commonly perfectly intact. A certain amount of shrinkage has occurred in the body. Coloring varies between black, dark brown, and dark green. Usually the flesh is leatherish and brittle. The motive for the desecration of so many mummies is revealed in the gold and semiprecious stones of

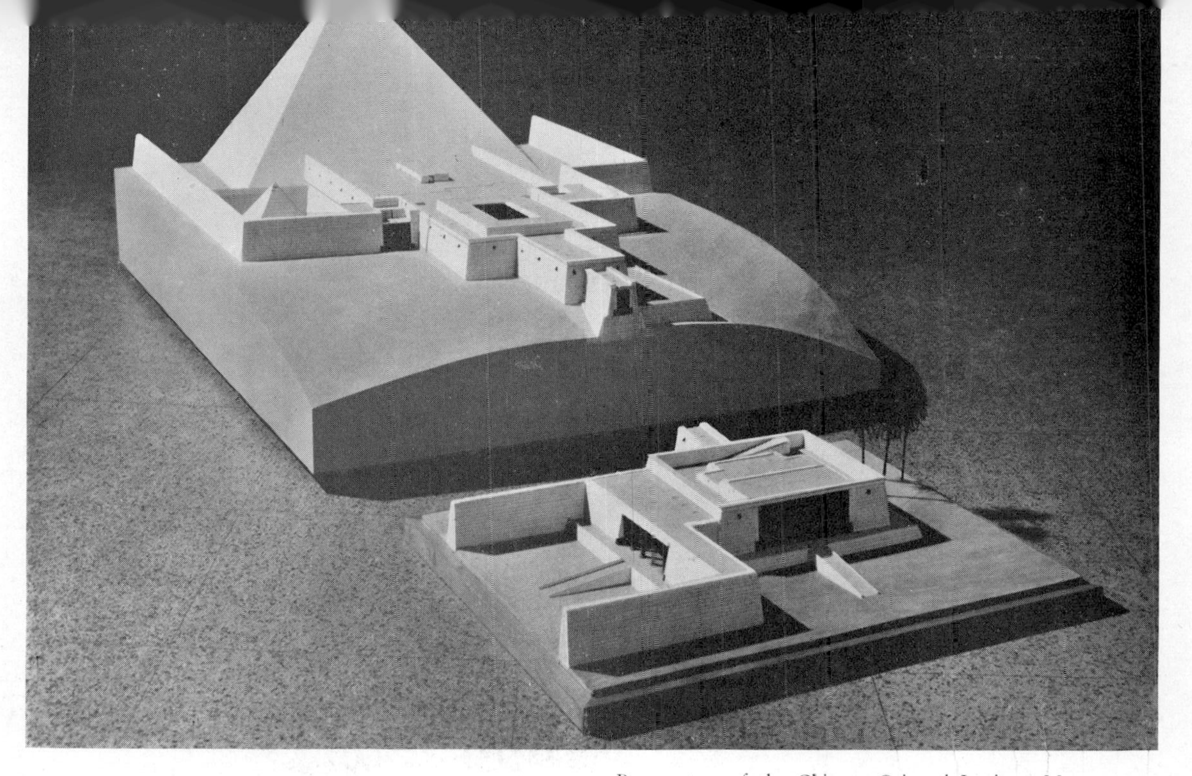

By courtesy of the Chicago Oriental Institute Museum

Fig. 17. A Pyramid and Adjoining Structures

In this reconstruction a covered causeway leads from the landing stage on the Nile to the mortuary chapel. Beside the chapel rises the small pyramid of the queen. On the western face of the great pyramid is cut the door to the secret passages which finally open into the tomb chamber of the Pharaoh.

By courtesy of the Chicago Oriental Institute Museum

Fig. 18. Preparing Bread for the Tomb's Tenant

With Pharaoh or noble were buried statuettes of servants, which were believed to be magically animated to attend him in the Afterworld. Here the process of bread-making is gone through the necklaces, rings, and magic amulets with which the body is adorned.

Two indispensable paintings on mummy coffins were an eye and a false door, both looking eastward. This was a bit of psychological naïveté expressive of the belief that the mummy might look out complacently upon his well-furnished room or even come out of his case and enjoy the useful and pleasurable objects the room contained. Enough has been said about the elaborate mural paintings which satisfied the dead man according to the law of magic: "The image supplies for the reality." The realities themselves, however, were added, even to the overcrowding of the narrow vault.[1] If inclined to rest, the spirit of the dead had his choice of splendid chairs, couches, and beds — a royal throne, too, if he had been a Pharaoh. He might mount again his favorite chariot, for it was at hand, or seat himself again in the Nile boat for a pleasure trip or a duck-shooting expedition. Wardrobe chests furnished change of raiment; walking staves and weapons leaned against the wall. To satisfy his hunger there was a sufficiency of grain and of embalmed beef, venison, ducks; while table furniture was complete, even to the napkins, flowers, and candlesticks. Reed mats protected his feet from the chilly stone floor. Finely wrought vases and jewels gave aesthetic enjoyment.

Of especial religio-magical import are the portrait statues of the deceased and certain doll-sized figures. The common material of the portrait statue is wood, which is carved and painted into some of the most lifelike representations of ancient times. In the statue the spirit of the dead man was thought to reside, which was probably the reason why tomb robbers superstitiously crashed in the statue's eyes, lest their

[1] The sepulchral room was never large, twenty-five by twelve feet being about the average. Sometimes, as in the case of Tutankhamen's tomb, several connecting rooms were cut in the rock to accommodate the great amount of sepulchral furniture.

sacrilege be seen and punished. Statuettes might replace or supplement the life-sized figure. Statuette groups regularly were employed to represent the man's servants busily engaged in baking, brewing, cooking. On a scale still smaller than these statuette groups was molded the soul-house, a furnished dwelling which a two-inch Liliputian might inhabit. A final testimony to triumphant magic is to be noted in the *ushebtti*. These miniature human figures, the "respondents," carried the tools of various manual laborers and were magically consecrated to empower them to answer in the dead man's name and to do the work assigned him in the Afterworld.

The best preserved of all papyri finds come from the tombs. Their subject matter is, however, restricted to texts from the Book of the Dead, scenes of the imagined Afterlife, magical incantations. The production of papyrus rolls for the dead was evidently highly commercialized, for the text and the scenes are so uniform and stereotyped that we must conclude that the rolls were prepared in quantity and kept in stock. Blanks were left for the insertion of the name and figure of the purchaser. Some papyri, however, are highly individualized. We will take up the religious ideas found in the papyri in connection with Osirianism.

The supposed tenant of the tomb presents problems more complex than any connected with the furnishings of his house. The Egyptians, at least till they came in contact with Greek thought in Ptolemaic days, held a psychology more akin to the dreamy vagaries of their uncivilized African neighbors than to anything soberly rational. Egyptologists have attempted interpretations of the confusing mass of evidence, but the variety of these interpretations is a proof that we may not hope for clear ideas on the subject of what the Egyptian believed in regard to soul and body. As well try to reduce to scholastic propositions the psychology propounded by Mrs. Eddy in *Science and Health*.

Egyptian psychology, to dignify it by this term, was polytomic. (Scholastic psychology, in contrast, is dicotomic, holding man to be composed of the two parts, body and soul.) There was the flesh, *aifu,* or the material elements of the human body. There was further the "double," *ka,* of a more subtle matter. There was next the "shadow," *haibit,* still more subtle. There was the "ghost," *khu,* perhaps of a finer texture than the preceding three. And finally still other terms occur which either are synonyms of the above or are further complications. But let us be satisfied with four. The comparison of four envelopes of decreasing size and coarseness is clumsy, but may serve as phantasm to illustrate how the four parts mentioned were interrelated.

The coming into existence of a human being was equally complicated. A "creator" god, such as Ptah, pronounced the *ran* or name of an individual (e.g., Amenhotep), and so constituted the individual as one the god destined for human existence. Actual existence came through the operation of natural forces, but life properly so called was given to the *ran-ka-aifu-khu-haibit* compound when a god touched the nostrils with the "symbol of life."

Death may be best understood as the separation of the *ka* from the other elements. As a condition for the happiness of the liberated *ka,* or even for its survival, the mummification of the body was required. The *ka* seems to be the nearest approach to the concept of a soul surviving after death that the Egyptians knew. The *ka* lived in the region of the dead, the Tuat, but at pleasure returned to the tomb to enjoy the good things there set out for it. In the tomb chamber it reentered the body or took up residence in one of the portrait statues.

This chapter on sepulchral beliefs and customs may be fittingly closed and the next one on the Afterworld fittingly introduced with two quotations. The first is the advice given by the scribe Ani to his son:

I pray thee to set before thee the path that must be traversed, and let old age testify to thee this fact. Thou must be found to have prepared for thyself a fine tomb in the cemetery in the mountain, which shall be the Tuat that shall hide thy body. I pray thee to set it before thy eyes in the midst of thy daily occupations, even as did the very ancient ones who now rest in their sepulchres. . . . The messenger of death shall come to thee to take thee, he shall find thee provided with a tomb, assuredly thou shalt have no anxiety. Verily his terrifying form will come and set itself before thee. Say not: "I am too young to be snatched away." Death comes and bears away the child who is at the breast of his mother, as well as the man who has reached old age.[2]

Looking now beyond the tomb, the "Egyptian Job" speaks:

Death is before me today
Like the recovery of a sick man,
Like going forth into a garden after sickness.
Death is before me today
Like the odor of myrrh,
Like sitting under the sail on a windy day.
Death is before me today
Like the course of a freshet,
Like the return of a man from the war-galley to his house.
Death is before me today
As a man longs to see his house,
When he has spent many years in captivity.[3]

---

[2] Trans. by Sir Wallis Budge.

[3] Trans. by Breasted in *The Dawn of Conscience,* p. 178. By permission of Charles Scribner's Sons.

CHAPTER « 16

OSIRIS, ISIS, HORUS

THE science of History of Religions is not a branch of Christian Apologetics. In other words, the Catholic who studies pagan cults with the express purpose of defending or confirming the divinely revealed origin of Christianity is guilty of interpolating a formal object into his inquiry different from the true formal object of the science of the History of Religions. For this science aims at determining, by a method strictly comparative and inductive, what were the causes that originated and developed man's complex religious history. The certainties that will emerge in the progress of such a science can, of course, no more contradict the certainties we hold by revelation than can the certainties emerging from the progress of geology and astronomy. Now, Catholic geologists and astronomers do not turn their respective sciences into grindstones for their apologetic axes. Neither should the Catholic in the field of History of Religions, even though this field contacts the field of revealed religion, change the scientific attitude of mind and the scientific purpose for the apologetic.

To be sure, it may annoy a Catholic scholar to be met with assertions such as the following in works otherwise learned and judicious:

To mention first a fundamental point of theology, it is probable that the worship of the Egyptian triad Isis, Serapis, and the child Horus helped to familiarize the ancients with the idea of a triune god and was not without influence in the formulation of the doctrine of the trinity as set forth in the Nicaean and Athanasian creeds.[1]

Indeed her [Isis'] stately ritual, with its shaven and tonsured priests, its matins and vespers, its tinkling music, its baptism and aspersions of holy water, its solemn processions, its jeweled images of the Mother of God, presented many points of similarity to the pomps and ceremonies of Catholicism. The resemblance need not be purely accidental. Ancient Egypt may have contributed its share to the gorgeous symbolism of the Catholic Church as well as to the pale abstractions of her theology.[2]

The knowledge of the ancient Egyptian religion which we now possess fully justifies the assertion that the rapid growth and progress of Christianity in Egypt were due mainly to the fact that the new religion, which was preached there by St. Mark and his immediate followers, in all its essentials so closely resembled that which was the outcome of the worship of Osiris, Isis and Horus that popular opposition was entirely disarmed.[3]

Here is a familiar theme song. Whether blatantly proclaimed or artfully insinuated, hostility toward the supernatural is broadcast in most books on the history of religions. Christianity — so runs the burden of the bland indoctrination — must have derived from pagan prototypes and can have nothing transcendently divine in its origins. Osirianism, or Isaism, the particular phase of Egyptian religion now under consideration, is one pagan prototype confidently adduced. Trinity, Incarnation, Divine Motherhood, Resurrection of the body, Heaven and Hell are dogmas allegedly borrowed from the Osiris-Isis-Horus cult.

For reasons detailed in a preceding paragraph, we do not purpose an explicit refutation of the slanders just noted. An objective account, such as we do purpose to give, will adequately damn the preposterous assertion of Christian dogmatic borrowings. The question of liturgical and ritualistic

---

[1] *Survivals of Roman Religion,* Gordon J. Laing (Longmans, Green & Co., 1931), pp. 128, 129. Serapis is for Ptolemaic and Roman days the same as Osiris.

[2] *The Golden Bough,* Sir J. G. Frazer (Macmillan, 1935), Part IV, Vol. II, pp. 118, 119.

[3] *The Gods of the Egyptians,* Sir E. A. W. Budge (Methuen, 1904), Vol. II.

borrowings is of less importance, since there is, in general, no inconvenience in admitting that the Church took over from paganism certain decorous and expressive external forms.

The presentation of objective facts begins now with a narration of the Osiris myth. Osiris and his sister Isis were born of Earth and Sky. Wedding his sister, he became the first ruler of the then savage Egypt and taught the people reverence for the gods and for a wise code of laws. When Isis discovered wheat and barley, Osiris taught their cultivation to his subjects and so won them from their gorges on human flesh to a farinaceous diet. Teaching them, too, to grow fruit trees and to train the vine, he established Egypt as an agricultural land. In fact he made his agricultural zeal the occasion for a world tour during which he publicized the high vitamin value of cereals.

As too often happens, affairs at home went badly as a result of this excurrent missionary zeal. Set, his villain brother, ambitioned the kingship and with his henchmen plotted Osiris' destruction. At a banquet on the king's return there was brought in a precious casket, into which Set proposed that each of the guests should lie. He whom it fitted exactly was to receive it as a prize. The origin of the myth in a near primitive state of society is confirmed by the character of this contest, for only rustic bumpkins would think up such an idea. However that may be, when Osiris stretched his length in the casket, the conspirators nailed tight the lid and floated the casket on the Nile. Carried out to sea, it was cast up finally at Byblus in Syria, where a great tree grew miraculously to enclose the royal coffin in its trunk. But the king of Byblus was seeking fine timber for his new palace, so he detailed a group of his workmen to bring in the miraculous tree trunk to serve as one of the pillars. Osiris—let it be noted to keep the record straight—had given up the fight by this time against these extraordinary vicissitudes and lay peacefully dead in the coffin within the tree trunk in the palace in Syrian Byblus.

Isis searched in vain for the body of her spouse and so roused the ire of Set. By advice of Thoth she concealed herself in the papyrus swamps under the protection of the serpent goddess Buto, and there gave birth to the child Horus, the destined avenger of Osiris' murder. Learning at last the whereabouts of the fateful coffin, she journeyed to Byblus, where she took service as nurse to the king's son. As reward for her services she was allowed to remove the body of Osiris to her Delta refuge. New tribulations ensued when Set, on a hunting expedition, happened on the body and savagely rent it in fourteen pieces which he scattered along the Nile valley. The devoted Isis found the pieces and sat down to mourn with her sister Nephthys. Their grief moved Ra to send Thoth and the jackal-god Anubis, by whose magical aid the two sisters and the boy Horus reunited the members of the body. Isis fanned life back into the corpse, but it was a life to be lived henceforth in the Underworld, where he exchanged his role of an earthly king for that of a king and judge of the dead.

The last chapter of the myth treats the exploits of Horus. A vision of his murdered father enjoined on him, now arrived at manhood, the duty of revenge. He accordingly sought out his murderous uncle and they squared off in deadly combat, a combat which mythological fancy has adorned with bizarre details. Poetical justice, of course, won out as it always does in stories and all too infrequently in life, Set being conquered and yielding the kingdom to the young hero Horus. But Set took an appeal to the supreme court of the gods on the plea that Horus was no true son of Osiris. The august judges declared for Horus' legitimacy.[4]

A study of the characters who play out this myth drama

---

[4] Plutarch's *Isis and Osiris* is followed in the above narration of the myth, though some of his details are modified to conform to more recent findings of Egyptologists. Plutarch, writing early in our own era, learned the myth in a form that combined Hellenic mythological elements with those originally Egyptian.

will bring us nearer to a correct understanding of Osirianism. Osiris himself was an agricultural deity and personification of the nature-force that energizes growing plants. Such he was to his original votaries in Northeastern Libya. On his migration into Egypt, it became obvious to identify him with the Nile, whose waters there are the determinant of fertility. The Heliopolitans legitimized the popular Libyan god by spinning the myth that he sprang of Qeb and Nut. The Babylonian invasion, solarized him as Lord of the West and of the setting sun. As Osiris' popularity increased, the people hailed him as lord of all life and lord of everything. Parallel with these attributes, which we may say in general are those of a nature god, were his eschatological attributes. As far back as our written sources go, namely to the Pyramid Texts and the Memphite Drama, the passing of Osiris from the throne of Egypt to the throne of the Underworld is clearly narrated. The funereal preparation of a dead body was all in imitation and in magical union with the funereal preparation of Osiris' body as told in the myth. Though in Old Kingdom days Ra's suzerainty permitted Osiris only a secondary role in eschatological theology, the Middle Kingdom established Osiris firmly as king and judge of the dead.

In his character of fertility god Osiris is represented lying prone while plants grow from his body. Pictures of him in his solar role are rare, a testimony to the fact that his solarization was a vain syncretic adaptation and never a tenet of popular belief. The standard ikon is that of a human figure mummified, surmounted by the sugar-loaf royal crown, whose hands hold the scepter and the scourge. Symbolic representations of him are the tree and the pillar, reminiscent of details of the myth. At Memphis a sacred bull Apis was reverenced in the temple as a "god-body" inhabited by Osiris. From the name given this bull, combined with the name of Osiris, is derived the name Serapis under which the Egyptian god of the dead entered the Roman world. For the transitional stages see Chapter 32 on "Oriental Cults at Rome."

Whence Isis originally came and even what were her original attributes, it is impossible to determine. Possibly she was a fertility goddess imported in prehistoric days from Syria. In Egypt her earliest ascertainable character is that of the divine spirit which made fruitful the earth of the Nile's banks. Her marriage to Osiris, the Nile water, is a natural mythological expression of the respective functions of these two divinities. They were, as has been seen, introduced into the Heliopolitan royal family as grandchildren of old king Ra. Astronomically, too, the bond between Isis and Osiris was emphasized by the former's identification with Sothis, whose appearance as day-star coincides with the beginning of Nile's inundation. She successively absorbed the functions of Hathor, both procreative and celestial; of Maat, as principle of truth and justice; and finally of every important goddess in the Egyptian pantheon. In funereal preparations she was regarded as a kind of supernal undertaker, whose magical operation, much more than the material means employed by the earthly undertakers, prepared the mummy for a happy sojourn in the Land of the West. In the successive stages of the soul's judgment she assisted, to present it finally before the judge Osiris.

Says Professor Budge: "She was water goddess, earth goddess, corn goddess, star goddess, queen of the Underworld, a woman uniting in herself one or more of the attributes of all the goddesses of Egypt. . . . She was, besides these things, the highest type of a faithful wife and mother."[5]

Of Egyptian magic she was the patroness, and weird and unseemly are the myths told of her in this role. Finally, in Ptolemaic and Roman days, she became such an object of devotion as to relegate to the background Osiris himself. To understand what she meant to her votaries in those later times, one has only to read her address to the Lucius of Apuleius' *Metamorphoses:*

---

[5] Budge, *The Gods of the Egyptians,* Vol. II, pp. 203 sq.

Behold, Lucius, I am come; thy weeping and prayer hath moved me to succor thee. I am she that is the natural mother of all things, mistress and governess of all the elements, the initial progeny of worlds, chief of the powers divine, queen of all that are in the lower regions, the principal of them that dwell in heaven, manifested alone and under one form of all the gods and goddesses. At my will the planets of the sky, the wholesome winds of the seas and the lamentable silences of hell are disposed. My name and my divinity are found throughout all the world in divers manners, in variable customs and by many names. For the Phrygians that are the first of all men call me the mother of the gods at Pessinus; the ancient folk of Attica, Cecropian Minerva; the sea-girt Cyprians, Paphian Venus; the mighty bowmen of Crete, Dictynnian Diana; the Sicilians who speak three tongues, infernal Proserpine; the Eleusinians, their ancient goddess Ceres; some, Juno; others, Bellona; others, Hecate; others, Rhamnusia; while both the Ethiopians who dwell near the rising sun and the Egyptians who excell in ancient learning observe my proper ceremonies and call me by my true name Queen Isis. Leave off thy weeping and put away all thy sorrow. . . . Know for certain that the rest of thy life shall be bound and subject to me. Thou shalt live blessed in this world, thou shalt live glorious by my guidance and protection. And when after thy allotted space of life thou descendest to the underworld, there thou shalt see me in that subterranean firmament shining in the darkness of Acheron and reigning in the deep profundity of Styx, and thou shalt worship me as one that has been favorable to thee. And if I perceive that thou hast been obedient to my commandments and devoted to my religion, meriting by thy constant chastity my divine grace, know thou that I alone may prolong thy days above the time that the fates have appointed and ordained.[6]

On the monuments Isis appears in two forms. In the one she is the conventionalized female figure of Old Kingdom days, clothed in a long close-fitting gown, with the sistrum she carries and the Hathor crown she wears as her distinguishing marks. (The sistrum, of course, is the ceremonial rattle used in her cult; the Hathor crown is the sun-disk surmounted by a serpent head and set between the horns of a cow.) The

[6] *Metamorphoseon,* L. XI, pp. 83 sqq. Translated by W. Adlington.

second representation is of Isis in her role of mother, seated and holding the infant Horus. A cow sometimes appears as an Isiac symbol. In the later period of her immense popularity, Isis is decked out in the borrowed plumage of the divinities whose functions she has absorbed, but the two forms mentioned just now persevered as the standard and most common ikons.

The attributes of Horus rival in complexity those of his mythical parents. A brief outline will suffice, since he has been considered in previous pages. He was, then, a sun-god. He was the Egyptian Heracles or divine hero victorious in epic combats against men and beasts. He was the avenger of rebellion and murder, the restorer of right order. He was the type of filial piety. In Afterworld function, as in funereal preparation, he was prominent, being both magical embalmer and warden of the soul in its progress through the halls of judgment. Horus is pictured as a hawk-headed man, kirtled in the Old Kingdom style, sometimes wearing Egypt's royal crown: he holds various symbols or weapons according to the scene depicted. As the child of Isis he appears as an unclothed bambino. The Harpocrates of the later Isiac religion (*Har-po-ḳrat,* meaning "Horus-the-child"), is furnished with an abbreviated mantle and a Phrygian cap and habitually holds his index finger on his lips.

Egyptian religion offers its contribution to the history of dualistic religious belief in the person of Set. For he enjoyed full divine honors, while being recognized as wholly malignant. Some interpreters would have him as a nature god of the wild desert which seemed ever encroaching on Egypt's fertile ribbon and threatening the people's destruction, but the explanation is myopic. His malignity was far more universal. In its physical aspects it comprehended the power of darkness, of the killing heat, of clouds and rain, of storm and earthquake; in short, of everything which tended to reverse the course of nature to man's detriment. This satan role of

Set is not confined to the Osirian theology, for he was the Darkness struggling against an old god of Light named Horus the Elder. The Heliopolitans told of him "ganging up" with all noxious influences against the progress of Ra's sun-boat. To him was assigned astronomically the constellation of Ursa Major in the cold north, the Ox Leg in Egyptian terminology. From a moral point of view Set was the personification of sin and opposition to the will of the good gods, a role which he continued to play in the Afterworld by contradicting the soul as it strove to clear itself before Osiris and to secure a favorable judgment. Being such a character, Set came to be chosen by soldiers as patron of their rough profession, by magicians as god of the Black Art. To avoid being "hexed" by Set, the superstitious Egyptian felt it necessary to spit or curse or call him by some other name than his own as "that fellow" or "obscene serpent."

Scratched on the walls of prehistoric tombs occur pictures of Set in a strictly animal form, but just what animal is meant must remain uncertain. A head tending to the jackass type, set on a greyhound body, and further contradicted by the tail of a warthog, is a zoological nightmare. In much later time other animal forms are given him, such as those of the serpent or crocodile. In his standard presentment, however, Set is an okapi-headed man who carries bow and arrows, and sometimes wears the red crown of the Delta kingdom. Red is the color sacred to him. The Ox Leg, mentioned above, is found as his symbol on later monuments.

Of the minor characters of the Osirian myth — Nephthys, Anubis, Thoth — little need be said. Nephthys, being the consort of Set, had, theologically speaking, attributes akin to his and was "the type of death, decay, diminution and mobility" (Budge). But it is obvious that in the myth she has put aside these evil attributes to appear as a lady stooge for Isis. Anubis, it would seem, was originally a divine protector of the inviolability of cemeteries. He appears consistently with the head of a jackal. Thoth's attributes and pictured representation we have already studied. All three of these worthies were officers in the Osirian Afterworld, where the soul beheld Nephthys, a kind of pale double of Isis; came to Anubis to be weighed in the balance against the Maat-feather; and in the ensuing trial looked anxiously toward Thoth's inscrutable ibic countenance, as this scribe of the gods wrote his record of the progress of the judgment.

Evidence presented here, as well as in preceding chapters, shows how artificial a piece of theologizing is this group of Osirian gods. The myth-drama, to slip into Hollywood patois, has recruited its actors from various "lots." For the leading role is cast Osiris the favorite of Libyan colonists of the western Delta and the divine principle of the annual renewal and decay of vegetation. Opposite him plays the Isis-Hathor of an Asiatic people of the eastern Delta, a mother-goddess with attributes complementary to those of Osiris. Altogether too popular to be passed by, the young hero Horus receives a part, though he has no known affinity to the vegetation cycle of religious ideas. Rated a prize villain by his performance in the solar mythology, Set gets the call for the role of adversary of the "good god" Osiris. For ambassador of Ra and wise counselor of the afflicted Isis is chosen Thoth. Gods from still other cults — Buto, Nephthys, Anubis — fill out the cast as extras. It is significant that a small area of the Delta contained important cult centers of these individual gods and goddesses at the very dawn of Egyptian history. Busiris worshiped Osiris; Behbet, Isis; Hermopolis, Thoth; Pharbaethos, Set; several towns, Horus. It is not unlikely that this geographical propinquity influenced the association of such functionally diverse divinities in the one myth story.

Further light on Osirianism is shed by the annual festivals and other cult practices. Unfortunately, the state of the evidence at present compels us to rely largely upon such late sources as Herodotus (fifth century B.C.), Plutarch (A.D. first century), Apuleius (A.D. second century) and the Christian apologetes. The cult had gone through several millennia of change before the earliest of these writers described it, so that allowance must be made in reading their records for possible intrusion of non-Osirian elements from other Egyptian and Hellenic cults.

One Osirian festival, however, certainly dates back to nineteenth century B.C. The treasurer Ikhernophret executed for his lord Sesostris III (1887–1849) a commission at Abydos. After checking up on the priests' fidelity to their temple duties and embellishing the shrines with costly gifts, he took part in a religious pageant enacted on the river and on the littoral near Osiris' temple. We quote, giving in brackets necessary comments:

> I celebrated the feast of the Going Forth of Upwawet [an old god of the dead and here described as in league with Osiris] when he proceeded to champion his father. I repelled the foe from the sacred barque, I overthrew the enemies of Osiris. I celebrated the Great Going Forth, following the god at his going. [Here is meant, according to Breasted, the funeral procession of Osiris.] I sailed the divine boat of Thoth. [A dramatization, conjectures the same scholar, of the search for Osiris' body.] I equipped the barque called Shining in Truth of the Lord of Abydos [Osiris] with a chapel when he went forth to Peker, I put on his regalia: I led the way of the god to his tomb before Peker. [Still referring to Osiris' funeral.] I championed Wennofer [a name of Horus] at that Day of the Great Conflict; I slew all the enemies upon the flat of Nedyt. [Nedyt is a name for Abydos. The reference here is obviously to Horus' strife against Set & Co. to avenge the murder of Osiris.] I conveyed him into his barque called The Great when it bore his beauty; I gladdened the heart of the eastern highlands; I made rejoicing in the western highlands. [Because of what follows, these words are best understood of some triumphant flotilla bearing back to Abydos the image of Osiris supposedly revivified.] When they saw the beauty of the sacred boat as it landed at Abydos, they brought Osiris First of the Westerners, Lord of Abydos, to his palace, and I followed the god into his house to attend at his throne among his courtiers.

[Final act of the ritual drama: Osiris revivified and returning to power.][7]

The parts of divine beings in the above drama were taken by the cult statues, as appears from earlier lines of the inscription, but religious devotees seem to have an active part, whether in celebrating Osiris' triumphant return or in taking a cudgeling in the mimic conflict on the river and the flats of Nedyt. Another record of about the year 1700 narrates a similar myth-drama, while Herodotus furnishes us with an account of a third for about the year 430.[8]

The laments of Isis and Nephthys occur in the *Pyramid Texts* in a form that one suspects is ritualistic, but there is no positive evidence that they were employed at so early a date in an organized Osirian liturgy. Later, of course, the laments are elaborated into a kind of divine office to accompany the scenes of the ritualistic drama.

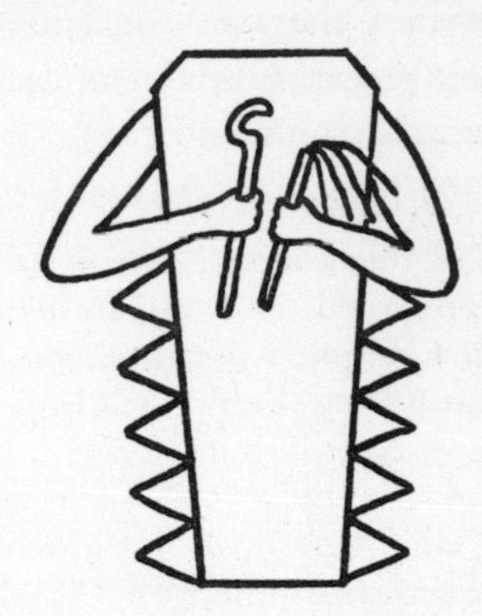

Fig. 19. The Zed Pillar

Every year the ruling Pharaoh solemnly set up this curious fetish of the god Osiris. The two hands hold the god's attributes of the scourge and the symbol of life.

A Theban tomb wall supplies details of the observance of an ancient Osiris festival, the setting up of the Zed Pillar. The event is dated certainly for 1375 B.C. This was the last year of Amenhotep III, who is shown in the relief

[7] From a memorial tablet erected at Abydos in 1868 B.C., now in Berlin.

[8] A stela from Abydos, now in Cairo, gives the first of these two accounts: it is dated in the second year of Pharaoh Nepherhotep, but he reigned during the chaotic thirteenth Dynasty when chronology is uncertain. Herodotus gives his account in the second book of his History.

raising up and setting this pillar in the ground. The queen and courtiers assist, while hymns are sung and oblations made. Osiris in his most fundamental attribute as a vegetation god may be said to be here honored, if we take for our interpretative cue the date of the celebration, namely January 19, when the beneficent effects of Nile's inundation are manifesting themselves in the lush growth of vegetation. However, there is likelihood that the ceremony commemorates the well-remembered mythical story of Osiris being enclosed in the pillar at Byblos.[9]

Herodotus, Plutarch, and Lactantius[10] offer details of two more of the cult's festivals. From November 14 to 17, the supposed time of Osiris' murder as well as the period when the inundation is waning, a golden ox or cow, richly caparisoned, was brought out of the temple and paraded while the attendant priests chanted mournful yet hopeful hymns. On May 14 the same priests carried a golden vessel to the Nile, filled it with fresh water and cried exultantly, "Osiris is found." They then formed a crescent of soil, spice, and incense, and richly adorned it. The symbolism of the crescent is dubious, but the rest of these rites are easily understood in the light of previous explanations.

When Ptolemy Soter (323–285 B.C.) effected a fusion of Osirianism with the Eleusinian religion of Demeter-Persephone-Dis, the ancient Egyptian cult became definitively a mystery religion. True, it had long before this time exhibited elements analogous to the "doctrine of the mysteries." For instance, the sacred myth-drama, staged in remote Middle Kingdom days, is akin to the Eleusinian pageants. Again, the belief that Osirian burial ritual was an indispensable condition for Afterworld felicity reminds one of the esoteric and semi-automatic salvation attainable by the *mystai* through the rite

[9] From the wall of tomb of the Theban noble Kheruf. The accompanying hieroglyphic text gives the date.

[10] Herodotus, Lib. II, 11, pp. 129 sqq.; Plutarch, *Isis and Osiris,* Ch. 39: Lactantius, *Divinae Institutiones,* Ch. I, lines 21 sqq.

of initiation. Finally, Egyptian sympathy for the tribulations and triumphs of Osiris and Isis parallels the emotions fostered by mystery devotees for Demeter and Persephone, for Cybele and Attis. However, it must be said that the religion of Isis which flourished under the Ptolemies and passed into the Roman world owed its mystic character — its initiation halls, its secret formulas and doctrines, its esoteric religious rites, its boast of irrefragable union with the goddess, its assurance of salvation — not to Egyptian sources, but to Hellenic.[11]

Osirian eschatology, though already treated in part, will be considered in the next chapter. To conclude and summarize our present subject:

Essence of Osiris Cult: Worship of divine energy manifested in plant life.

Development: Specification of this religious idea to fit Egyptian conditions makes of this energy the life-giving waters of Nile.

Primary Religious Expression: Rejoicing and thanksgiving at coming of inundation; contrary sentiments at recession.

Anthropomorphism: Osiris thought of in human form, wedded to Isis.

Myth: An aeitiological and syncretic myth spun on the theme of Nile's rise and recession, into which enter as anthropomorphic god actors not only Osiris and Isis, but also gods who originated from other cult ideas.

Moral and Eschatological Aspects: Osiris the good and beneficent opposed by evil Set: triumph of right: Osiris judge of men in Afterworld.

Cult Practices: Myth-drama: Zed Pillar: Isis laments: ritual for greeting the rising Nile, for mourning at its decline.

---

[11] The mystery religions will be found treated in the chapter on "Apollo and the Mystics." The Hellenic development of the religion of Isis is discussed in the chapter on "Oriental Cults at Rome."

CHAPTER « 17

JUDGMENT AND THE AFTERWORLD

THE odd fancy contained in the Osiris myth, of the god being restored to life only to become king of the dead, indicates an article of Osirian faith not formally examined in the preceding chapter. He was the dominant figure of the fully developed eschatology of the Middle Kingdom and the Empire. As early as 2000 B.C. he had replaced Ra as judge and vindicator in "the undiscovered country," nor did he relinquish his functions till Hellenic ideas magnified Isis in later Ptolemaic times.

Belief in a future life is attested by the earliest finds in the Nile valley. Prehistoric graves of an undeterminable antiquity offer the evidence of food, utensils, and weapons that is usually turned up in ancient burials all over the world. What the mastaba tombs and the pyramids teach in their arrangements and furnishings, has been studied. However, the spoken testimony of the *Pyramid Texts* must here be added to the information supplied by these silent witnesses. Professor Breasted names as the purpose of the *Pyramid Texts* "the insuring of the king's felicity after death," and as their theme song "a passionate protest against the fact of death."[1]

The royal scribe, then, sweating away at his hieroglyphics in the galleries of the pyramid, wrote how his master was entitled to his heaven for that he was the offspring of gods.

---

[1] *The Dawn of Conscience,* pp. 67, 70. Acknowledgment is made to this work for factual data and, to a certain degree, for interpretation in the composition of the present chapter.

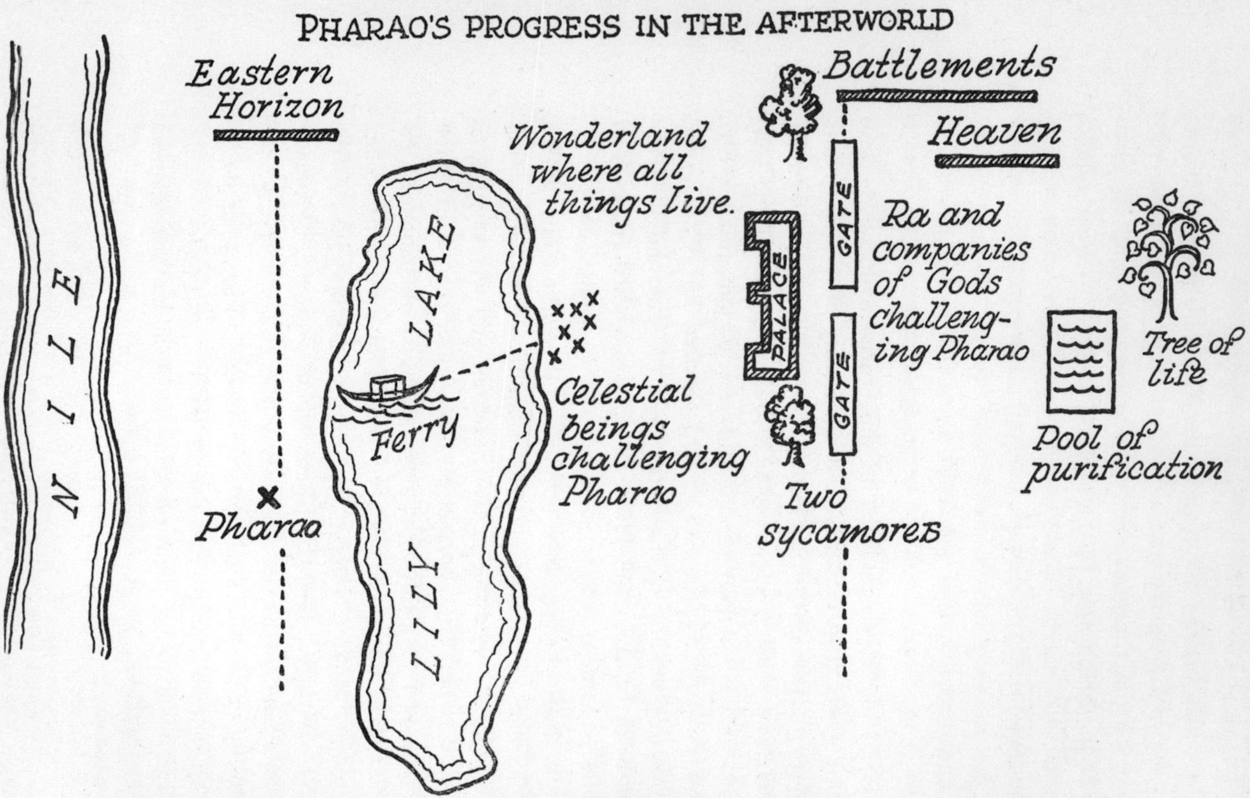

Fig. 20. Pharaonic Celestial Afterworld

There was, besides, the item of the Pharaoh's personal merits for he had been a fountainhead of beneficence to his subjects. Should the gods still wish to blackball him, let them look to themselves, for he was advancing to their citadel armed with magic charms potent to undo their envious exclusiveness. Let them, at most, subject him to a purificatory bath at the portals of heaven and so take him in.

Joined to manifold solicitude as to the dead man's future state, a solicitude in which one recognizes uncertainty as to a favorable judgment, there is protest against death. The grim fact is ruled out of court by the reiterated: "He lives" and by refusal to speak of his death save in euphemisms. A nostalgic longing is expressed for a lost better moral and physical age in which lived "the first company of the just, born before came strife, blasphemy and conflict, before death came forth." These striking words of the *Pyramid Texts* are Egypt's contribution to the widespread belief of ancient man in a vanished Golden Age.

On page 148 has been sketched The Pharaoh's Progress. The locale must be conceived as celestial, for he starts from the horizon and passes upward through the several spheres to the high heaven of the gods. The progress is essentially an obstacle race.[2] By cajolery, magic, bravado, as well as by the asseveration of his sinlessness and divine descent, must the Pharaoh win his way. To the silent ferryman, old "Averted Eyes," he says, among other things equally mendacious, "I am the dancing dwarf for whose arrival Ra is impatiently waiting." If the ferryman is obdurate, he casts a spell on him or on his long sweep and the boat draws to the shore. Against the challenge of the watchers on the eastern shore of the Lily Lake he must justify himself before they receive him and

---

[2] Among the adverse agencies are named Osiris and the Osirian gods. It is to be remembered that the heaven here described is that of the sun-god, and that at a period before Osiris had been fully recognized by the official theology. Still other of the *Pyramid Texts* speak of Osiris and his suite as among the gods surrounding Ra and welcoming the Pharaoh.

permit him to take possession of the Wonderland palace. But the Wonderland is only an intermediate heaven, above which hang Ra's battlements. In the sight of the companies of the gods he must undergo another examination before he may pass between the two sycamores through the eternal gates. Within awaits him the last rite of his probation, a purifying and perhaps immortalizing bath.

Mythological imagination is given full rein in describing the manner of life in Ra's heaven. Two ideas, however, may be said to dominate — a sublimation of earthly joys and a metamorphosis into an astronomical divinity. Thus Pharaoh appears as the center of an obsequious court life quite on the model of his grand life at Memphis. The Field of Rushes affords needed relief from cares of state, for in that pleasant playground he may shy his boomerang at celestial ducks, harry wild oxen in the chase, and generally boondoggle a holiday. For commissariat he has the food and drink of the gods supplemented by the aliments regularly renewed at his pyramid and forwarded by the magical parcel post. Other pictures different from these human ones, and inspired by astronomical religion, show Pharaoh riding the daily course in Ra's sun-boat or eating fruit from the Tree of Life to effect his metamorphosis into an imperishable star. Yet, lest even this grandiose horoscope seem meager praise when Pharaoh comes to inspect the pyramid, the scribe again dips his reed pen and adds more lines of royal flattery. The hieroglyphics run on to explain how the Pharaoh will assimilate the powers of all the gods by banqueting on their bodies, how he will relieve his father Atum of his functions as principle and origin of all things.

The position of Osiris in the *Pyramid Texts* is peculiar. Recognized as a god of the dead, he is propitiated, yet no one desires to fall into his power after death. Magic spells are inscribed in the pyramid to prevent him and his circle of gods from entering to disturb the mummy, while one of the triumphant assertions of the Pharaoh's Afterworld felicity is: "Thou, O Ra, hast not given him over to Osiris." It is conjectured, not unreasonably, that the Heliopolitan theology regarded Osiris' realm, the regions beneath the earth, as a place of darkness and unknown terrors, and hence provided apotropaic means to prevent the dead man being hurried away thither. However, so potent an eschatological figure could not be neglected, so that even the earliest of the *Texts* represent him in the receiving line of the celestial gods when the Pharaoh approaches heaven's battlements. In later *Texts* he is obviously growing in importance and fairly on the way to usurp Ra's eschatological suzerainty.

We have merely theory and the analogy of other Mediterranean religions to serve as guides in the problem of the relation of Osiris' agricultural attributes to his eschatological. The following solution is offered tentatively:

a) An agricultural people of eastern Libya worshiped the principle that restored and maintained the life of the fields.

b) This principle or god was taken as that personal being to whom man refers his origin and to whom he feels responsible.

c) This god, naturally, would take care of his faithful votaries in some kind of an hereafter.

d) Migrating with his people into Egypt, this god became associated, for reasons suggested in the preceding chapter, with Isis, Horus, and other gods. As god of the dead, too, he was given the form of the mummy which Egyptians associated with death.

e) Mythographers set to work to express in an apologetic story the cult facts of the worship of the vegetation spirit Osiris and of his association with Isis, Horus, etc. It is probable that this myth spinning had for prototype the very ancient Mediterranean myth which is familiar in the variant forms of Cybele and Attis, Venus and Adonis, and the like.

f) The details of the Osirian Afterworld are imaginative,

men having at the same time a strong belief in retributive justice and a curious longing to know what secrets the future life holds.

The celestial hereafter fades with the passing of the Old Kingdom. As written and pictured records begin to illuminate the Egyptian scene after the five hundred years of the Dark Age (about 2500–2000), man's future lot is described as cast in the subterranean regions. Thither have been brought down from the heights many of the eschatological figures imagined by the ancient theologians and scribes. Yet there appear radical changes which cannot be well explained except as contributions of a strictly Osirian theology. The geography of the region is an imaginative projection of that of Egypt. Along the shores of a subterranean Nile lie various districts, just as in Egypt there are the various nomes or administrative districts. These districts are populated by the dead who enter the land of shadows through a gate lying back of their tombs in Egypt's western desert. The district assigned everyone depends upon the judgment of Osiris-Ra. His sun-boat enters the current of the subterranean Nile every evening and illumines the antipodean Egypt. The dead crowd to the shore, to hear their sentences. If their lives meet the god's approval, they are districted in pleasant places along the banks or even received as companions in the sun-boat. Eager demons await those on whom Osiris-Ra frowns, to snatch them off to torture regions for hacking, beheading, burning.

In the third visualization of the Afterlife, Osiris appears as the supreme judge.[3] The soul entering the subterranean country is taken in charge by hawk-headed Horus and brought into a great judgment hall where sit the Forty-Two Assessors. To them the soul protests its innocence in terms of the Negative Confession. Horus then places the dead man's heart in one pan of a balance, and in the other the Maat-feather,

[3] To insure the favor of both Osiris and of Ra, the proper eschatologies of each were sometimes inextricably mixed in tomb papyri and carvings.

symbol of righteousness. Anubis holds the balance, while Thoth assists to write down the result of the weighing. If the heart is found wanting, a fantastic animal called the Swallower stands ready to seize it. But if his heart stands this test of righteousness, the soul is conducted by Horus into the presence of Osiris enthroned and attended by Isis and Nephthys. To him Horus announces that the soul is pure and the great god ratifies the sentence. Reward is pictured both as immediate companionship with, even identification with, Osiris and as the enjoyment of that sublimated human life already described. On his way to the happy hunting grounds, however, the soul must yet be barked at and threatened by a variety of zooform demons. Against these he will prevail, provided the potent papyrus of the *Book of the Dead* has been placed in his tomb. To repulse them, the soul need but read the specific charm against everyone from that curious magical document.

With the very considerable body of evidence, developed in the present chapter and the two preceding chapters, now before us, we are in a position to form our judgment on several important phases of Egyptian religious belief. What did the people hold on personal immortality? How comprehensive was their moral code? Was moral conduct's sanction the pleasure or displeasure of the gods? We purpose to answer these questions in the order given.

Three future states were visualized by the Egyptians: the life in the tomb and its environs, the celestial life beyond the eastern horizon, the life in the Osirian Netherworld beneath the earth. Of the first belief parallels among other peoples are numerous, for a superstition of wide ethnical diffusion fancies the sepulcher inhabited by the dead man's spirit. A peculiar development, however, of the general superstition is noted in Egypt, a development traceable to native African sources. Among low-culture peoples of that continent it was and is common doctrine that a man's "life" or soul may be conjured into an inanimate object. A colored gentleman in his homeland, who suspects that his enemy is stalking him in the jungle, will deposit his soul for safekeeping in a tree trunk by means of proper magical hokum, or by like means conjure his enemy's soul into a mud mannikin and impale the same.[4] Egyptian ceremonies for "Opening the Mouth" of mummy or portrait-statue, as given in the *Book of the Dead,* are nothing but more highly ritualized magical formulas for producing the same result. In obedience to the spells the dead man's *ka* entered these inanimate objects. How long the animation of mummy and portrait-statue was to endure is indicated by perpetual endowments for tomb-offering and tomb-services.

A great body of superstition also bears testimony to belief in the spirit inhabiting the Egyptian sepulchers. Ancient ghouls would take the precaution of bashing in the head of the portrait-statue or of covering it with a sack before helping themselves to the valuables in the tomb-chamber. Romancers such as Poe have told of ill luck pursuing the possessor of tomb-objects, while in the British Museum there is a malevolent lid of a mummy case with a long record of misfortunes brought on those who have handled it. A revival of these curious superstitions, all founded in the old Egyptian faith in tomb inhabitation, has followed on the series of coincidental deaths among the explorers of Pharaoh Tutankhamen's tomb.[5]

Assertions that Christian doctrine found its prototype of corporeal resurrection in the reanimation of portrait-statue or mummy are made only by those who, knowing a little of Egyptian superstition, know less of Catholic teaching. Nor do

[4] The older Egyptologist Maspero proposed the theoretic basis for the explanation here given. One of his pupils fully developed the explanation in a publication, 1926, of La fondation Egyptologique Reine Elizabeth. The title is *Les Statues Vivantes,* by M. Weynandts-Ronday (Bruxelles). Some of the authoress' conclusions are doubtful, but she proves her point in the matter which is here under discussion.

[5] Cf. Mr. Arthur Weigall's *Tutankhamen* (G. H. Doran Co., 1924), especially Ch. VI.

such assertions gain any color of probability from the obscure Chapter 89 of the *Book of the Dead* entitled "For Uniting the Soul and Body." To quote:

> Hail, great god! Grant that my soul may come to me from wheresoever it may be. . . . Let me not lie down in death among those who lie down in Annu, the land wherein souls are joined to their bodies even in thousands. . . . Hail, ye gods who make souls to enter into spiritual bodies, destroy ye the enemy! Grant that my soul may come forth triumphant before the gods in the region of peace. Grant that it may look upon its material body, may rest upon its spiritual body; and may its body neither perish nor suffer corruption for ever.

That a large part of heaven's joys was corporeal, is only too clear from previous explanations. For the enjoyment of these, it is not surprising that the fertile eschatological imagination of the Egyptians forwarded the body by magic express into the Afterworld. The whole idea is obvious and crudely material, nothing more than "flesh and blood possessing the kingdom, corruption possessing incorruption."[6] But in the Christian resurrection the body "is sown in corruption, it shall rise in incorruption. It is sown in dishonor, it shall rise in glory. It is sown in weakness, it shall rise in power. It is sown a natural body, it shall rise a spiritual body."[7]

Since Rationalistic capital is made of such phrases as: "Just as Osiris did not die, so this Sety shall not die," it is as well briefly to dispose of the "resurrection" of this god. Neither in the myth nor in the ritual can there be found evidence to justify a comparison of him to the risen Christ, "the first fruits of them that sleep."[8] After being murdered, Osiris never returns alive to the land of Egypt. What the myth narrates is how Isis finds the scattered members of his body, joins them together, mummifies the body and then fans life into the mummy. But what manner of life? Certainly not that of a living king of Egypt, much less that of a glorified body. Osiris receives that fanciful animation effected by Egyptian mortuary

[6] I Cor. 15:50.
[7] *Ibid.*, 42–44.
[8] *Ibid.*, 20.

priests when they "opened the mummy's mouth." Osiris himself, like every right-thinking dead Egyptian, has departed for the Netherworld when done to death by Set and there he stays. The great ritual drama and other ritual observances do nothing else, as has been shown in the preceding chapter, save ring the peculiar Egyptian change on the old Mediterranean theme of the vernal rebirth of vegetation.[9]

Tolerably clear is it that blissful life both in the upper (Ra's) and the nether (Osiris') heaven was endless. Eternity, to be sure, "is a long time" and a hard concept for man's mind unillumined by revelation, so that it is likely that the people's ideas in this regard were vague enough and imperfect. Whether the atrocious pains inflicted on the condemned in the Osirian Afterworld ended in the soul's annihilation or whether we are to understand an eternity of pain, cannot be determined with certainty. Of a purgatory of penal ordeals to be followed by the admission of the purified soul into bliss, a few texts make mention.

From the same tombs that tell so much of Egypt's gods and of hope of immortality, there come echoes of the voice of conscience. The merit of good deeds is a title advanced by the Pharaoh to secure entrance into that earliest heaven described by the *Pyramid Texts*. In the same texts are found the dead man's pleas of "Not Guilty" to specific moral lapses, pleas already so stereotyped in expression as to indicate a written or verbally formulated "code of morals." The suspicion of such a formulary becomes a certainty as Middle Kingdom documents appear, for in the *Book of the Dead*[10] the scattered pleas of innocence are catalogued in the forty-two points

[9] Cf. P. de Grandmaison, *Jesus Christ,* Tome 2, pp. 511 sqq.

[10] The earliest complete text of the *Book of the Dead* is from a tomb papyrus of about the eighteenth century B.C. and is taken to be a recension by Theban priests of the undoubtedly much older original. The *Book* has been rightly described as the Baedeker of the Netherworld. It directs how the mummy is to be prepared, describes the geography of the region of the dead, names the gods and demons to be encountered, prescribes the prayers, spells, and declarations necessary to pass the soul through every challenge and obstacle.

of the Negative Confession. How comprehensive was the code of morals may be judged by a selection we have made from the forty-two "alibis." In citing them here we omit the invocation of the god which precedes each member. These gods were in general the local gods of the forty-two nomes or administrative districts of Egypt; they are pictured in the vignettes which illustrate the text of the Confession as seated in the great hall of judgment, holding each one the familiar Maat-feather or symbol of truth.

2. I have not robbed with violence.
4. I have not stolen.
5. I have not slain men.
7. I have not acted deceitfully.
8. I have not stolen the property of the god.
9. I have not uttered lies.
10. I have not uttered words of blasphemy.
11. I have not played the spy.
19. I have not committed adultery.
20. I have not been guilty of private vice.
21. I have not terrified any man.
22. I have not attacked any man.
25. I have not stirred up strife.
26. I have made no man to weep.
27. I have not been guilty of sexual impurity.
28. I have not cherished resentment nor envy.
29. I have not cursed.
31. I have not judged hastily.
33. I have not talked overmuch.
39. I have not behaved with insolence.
40. I have not sought distinctions for myself.

If we add to these moral ideas the repeated injunctions on reverence toward parents and all in authority which are found in the Egyptian "sapiential writings,"[11] we must concede the correctness and comprehensiveness of this ancient code of conduct. Right reason had led the people to an approximation to that law of right and wrong which God was later to

---

[11] Cf. *The Teaching of Amen-em-apt,* Sir E. A. W. Budge (London: Martin Hopkinson & Co., 1924).

formulate as the Commandments and sanction by his revealed authority.

The luster of Egyptian moral teaching is, however, considerably dimmed by what we know of practical applications of their code. For instance, the strange gods forbidden by Jahve's revealed Law were the rule in Egypt. Graven images were worshiped. Magic was deemed often more useful for salvation than a good life, more potent than the very divine will. Polygamy through secondary wives and concubines flourished in all periods. Many a Pharaoh married his own sister. There is noticed, finally, in ancient Egyptian religious psychology a singular lack of the sense of personal sin, evidenced in self-justification, in recourse not to a contrite heart and restitution for wrong done but to the alibi and to magical insurance against the displeasure of the gods.

The earliest coherent expressions of moral standards—*Pyramid Texts,* sapiential writings, the *Book of the Dead*—propose the gods as the sanctioners of human conduct. Osiris, Ra, and the Forty-Two Assessors quite obviously assign man his future lot according to moral demerit or merit.

"Remember the Assessors," says Pharaoh Khati to his son, "who judge wrongdoers. Know that they will not be lenient on that day of judgment of wretched man. It is a terrible thing for a man who knows his sin to be charged with it. Fill not thy heart with hope because of length of years, for they regard a lifetime as a single hour. . . . There in the other world existence is everlasting. A fool is he who has put the remembrance of it away from him. The man who attains to that place without wrongdoing has an existence like that of a god" (Text of about 2500 B.C.).

Two pet theories, then, of evolutionistic rationalism find no support in the facts of Egyptian religion. First, the third millennium in the Nile valley exhibits not any "dawn of conscience," but a quite luminous daylight. Second, religion and morality are not at the same early date two independently developing forces, but are and seemingly always have been inextricably interrelated.

Scholion on Contacts of Biblical with Egyptian History

Here it is opportune to indicate briefly what confirmation the inspired history of the Jewish people has so far received from the finds of Egyptologists. The confirmation, it will be seen, is almost wholly negative, consisting as it does in harmony between the Hebrew chronicler's account and the ascertained facts of Egyptian life, not in Egyptian documents which narrate the same facts as do Genesis and Exodus. Perhaps archeology will yet uncover an Egyptian account of the Hebrews' stay in Egypt, but, apart from such confirmation, a reason for the silence of Egyptian records lies perhaps in the unimportance of the Jews to an Egyptian mind and in the fact that the manner of the exodus was a disgrace to the Pharaoh and therefore a thing to be hushed up. For the following table we stand largely indebted to the article "Egypte" in the *Dictionnaire Apologetique de la Foi Catholique.*

Biblical Narrative	*Egyptian Documents*
Abraham, about 2000 B.C. descends into Egypt because of a famine in Chanaan. Sara is taken to wife by Pharaoh, but God afflicts him for this and he sends Abraham and Sara away.	On tomb wall of Knumhotep, a twelfth-dynasty noble, is carved a Semitic caravan entering Egypt, just such a caravan as Abraham might have led. The leader Abspa asks and obtains from Knumhotep permission to sojourn in Egypt. Many instances of foreign women being taken as wives by Pharaohs. Egyptian moral code on taking wife of another man was very severe, hence Pharaoh's horror on learning that Sara is Abraham's wife. Among the cattle of Abraham so exactly inventoried the horse is not named: the horse came into Egypt probably only with the Hyksos.
A caravan brings Joseph into Egypt and sells him into slavery. Solicited by	At this period, about 1800, caravan trade between Syria and Egypt flourished. Several centuries after Joseph

Potiphar's wife, he is imprisoned on her false charge. Interprets Pharaoh's dream and is made grand vizier. Seven year plenty, seven year famine. The land of Gessen assigned to Hebrews.

the Egyptian tale of Anpu and Bata was composed, bearing a marked resemblance to the early part of Joseph's Egyptian experience. Magicians and dream interpreters are characteristically Egyptian. On record are several famines in the Nile valley, as also the storing of grain in anticipation of famine years. At court of Pharaoh Merneptah a Chananean held an office analogous to one held by Joseph. Land of Gessen and city of Pithom are mentioned in records, as also the fact that Merneptah, who would have been Pharaoh shortly after the Exodus, found Gessen unpopulated and established a colony there.

Israel grows into a great people. A Pharaoh who knew not Joseph enslaves them. Moses. "Bricks without straw." Plagues. Magicians' *mira.* Route of exodus. Red Sea. Dates about 1537–1437.

The settlement in Egypt of the sons of Jacob was probably under the friendly Semitic (?) Hyksos Pharaohs. Thebes after fierce struggle drove Hyksos out of Delta. What more natural than that native Egyptian Pharaohs should suspect the growing strength of the former favorites of the Hyksos, especially since they were colonized in the frontier region beyond which the Hyksos power still flourished? Large scale slave labor on public works begins in Empire. Bricks without straw found in part of Pithom monuments. Plagues such as would be most grievous to Egyptian life. Fleeing people would have shunned Isthmus of Suez because of Egyptian garrison. Shortly after 1400, when Josue would have been conquering Palestine, vassals there write urgently to Pharaoh for help against invading Habiri. Merneptah (1225–1215) mentions Israel as one of people beaten in his raid in Palestine.

CHAPTER « 18

AMON AND ATON

THE Middle Kingdom (2160–1788) disintegrated from the same causes as the Old Kingdom (3400–2475). Powerful nobles in each case asserted the autonomy of their own districts when weak Pharaohs let the rod of command totter in their grasp. There followed in each case, at least as far as meager records allow us to infer, a period of disunion culminating in a struggle between rival claimants for supreme Pharaonic power. In the Dark Age which followed the Middle Kingdom's decay the situation was further complicated by the Hyksos' conquest of Egypt. They were probably Semitic raiders whose methods resembled those of the followers of Gengis Khan, in that they overran vast territories and maintained them ephemerally in a loose sovereignty. Archeological research is beginning to show that at one time they ruled from the Nile's first cataract on the south to the Euphrates and central Asia Minor on the north. From their eastern Delta Hatwaret (the Avaris of Manetho), a strongly fortified camp, they sent forth their cavalry columns and their tax gatherers to prey ruthlessly upon unwarlike and disunited natives.

Only in far southern Thebes was patriotic resistance effectively organized. The ruling house of the Middle Kingdom had been Theban and it seems that the Theban princes were regarded by Egyptians as *de jure* Pharaohs even during the Hyksos interlude. Shortly after the opening of the sixteenth century one of them, Ahmose by name, made himself *de facto* Lord of Upper and Lower Egypt by capturing Avaris and chasing the Hyksos over the northeastern frontier. He and his next two successors, Amenhotep I and Thutmose I, secured this same frontier, emphasized the superiority of the white race by raiding the Nubians, restored administrative order in the Nile valley.

Egypt's first cycle of expansion was now to begin. After a brief reign by the almost unknown Thutmose II, Queen Hatshepsut and the third Thutmose appear as joint sovereigns. The latter, it appears, was not of the direct line of Theban royalty, so was forced by the conservative tradition of the time to be tied to Hatshepsut's apron strings while that royal lady lived. Dreams of world power were germinating in his restless and able mind during these years of ungrateful restraint, and his queen was no sooner properly mummied and domiciled in the western cliffs than he was off on the first of the seventeen brilliant campaigns which were to establish him as the peer of the world's greatest strategic geniuses.

Hitherto, Egypt's foreign wars had been little more than sporadic punitive expeditions against Nubians, Libyans, Bedouins, who had raided her three frontiers. Now Nubia was definitely beaten into submission and contributed her harvests and her levies of "big, black, bounding beggars" for Thutmose's more serious campaigns in the north. His war galleys patroled the eastern Mediterranean, to secure his lines of communication. He personally led the new Egyptian chariotry, the phalanxes of spearmen, the companies of bowmen in an unchecked series of sieges and pitched battles characterized by methodical planning and daring execution. It is generally accepted that it was the Hyksos Empire that he was shattering. But, be that as it may, he made tributaries of both Palestine and Syria and enjoined on their rulers to bring annually to his coastal depots the supplies he needed for his further campaigns. Quite insatiable, he returned from Egypt each spring with fresh troops, landed them at a Syrian port and pushed his Empire's frontier still farther north and east. He conquered strange tribes which are to modern research scarcely more than names. He rested only when, as an old man, he set his victory stela on the eastern bank of the Euphrates.[1]

The prestige of Egyptian arms won by the great conqueror assured his immediate successors a steady flow of tribute from the subject nations as well as the deferential regard of the other powerful rulers of the time. The luxury of Pharaonic and noble life showed a sharp upcurve, as the choicest foreign products poured into the Nile valley and as the most skilled artisans of the age transferred their talents to the new center of empire. A down curve seems to have begun in the economic condition of the native *fellahin,* for captives of the foreign wars were brought in to take over the manual labor that was the poor Egyptian's only means of livelihood.

Thebes was supreme. Her princes had led the patriotic uprising which expelled the tyrant Hyksos, had founded a new dynasty, had won an empire extending from the third cataract to the upper Euphrates. Thebes' god, Amon, was hailed, according to the custom of the age, as the one who had prospered all these splendid achievements, nor were his alert priests minded to allow forgetfulness of this manifestation of his might to seize upon the Pharaoh. No mere tithes nor presents from the fruits of victory would suffice, but wide districts in the newly acquired regions must be permanently sequestered as cult endowments.

The records of Rekhmire, Grand Vizier under Thutmose III, reveal how vast the religious "racket" had grown, how shamelessly the Theban priesthood importuned the aging hero in the name of "his father Amon." Karnak, the Theban suburb and cult center, became during this and the three subsequent reigns a state within a state. Uncountable wealth in precious stones and metals was here hoarded, thousands

---

[1] The annals of the reigns of Hatshepsut and Thutmose III rank with the great literature of the world. They may be read in Professor Breasted's translation in his *Ancient Records of Egypt,* Vol. II.

of slaves were assigned to the temple property, herds of cattle grazed on the sacred estates, the docks and warehouses were filled with tribute of the Empire's choicest produces. Archeology is only now beginning to realize the extent and splendor of the Karnak Temple itself, the house built for Amon in these days of his aggrandizement. Before the portal of St. John Lateran, *mater et caput omnium ecclesiarum,* stands the obelisk which the most illustrious of Egypt's rulers erected before the entrance to this grandest of her pagan temples. Its still legible inscription is translated as follows:

> Thutmose III, rich in monuments in the house of Amon; making his monuments greater than those which the ancestors made, who were before; exceeding that which ever was, not resembling the likeness of anything that was made in the house of his father, Amon.[2]

The original attributes of Amon were probably those of a god of procreation, and there is sound reason for saying that he was the same as the ithyphallic Min who came into the Nile valley from the southern shores of the Red Sea. Etymologically, *Amon* means "the hidden one," but this cryptic meaning helps little. In form he is human, or human with a frog head or a serpent head. Though the ape and the lion were animal symbols of him, the commonest of these symbols is the ram. For female counterpart he had Mut (the mother), a mother goddess who conceived and brought forth all that exists. The Theban triad was completed by Khonsu (the traveler), the son of Amon and of Mut. Probably a moon-god, Khonsu was assigned a role of influence in effecting generation and growth. He was hawk-headed, winged, and bore the lunar crescent and the scourge.

The ascendancy of Ra of Heliopolis and of Osiris of Abydos was, of course, challenged by Thebes' favorite. To the theo-

---

[2] Thutmose set up five obelisks at Karnak and two at Heliopolis. It is one of the latter pair that stands in Central Park, N. Y. The Lateran obelisk was brought from Karnak to the Circus Maximus in Rome by Constantius in 357. Pius V, in 1587, had it removed to the Lateran.

logians fell the task of working out formulas of reconciliation. For Osiris, who through the Middle Kingdom had been steadily progressing toward recognition as the great god of all Egypt, the theological solution was a restriction of his functions to the Afterworld, since Amon made no claim to sovereignty there. The heavens and the earth thus remained for division between Amon and Ra. Now, the Egyptians were inveterate worshipers of the sun, and Amon was no sun-god. Hence, the solarization of his attributes was requisite to his popularity. The whole titulary of Ra, the sun-god, was accordingly borrowed for the Amon ritual. The next step was only too obvious. Heliopolis had always been the chief center of theology in Egypt, and her teaching had extraordinary weight. The Heliopolitan priests accepted Theban Amon as a god to be equated to their own Ra and coined the syncretic name Amon-Ra. The ancient seat of sun worship in northern Egypt became now a center of Amon cult second in importance only to Karnak in the south.

To the cult of Amon-Ra belong the series of Egyptian Hymns to the Sun which of all documents speak the most explicitly of the divine attributes. The various recensions of the hymns differ considerably in detail, but the following may stand as a fair example of the content. It is from a stela of Amenhotep III (1411–1375), now in the British Museum.

> Thou art a craftsman shaping thy own limbs;
> Fashioner without being fashioned;
> Unique in his qualities, traversing eternity;
> Over ways with millions under his guidance.
> When thou sailest across the sky all men behold thee,
> Though thy going is hidden from their sight.
> Thou traversest a journey of leagues,
> Even millions and hundred thousands of time.
> Every day is under thee.
> When thy setting comes,
> The hours of the night hearken to thee likewise.
> When thou hast traversed it,
> There comes no end to thy labors.

All men see by means of thee.
Thou art creator of all and giver of their substance,
A mother profitable to gods and men,
A craftsman of experience,
A valiant herdsman who drives his cattle,
Their refuge and giver of their sustenance.
Thou beholdest that which thou hast made,
Sole lord taking captive all lands every day,
Alone beholding them that walk therein;
Shining in the sky as the sun.
Thou makest the season by the months,
Heat when thou desirest,
Cold when thou desirest.
Every land is in rejoicing
At thy rising every day, in order to praise thee.[3]

Though the concept of divinity here expressed is relatively high, it is not necessary to seek its explanation elsewhere than in the purer streams of Egypt's immemorial religious thought. Dominant, obviously, is the naturistic worship of the sun's might and beneficial power. Self-production and "creation" of all things else were attributed from earliest times to several of the gods, notably Ptah. The depth and warmth of personal religious feeling in the phrases "a mother profitable to gods and men" and "a valiant herdsman the refuge of his cattle" are indeed striking, but Egypt's Wise Men had spoken so of the great gods in previous centuries. Certain Egyptologists would have these sun-hymns as the people's first expressions of realization that a god was more than a local or national force. Universality of dominion, they say, was attributed to the god only when his power was manifested in the conquest of foreign nations. True it is that before Thutmose's great adventure Egypt's mentality was rather self-centered and that there was not occasion to think of the gods save as the tutelaries of the Nile valley. Yet, in the earliest records of

[3] Breasted's trans. quoted by permission of Charles Scribner's Sons from *The Dawn of Conscience.*

the worship of Ptah, Osiris, and Ra there are unequivocal statements that these gods, at least, held universal sway.

For more than a hundred years Amon-Ra, and the two priesthoods which so faithfully publicized his merits, continued in the ascendant. In 1375 the fourth Amenhotep succeeded to the double crown of Egypt. The many statues and pictures of this remarkable Pharaoh bring him before us as a man of delicate physique with the countenance of an idealistic dreamer. His ideal was the religious one of supplanting Amon cult with the cult of Aton. Toward the other gods his attitude cannot be known with certitude, but was probably one of indifference, provided only that he could pull Amon down from his pedestal. Genuine devotion to Aton must be recognized as the master-key to his psychology, though other elements, such as irritation at the political pretensions of the Amon priests and complaisance to the will of his foreign-born and forceful queen[4] probably motivated in part his intolerance of Amon.

Besides applying the exquisite torture of the tightly drawn purse string to the overgrown priestly establishments at Karnak and Heliopolis, Amenhotep IV directed the despotic pharaonic power toward undoing the publicity they had built up for Amon. Throughout Egypt and the provinces Amon idols were systematically smashed, while the same scribes who had chiseled the god-name or image on tomb and temple walls now earned their bread and beer by defacing their handiwork. We must recognize in this iconoclasm an interesting illustration of a widespread pagan superstition which attributes magical potency to divine names and images. For the old, the new god-name and image were substituted, although it does not appear that Amenhotep IV dared so far to defy the Amon priests as to order this done in the sacred Karnak temple. Instead, he built early in his reign an Aton

[4] Tadukhipa, daughter of the king of the Mitanni. Amenhotep IV was the third successive Pharaoh to marry a princess of this line.

temple at Thebes, naming it "Brightness of Aton the Great" and renaming the city "City of the Brightness of Aton." His own name *Amen*hotep he changed officially into Ikhn*aton* or "Spirit of Aton" and named all his daughters by analogous Aton derivatives.

Friction with his religious adversaries as well as desire to build for Aton a holy city which would rival Amon's Karnak motivated Ikhnaton's next step. Abandoning Thebes he transferred the seat of government to a site about one hundred and fifty miles south of the Delta, where the eastern and western cliffs form a kind of amphitheater, five miles in length and close to sixteen in width. Here on the eastern bank he built a splendid new royal city and on the western bank an equally fine nekropolis. He seems to have made a vow never to leave this Akhet*aton* (Horizon of Aton), but shut himself up with his family and his favorites, very much as did the disillusioned last of the Romanoffs. Affairs of state he let slip, till the foreign conquests were lost and internal economics fell into confusion. Apart from the persecution of Amon, his sole interests were his family, his courtiers whom he prodigally enriched, the beautification of his city, the daily hymns and offerings in his gorgeous Gem-Aton (Brightness of Aton) temple.

Had it not been for the rise of this royal idealist, Aton would have come down in history merely as one of thousands of god-names of the ancient days. Among the gods of Egyptian Heliopolis he is mentioned occasionally in documents antedating the reign of Amenhotep IV, but always in an undistinguished position in the litanies of divine names. The probability is that he originally was a local sun-god of some forgotten Delta town, whom Ra early absorbed. So far as we know, his specific attribute was the naturalistic one of "beneficent heat of the sun." Whether he ever had an anthropomorphic or thermiomorphic representation, we do not know. After the ephemeral exaltation procured for him by

Cast in Chicago Oriental Institute Museum from original in Berlin Museum

Fig. 21. Nofretete, Queen of Ikhnaton

This forceful daughter of the Aryan King of the Mitanni, who married Pharaoh Ikhnaton, is conjectured to have influenced that reformer's religious ideas.

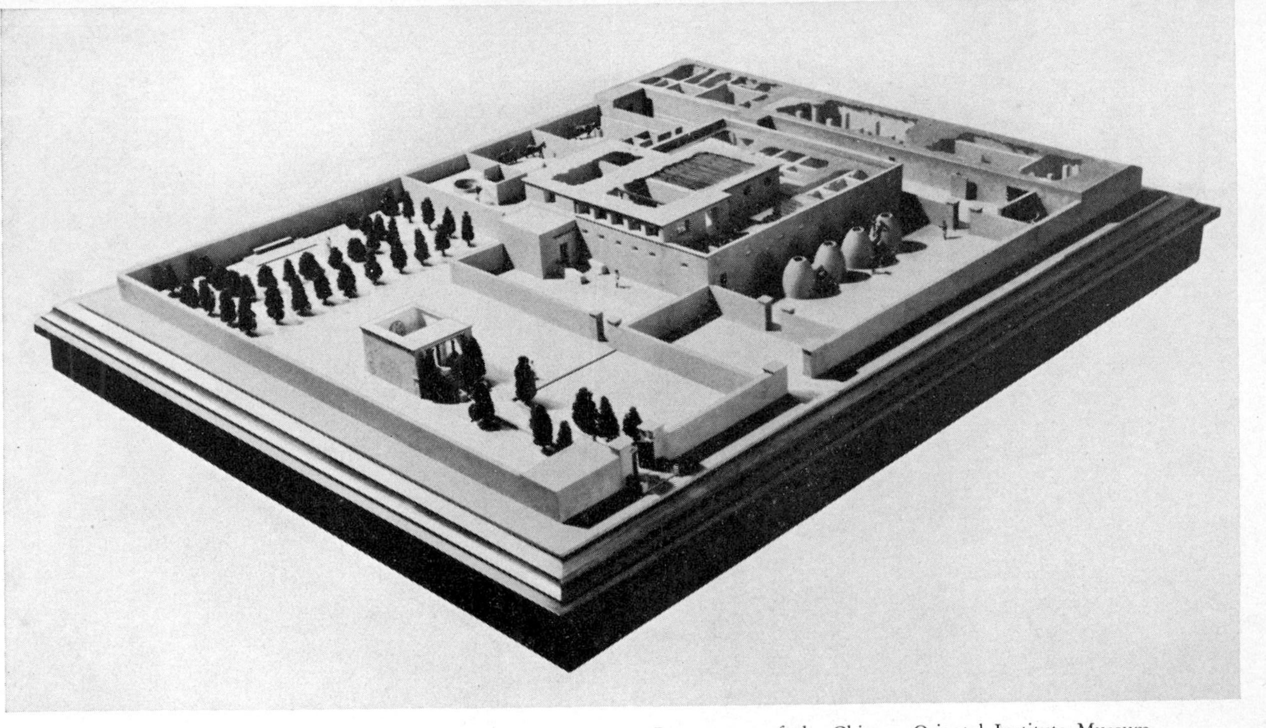

By courtesy of the Chicago Oriental Institute Museum

Fig. 22. Model of Dwelling in Aton's Holy City

Entering at the porter's lodge of his estate, the owner performed his devotions in the Aton chapel before going to his well-appointed house. Slaves stood ready to pour bowls of water over him in a neat shower room. Refreshment awaited him in the dining hall, rest in his darkened bedroom. Grouped about the apartments of the master and his family were servants' quarters, kitchen, and storerooms, while at a little distance stood the stables.

Ikhnaton's revolution, he sank into even greater obscurity, for his cult was then positively proscribed by the restored and revengeful priests of Amon.

On the monuments of Akhetaton, Aton appears in symbol and not in idolic form, the symbol being the sun-disk and rays, with each ray terminating in a human hand. To these same monuments, especially to the highly artistic tombs of Ikhnaton's courtiers, archeology turns to learn the precise content of the Aton religious teaching. It is interesting to note that the "doctrine" or "teaching" is explicitly proposed as a "revelation" given to Ikhnaton and to be propagated by him. Courtly flattery, which in the normal tomb of a Pharaonic noble dwells on the themes of the Pharaoh's conquests and wise administration together with discreet references to the number of Nubians and Syrians smitten by the noble himself and his own canny discharge of official functions, harps in the Akhetaton monuments almost exclusively on the Pharaoh as a religious prophet and on the delight of his court in his doctrine. However, it is time that we offered a specimen of the Aton *Credo.*

How manifold are thy works! They are hidden before men.
O sole god, beside whom there is no other.
Thou didst create the earth according to thy heart.

Creator of the germ in woman, who makest seed into men,
Making alive the son in the body of his mother,
Nurse even in the womb.

Thou setteth every man in his place,
Thou reckonest his days,
Thou suppliest his necessities.

When thou alone wast, thou didst make all living things,
All herds upon the earth, that walk on their four feet,
All birds, that course the air in their flight.

Thou dawnest beautifully in the horizon of the sky,
O living Aton who wast the beginning of life,
Filling every land with thy beauty.
Thou makest the seasons,
In order to make develop all that thou hast made,
Winter to bring them coolness, and summer that they may taste thy heat.

All men are fallen asleep, whose faces thou hast made
That thou mightest no longer see thyself alone.
Yet thou art still in my heart.

There is no other that knowest thee save thy son Ikhnaton;
Thou hast made him wise
In thy designs and in thy might.[5]

The above strophes are selected from the Royal Hymn attributed to the Pharaoh himself. His personal devotion to the living Aton, sole god, is as clear as is his confidence in his own prophetic relation to the divinity. We do not believe that pagan literature offers a better example of a worshiper's approach to God in the spirit of selfless love than Ikhnaton's prayerful review of the benefits of creation, conservation, and providence. The phrases "creating according to thy heart" and "making men that thou mightest no longer see thyself alone" are such fine flashes of religio-philosophic intuition that one is tempted to suspect the accuracy of the translation. Unicity, with its connotation of a monotheistic cult, is of course, unequivocally expressed throughout, but especially in the first strophe. However, against a monotheistic interpretation of Atonism militate the naturalistic identification of Aton with the material sun, as well as the persevering doubt mentioned above as to whether Ikhnaton disbelieved in the other Egyptian gods.

The New Deal in Egyptian religion collapsed with the

[5] Breasted's trans. quoted by permission of Charles Scribner's Sons from *The Dawn of Conscience.*

death of the striking personality who initiated it. The starved Amon-Ra priesthood brought to bear their whole power upon the more compliant Tutankhaton who now bore the double crown by reason of his marriage with Ikhnaton's daughter. They forced him to substitute an "m" for the third "t" occurring in his royal name (Living Image of Aton), as a symbol of his return to orthodoxy, and to remove the royal court to Thebes. Aton records and monuments, outside of the abandoned Akhetaton itself, were destroyed or defaced in the name of the once more triumphant Amon-Ra. After Tutankhamon's brief reign and the three years of the Pharaoh Eye, the illustrious Thutmosids pass from the Pharaonic power, to give place to the forceful Ramsids who reorganized the land and won back the Empire.

A brief judgment must be passed on Atonism. It was a high type of natural religion, owing its form to the efforts of a religious genius whose sensitive ear picked out the finer strains from the discordant concert of Egyptian polytheism, who contributed something from his own originality, and combined these elements into a symphony. Yet his masterpiece, as others of a like kind in the history of natural religions, influenced only a small group and was forgotten shortly after his death. Finally, of moral content in Atonic doctrine, we have no evidence.

That Ikhnaton's monotheism could have been the fount from which flowed the monotheism of the Hebrews, is impossible. Genesis definitely ascribes the Hebrew belief to a revelation divinely given and divinely conserved in a world growing progressively polytheistic. Secondly, Hebrew worship was never naturistic, but had for its object a personal Being who transcended all nature forces. Thirdly, Hebrew religion was highly ethical, while Atonism has as yet to show moral content, if it possessed any. It is probably true that the Hebrews were domiciled in Egypt during the Aton Movement, for the more probable theory on the exodus date makes them quit Egypt under the Ramsids. But what likelihood is there that a colony of foreigners living in bondage in Gesen two hundred miles to the north of Akhetaton would have profoundly changed their ancestral religion into the esoteric cult of the shut-ins of Ikhnaton's court? Finally, Moses led the Hebrews out of Egypt either about a century before Atonism's rise or about a century after its total collapse (these being the two possible dates assigned by scholars). Hence, that he could have known Atonism or been the prophet of its doctrines to his people, is either impossible or highly improbable from the standpoint of purely secular history.

PART FOUR

RELIGION OF THE GREEKS

CHAPTER « 19

ORIGINS OF GREEK RELIGION

"The study of Greek religion," says Professor Farnell, "is almost coextensive with the study of Greek literature." A gifted race intellectually and esthetically, this people in all periods was inquisitive about religious truth, appreciative of man's need for religion. It was indeed an intellectual and esthetic preoccupation which rather failed to generate personal piety, since the clever Greek took occasion of the absurdities and indecencies of paganism to play the skeptic and the dilettante. Yes, his keen curiosity has preserved for us in his literature an observant record of the growth of the syncretic medley which was Hellenic religion.

For the reconstruction of the nation's sacred history, written Greek offers almost a millennium of documents. At one extreme Homer pictures the gods rising from Olympian council table, to don armor and settle the question at issue in combat beneath Ilion's walls. At the other, an obscure scholiast of the second century grinds out footnotes on yet more obscure cult-practices. The three great dramatists control the action of their masterpieces by a mechanism frankly divine, while Pausanias pens a didactic treatise on Grecian religious antiquities. Herodotus qualifies as a comparative religionist by his first-hand observation of foreign worship and interpretation of it in the light of Hellenic thought. The philosophers theorize on the origin of religion, while their three leaders think through to the purest theologic concepts which unaided reason has ever attained.

Add to the literary sources a profusion of inscriptions regulatory of public worship or expressive of private devotion. Add the mute witness of temples still standing on every shore of the old Magna Graecia. Add, finally, the fact that the mythological theme was the commonplace of the brush and chisel of Hellenic art. There is good hope that such abundant source material will ground a fairly adequate appraisal of the religious soul of Hellas.

Greek religion is a blend of simpler and more primitive forms of cult. The statement applies even to the Homeric Olympus. To hold that the hierarchical polytheism and the fairly developed ritualistic system pictured in *Iliad* and *Odyssey* are original types is as naïve a position as to hold that the epics themselves sprang full-panoplied and without dependence upon previous compositions from the creative fancy of the blind poet. Kipling sings on this head:

> When Homer smote his bloomin' lyre,
> He'd heard men sing by land and sea;
> And what he thought he might require,
> He went and took, the same as me.

The jingle may be applied to suggest how the Argive religion had borrowed from others. For this cult of the beginning of the first millennium B.C. is now known to plunge roots deeply into second millennial and earlier strata of ideas. It is proposed at present to trace this dependence.

An ascertained fact of archeology, another of anthropology furnish us with orientation. Anthropology testifies that the Hellenes were not the aborigines of Hellas, but were tribes which migrated down through the Balkans to fuse with the established natives of the land. Whether the natives, in turn, were themselves aboriginal, is another question. Fine archeological discoveries, from 1871 to the present, have authorized a partial reconstruction of the Cretan or Minoan-Mycenean civilization which the invading northerners found. The orientation mentioned above consists in the known confluence during the second millennium of two distinct culture-streams. What we know of the respective characteristics of each serves

From Sir A. Evans' *Earlier Religion of Greece*. By permission of The Macmillan Co.

Fig. 23. Sanctuary in Cave near Cnossus

urrounded by a wall of masonry stands a stalagmite pillar which was probably an
bject of worship. Numerous remains of votive offerings from all periods of Greek
istory attest a popular cult. The location of the cave, too, recalls *Odyssey,* XIX, l.
38: "He stayed his ships in Amnisus, whereby is the cave of Eilithia." Sir A. Evans
interestingly argues that here we have the Dictaean cave where Zeus was born.

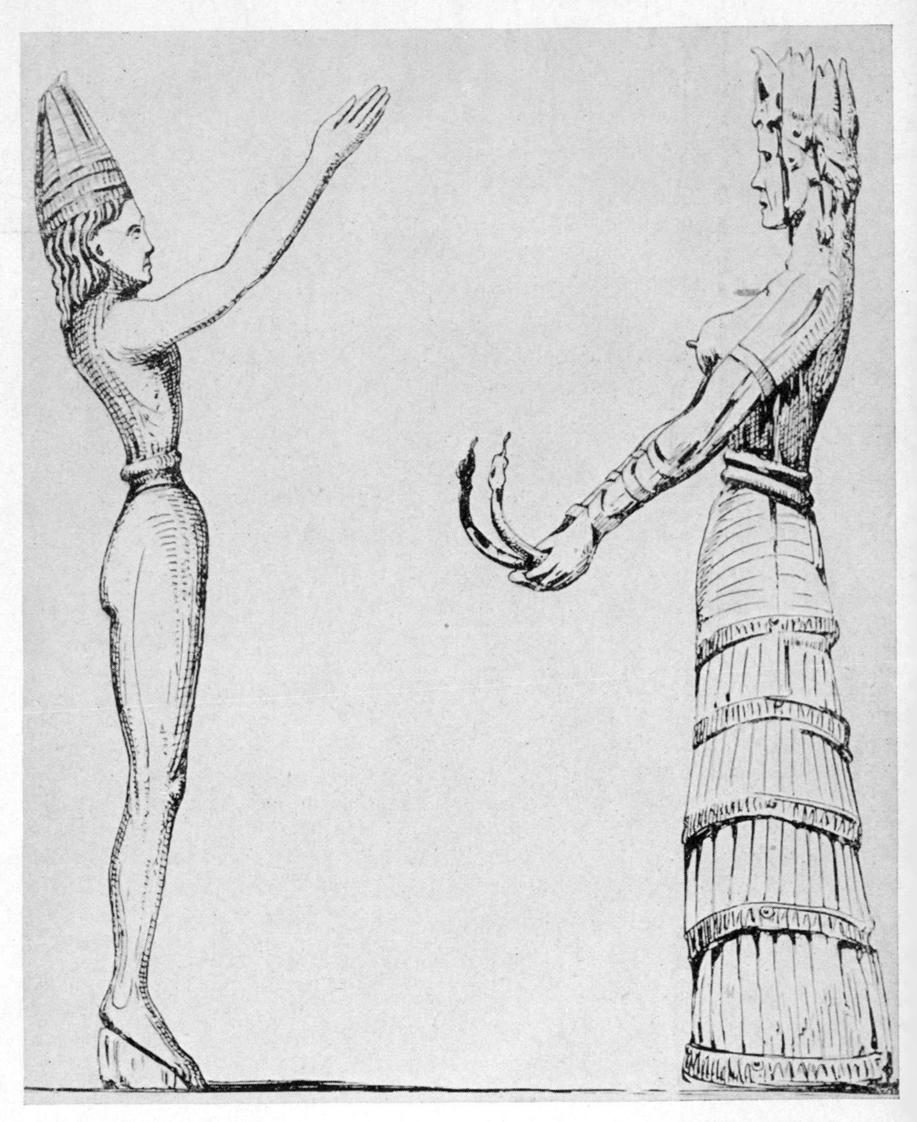

From Sir A. Evans' *Earlier Religion of Greece*. By permission of The Macmillan Co.

Fig. 24. Cretan Mother-Goddess and Boy-God

The mother-goddess and her associate or child occur in myth and monument throughout the old Mediterranean world. They were the tutelary divinities of the fruitfulness of nature.

as a norm in the interpretation of the characteristics of the composite stream which we first perceive in Ilian and Odyssean pantheon and worship.

The civilization which the Hellenic invaders supplanted extended from Mount Olympus in Thessaly, where ruled Zeus the father of gods and of men, down through Boeotia, Attica, and the Peloponnese to the Dictean cave in Crete, where the infant Zeus was born. The cult evidence now to be introduced is drawn from archeological finds all along this culture-chain—from Dimini in Thessaly, Orchomenus in Boeotia, Menidi in Attica, Tiryns and Mycenae in Argolis, Vaphio in Laconia, from the splendid royal palace at Knossos and the cave shrines in Crete.

It is interesting to note the prominence of fetishes in the Aegean cult. In shrines actually uncovered by excavations and in scenes depicting worship there are found uniformly sacred stone-pillars. They occur sometimes singly, sometimes in groups of three, sometimes poised one upon two others to form an arch after the manner of the Stonehenge in England. They are admitted now by all investigators to be objects of worship. The evidence compels this admission, for the pillar appears in the record immediately adored by votaries, emitting rays of light, accompanied by the sacred dove, lion, or bull, in conjunction with the divine symbols of the double-edged ax, swastika or cross.

The phenomenon of sacred-stone worship, noted throughout the whole of Greek religious history, has thus in pre-Homeric days a distinct analogue, if not in fact a causal prototype. One difference must be remarked. The Aegean stone is revered in a generic way as a dwelling-place of an undetermined divine spirit, while the Greek of classical days associated particular stones with the persons of particular Olympians. Among the sacred stones of classical Greece we have those sacred to Aphrodite, to Cybele, to Eros, to the three Graces, to Heracles. They are more varied in form, too, than the Aegean stones, for they appear as boulders and aerolites, cones, and pyramids, even as grotesquely carved figures. The constancy of the phenomenon of reverence paid to these stones and the like constancy with which they are referred to divinities point convincingly to Fetishism as the underlying religious motive.

One may well pause and mark with interest the occurrence of the same cult practice among Africans, Australians, Amerindians, early Cretans — races which even Reinach will hesitate to pronounce interdependent. The reasonable conclusion is that the uniformity of certain religious manifestations is sufficiently explained by the unity of the human species. Fetishism grows from a natural human desire to localize the divinity, to appropriate it, even to make it portable.

Other cult-objects which the excavations offer in abundance are the labrys or double-edged ax, the *taurokerata* or bull's horns, the swastika or *crux gammata,* the Greek cross. Of these the first is a fetish, but its precise symbolism is puzzling. *Taurokerata* are no more than conventionalized symbols of the sacred bull, but have become so usual as to be probably purely decorative. Of the meaning of the various cross forms, savants offer divergent explanations (cf. *Catholic Encyclopedia*); however, the opinion may be hazarded that in the Aegean monuments they are symbols held over from star-worship which formerly dominated that cult.

Another feature of pre-Homeric religion may be arrived at partly by comparative conjecture, partly by direct testimony. The conjecture rests on two facts. In historic Greece Zeus, Pallas Athene, and Apollo all had their cult symbolized by sacred trees — the oak, the olive, the bay-tree — while a whole class of minor divinities were the wood-sprites or Hamadryades. These two facts lead to the inference that a source-religion of ancient Greece was dendrolatrous. Seeking direct evidence in the Minoan-Mycenean discoveries, we are not disappointed, for the tree no less than the stone was held sacred. The palm, the fig, and the cypress stand near the altar or grow from it. The Aegean goddess is seen seated beneath the tree with votaries approaching to worship. She and her consort god regale themselves on the tree's fruit.

Dendrolatry is a fairly widespread pagan superstition, whose explanation varies for different peoples. No universal explanation suffices, such as remembrance of Eden's fateful tree, or the legend of a mighty tree whose roots held the earth together and whose branches supported the heavens. For the Aegean worshipers of the principle of life, the explanation seems to be that the perennial vitality of trees led to association of them with the workings of that principle. Under the influence of religious myth and poetry trees were personified as Dryads, while suitable species were taken as symbolic of the attributes of particular great gods.

Discoveries in the palace at Knossos appear to establish Minos and his Minotaur as historical figures. The palace's antiquity and splendor fit well with the legend's account of the Cretan king's dwelling. More curious still is evidence uncovered of a real labyrinth. Most remarkable are representations of the Minotaur and scenes which seem to be sacrifices of youths and maidens tossed to the mercy of sacred bulls. The half-human form of the Minotaur may well have been created by fear of the animal which roamed the labyrinth.

Other animals — serpents, doves, lions, goats, griffins, and sphinxes — are represented in cult scenes as companions and guardians of the Cretan goddess. The association of animals with gods passes on into historic Greek religion, which assigned the eagle to Zeus, the ox to Hera, the owl to Athene. For Reinach the presence of animal cult proves that the Greeks were originally totemists, that is, that early Greek tribes or families worshiped particular animals as their ancestors and protectors. By a parallel argument, some future scholar will conclude that our present-day North American culture was totemic because of the annual turkey sacrifice and the exaltation of the symbolic animals of our two political parties. Greek society offers no evidence of Totemism, while the assumed evidence of sacred animals can be otherwise explained. The early Aegeans probably thought the divine spirit of fecundity peculiarly manifested in animal life, while later Greeks associated special animal with special god because of some mythological story, or because the animal's qualities seemed to symbolize the god's attributes. The animal was rather a fetish than a totem.

Funeral pyres, so familiar in *Iliad* and *Odyssey,* were not the rule in Minoan-Mycenean civilization. The dead were either inhumed or placed in shaft-graves cut in the side of a cliff. Offerings to the dead are found uniformly within the graves. From the shaft-graves at Mycenae, for instance, archeologists have removed finely wrought daggers with embossed hilts and blades adorned with scenes from the chase, mighty broadswords which an Ajax might have wielded, inlaid silver and gold goblets whose gracefully turned handles invite the touch of a Ganymede. Altars stood near the graves, while such numbers of animal bones have been uncovered in the vicinity that we must infer that the holocausts were frequently repeated. It is clear that in earliest times Greece cherished a belief in survival after death.

What was the nature of the divinity to whom Aegean cult was directed? The answer to the question was delayed for a time because archeologists at first found neither idols nor pictures of gods. With these now available and with the whole mass of cultural facts to judge from, the Aegean concept of deity may be inferred.

The Aegean deity was a goddess. Accompanying her is occasionally depicted a male divinity, seemingly a child, who shares the worship, but obviously in a minor role. In cult-scenes carved on gems the goddess appears seated beneath the sacred tree and surrounded by other cult-objects, receiving the homage of votaries. She walks between protecting lions, while the dove circles above her head. She brandishes the double-edged ax. The idols of her range from crudely molded busts of clay, through a group of marble figurines, to the really artistic statuette from the sanctuary of the Knossan palace. The statuette is of a native clay overlaid with white enamel. The costume, neatly painted in several colors, would have been pronounced quite up to date at the turn of the last century. Entwined around the headdress and raising its head threateningly above it is a spotted snake, while similar snakes form the girdle of the figure and twist down each extended arm. Sir Arthur Evans unearthed this greatest of his treasures from soil impregnated with the fat of sacrificed animals and filled with votive offerings and cult-objects.

We do not know the goddess' name, for Aegean civilization is at present a "picture book without text," since philologists have found no clue for deciphering Aegean writing. Names of gods, however, are of secondary importance: what is desired is to get at the religious idea embodied in the goddess and her little attendant god. There would not be much evidence on which to base a theory, did the Minoan-Mycenean finds stand alone, but these finds compared with later Greek religion and with various ancient Mediterranean cults furnish an identification of the goddess and her little fellow. They are the counterparts of Phenician Ashtaroth and Tammuz, Pessinus' Cybele and Attis, Egyptian Isis and Horus. All these dual cults have a common meaning. The goddess stands as a personification of the force of vegetation which man made into a god because of his intimate dependence upon it. The male divinity, who is personified as child or lover of the goddess, signifies the fresh vegetation of springtime. Explanatory myth tells how the godlet is slain, how the goddess seeks him in the Netherworld and brings him back to earth. In later Greece this kernel of religious belief grew into the Eleusinian Mysteries.

The following table outlines the subject just discussed:

AEGEAN CULTURE AND RELIGION

Time: Prior to 1200 B.C.
Area: Thessaly, Boeotia, Attica, Argolis, Laconia, Crete.
Characteristic: Worship of fecundity-spirit.
Cult Objects:

1. Sacred Pillars (fetishistic in significance).
2. Sacred Trees (fecund objects, naturally revered as manifestations of fecundity spirit).
3. Sacred Animals (interpretation same as for 2).
4. Theriomorphic human figures (such as minotaur, probably an adumbration of anthropomorphism).
5. Horns of consecration (conventionalized symbols of sacred bull); Swastika and Cross (probably symbols of stars from an earlier astrology); *Labrys* or bipennis or double-edged ax (a cult object of undetermined significance).

Burial Customs and Belief in Hereafter:

a) Inhumation or shaft-grave burial prevailed.
b) Useful articles and treasures placed near the body.
c) Sacrifices offered at the grave, at burial and afterwards.
d) Clear evidence of belief in survival after death.

Divinities:

a) Fecundity-spirit (represented as a woman).
b) Small male god attendant on her (either a child or a lover).
c) Ascertained connection between this pair and many Mediterranean pairs.

Homeric society is an amalgam of the civilization of the Minoan-Mycenean with the civilization of Hellenes and Dorians who entered the land in two great migratory waves from the north. That Hellenes and Dorians were Indo-Europeans, ethnologists no longer doubt, but a brief summary of the arguments for this identification is in order.

Greek tradition on the making of the nation particularizes an original period of domination by the Minoan dynasty of Crete; then the fusion of the families of the Minoan lords of the mainland with god-born heroes from overseas; finally, two great invasions from the north effected respectively by the "sons of Hellen" about 1360 and "the sons of Dorus" about 1100. Both invading hosts, the tradition states, came from the northernmost borders of Thessaly. Now, we know that in the second millennium B.C. it was the Indo-Europeans who were surging restlessly through the Balkan lands north of Thessaly.

Philology definitely assigns classical Greek language to the western group of Indo-European languages, a group which embraced the speech of peoples anciently situated north and northwest of Hellas. We do not know positively to what language group the Minoan-Mycenean speech belonged, but best critical opinion (for example, Edmund Power, S.J., in *Biblica* for 1929, pp. 129–169), holds that Minos and his vassals spoke a language akin to the Cyprian. Hence, the Indo-European basis of Greek speech is to be attributed to the invading Hellenes and Dorians.

Some further light is thrown on Greek origins by physical anthropology. In general, the Minoans are classified as Mediterraneans on the evidence of Cretan skeletal remains and pictures. Turning to Homeric and later testimony, we find not Mediterranean, but rather Indo-European physical characteristics in the ascendant. The Olympians, for instance, are fair-haired; Achilles, the Homeric ideal of manhood, yellow-haired; his son Neoptolemus, even red-headed; Spartan athletes, blond. From literary and pictured sources there is ample testimony to the prevalence of light complexion, of gray and blue eyes. What evidence is available from comparative study of skeletal remains indicates a wide diffusion of the Indo-European type alongside the indigenous Mediterranean.

The Indo-European Theory is an epic of anthropology composed during the past century and more. Inspired guessing and tireless research have established kinship of language, social culture, and religion between peoples superficially so different as are Greeks, Italians, Scythians, Thracians, Indians, Persians, Germans, Scandinavians, and Slavs. The common fund of Indo-European religious ideas must be summarily studied, since these constitute the second of our two sources of Homeric religion.

Though polytheists, the Indo-European worshiped a Supreme Being, whose relation to the other gods was that of master. His attributes are exalted dignity, sanctity, justice, and benignity. Toward men he shows himself to be a father, and is called such. Among warlike tribes, he is the one who directs the battle and gives victory, while peoples fairly advanced in the formation of a civil society conceive of him as head of the state and sanctioner of its ordinances. Though clear ideas of creation are not found where polytheism prevails, yet the Indo-Europeans with various degrees of clearness understand the Supreme Being as transcendant and as the first origin of all things.

The other gods are, to speak in general terms, personifications of natural forces such as earth, sun, moon, water, fire, storm. Their attributes, however, are borrowed in part from the supreme god. Myths, which at first tell in naïve allegory of the operation of these natural forces, gradually humanize and cheapen the persons of these gods. Three causes, therefore, may be said to produce the typical Indo-European god. There is the decay of monotheism, though the Supreme Being is never wholly obscured. Then, superstitious attention is directed to the natural objects and phenomena which attend and influence human life, and these are thought to be gods. Anthropomorphic myth paints the final humanized portrait of the supposed divinities.

A selective levee of Indo-European gods will serve as illustration. Ahura Mazda of the Persians is peculiarly resident in the illimitable and luminous sky. The Norseman's Thor clouds the heavens by shaking his red beard, drives across them with thundering chariot wheels, hurls his hammer to produce the lightning. Eostre of the Anglo-Saxons is the mild goddess who awakens vegetation from its winter sleep. Two divinities of fire, Hestia of Italy and Agni of India, typify the sanctity respectively of the domestic hearth and the sacrificial fire.

The moon stood as a symbol of death in the Indo-European mythology. That the moon was regarded as a god of the dead in any personal sense, cannot be shown. Rather was there an amorphous apprehension of a connection between "the inconstant moon" and the passing and future state of mortal man. A variety of ritualistic practices attest this. The human soul itself, while it tenanted the body, was for the folk we are considering a robust principle which battened upon the body's blood. Through death the personal identity of the soul was not lost, but its nature was transmuted to a shadowy vestige of itself. Special divinities grew up in mythology to take charge of human wraiths in the Afterworld. For instance, Odin of the Norsemen is primarily a god of the dead. A future state of punishment is not always grasped by the Indo-Europeans, nor are their beliefs always precise in regard to an aftertime of reward for right conduct. Ancestors and racial heroes might be accorded apotheosis.

The two main sources of Homeric religion may be thus summarized.

Aegean Religion	Indo-European Religion
Goddess personifying the principle of natural fecundity.	Supreme Being, benign, holy, just, sanctioner of moral order, support of social order.
God, offspring of goddess, personifying vernal rebirth of vegetation. Cult of "god-bodies" or fetishes regarded as residences of fecundity goddess: such as trees, pillars and stones, animals.	Nature cult: gods of sun, moon, fire, storm; nature-myths allegorizing natural phenomena and humanizing nature-gods.
Survivals of star-worship: such as cult of labrys, of swastika, of Greek cross.	Cult of dead: personal survival in shadowy existence; gods of the dead; hero and ancestor apotheosis.
Belief in future life attested by offerings in graves and sacrifices near graves.	

CHAPTER « 20

THE GODS OF HOMER

SINCE the ideas of the preceding chapter have prepared the way, we may observe now the Homeric method of rushing *in medias res*. The gods of Olympus who appear in *Iliad* and *Odyssey* will be first treated. Then Mythologism and Anthropomorphism will be analyzed, to secure a right understanding of the gods. Finally, the religious picture of the epic age will be completed by a sketch of the relations of men with gods.

Phidias is said to have modeled his statue of Zeus upon Homer's description of the father of gods and of men. Truly, the religious-minded Greek who entered the temple at Olympia, when the rich veil was drawn aside from before the sanctuary, must have recognized in the majestic figure the identical attributes of divinity which had been crystallized in verse at the crisp dawn of Hellenic thought. Majestically enthroned, crowned with olive leaves and bearing a scepter surmounted by the emblematic eagle, the god's statue towered almost to the top of the shrine. A golden robe draped the lower limbs, while the noble lines of the torso were worked in pure ivory. Benign power spoke in every feature of the countenance. Statuary art had translated into its own language what poetry had sung of Zeus:

> Kronion spoke, and bowed his dark brow, and the ambrosial locks waved from the king's immortal head; and he made great Olympus quake.[1]

Sovereignty is the characteristic note impressed upon us

[1]Translations throughout this chapter will be those of Professors Butcher, Lang, Leaf, and Myers. Here *Iliad,* Bk. I, lines 528–530.

in every Homeric statement of Zeus' thoughts and actions, whether these concern plans for the war about Ilion's walls, missions entrusted to other divinities, reproof of even the greatest of them, or the more properly universal functions of weighing out men's destinies in golden scales, distributing to them good and evil gifts from his fateful urns, sanctioning by his judgments their right or wrong conduct. No god dared gainsay his determined will for, to quote the lame Hephaestus' advice to Hera, he was too hard a foe to face. From his palace on the peak of Olympus he directed the change of seasons, gathered the storm clouds like sheep around his feet, or drove them forth to cover the firmament and hurled his vengeful lightning-bolts. He was ruler not alone of present but of the future also, whose secrets he read and communicated at will to man. To the dying Hector he reveals the fate of Achilles:

> Take heed now lest I draw upon thee the wrath of gods, in the day when Paris and Phoebus Apollo slay thee, for all thy valor, at the Skaian gate.[2]

Yet his power is tempered with benignity. Pitying the distress of Andromache, of Priam and Hekabe over the death of husband and child, he arranges an artful plan to move the heart of dire Achilles to the rendering up of Hector's body for burial. He takes under his special providence the wanderer and the friendless, is zealous for the cause of humble suppliants, grants pardon and averts threatened doom in view of propitiatory sacrifices. With a naïve inconsistency, Homer represents the all-powerful and all-seeing one as worried over the course of his children's affairs and as tossing sleepless on his Olympian couch while he meditates a suitable remedy for their relief.

Some strokes of drab shade will be added to this bright picture of the Greeks' chief god, when we come to speak of

---

[2] *Iliad,* Bk. XXII, ll. 358–360.

Anthropomorphism and Mythologism. However, an identification of Zeus may be presented at once without fear of doing violence to the evidence. He is essentially the Indo-European Supreme Being. His cult had been retained by the northern invaders at the various centers of their settlement in Greece, a fact attested by a number of local appellations added to his name. The very choice of Olympus as his throne points to Indo-European derivation, for it was in the neighborhood of this impressively lofty mountain that the sons of Hellen and Dorus fixed their first abode before proceeding to the conquest of the lands lying to the south. A fusion, however, of the concepts of the Indo-European Supreme Being and of the little god of the Aegeans must be admitted. For, in the first place, Zeus' origin was assigned in mythology to birth from Kronos and Rhea in the Cretan cave. Secondly he appears in Homer as the prolific parent of gods and heroes, which idea seems to be an adaptation of the attributes of a fecundity spirit.

Zeus' supremacy is emphasized by contrast with other Olympians. Mythologically, Poseidon is Zeus' brother, to whom after the struggle which established the reign of the Kronidae was assigned the empire of the sea, just as to Hades was assigned the region beneath the earth and to Zeus the heavens and earth Yet, Poseidon is definitely a subordinate. He dwells in the sea and owns no palace on the slopes of Olympus, though he is summoned thither for council meetings. He lacks the judicial calm and impartiality of Zeus, being, like his element the sea, changeable and violent. He knows his subjection to the will of his greater brother, but nonetheless schemes to work private spite upon mortals whom he dislikes and for whom good destinies have been appointed by the father god. Thus, he hinders by wind and wave the return journey of Odysseus. Poseidon is undoubtedly an Aegean, not an Indo-European, divinity. Aegeans doubtless associated closely the divine principle of vegetation with the waters, so anthropomorphism supplied in Poseidon a personification of water's fertilizing power.

The son of Leto and Zeus, far-darting Apollo, is not only the god whose wrath sets going the divine and human mechanism of the *Iliad,* but he plays throughout an important role which is a forecast of the aggrandizement of his cult in later Greece. In his Indo-European original, he is a nature-god, specifically a god of fire. Fire's destructive might is typified in the arrows he pours on his enemies and in his proper epithet "the far-darter." An idea more strictly religious underlies the Homeric picture of him as sharer of Zeus' counsels in regard to men and as principal envoy between the father god and mortals. Such functions as intermediary between god and man belong in Indo-European religion to the sacrificial fire. Phoebus, then, "the gleaming one," stands forth in his higher attributes as a symbol of light, spirit, purification from defilement, sacrificial atonement.

On a like high level are the attributes of Pallas Athene. An Aegean origin is indicated for her. In Mycenean days cult addressed almost exclusively the goddess who personified nature's power of fecundity. On her favor depended the welfare of the individual and the family, of the city-states Cnossus, Mycene, Tyrins, and the rest. It goes without saying that the Hellenic invaders could not eradicate a cult so intense unless they were minded utterly to destroy Aegean folk and civilization. In the fusion of Hellenic and Aegean stocks, religious syncretism found a way to save reverence for the goddess. She might not supplant the Indo-European Supreme Being, neither would Aegean devotion brook her stepping down to a definitely subordinate plane, nor her being deprived of her function as fosterer of all human concerns. At first, it may be supposed, Zeus cult and the goddess cult developed side by side despite their logical mutual exclusiveness. Mythology then solved the contradiction by making her spring from the father god Zeus, not in commonwise, but from his all-ruling mind. Her Zeus clothes with the aegis, emblem of his own irresistible power. Her he dispatches to execute his determined counsels among mortals. She retains, moreover, her character as guardian of the city-state in her special function of warding off from the Argive community any urgent danger. She is the goddess of ordered battle, a Greek ideal from earliest times, potent to bring discomfort upon the madly valiant Ares. She bests him, and wounded and baffled he sits him down beside the son of Kronos and whines:

> With thee we are all at variance, because thou didst beget that reckless maiden and baleful, whose thought is ever of iniquitous deeds. For all the other gods that are in Olympus hearken to thee, and we are subject every one; only her thou chastiseth not, neither in deed nor word, but setteth her on, because this pestilent one is thy own offspring.[3]

In Zeus, then, and by a kind of emanation in Apollo and Athene, is to be recognized the sum total of attributes properly divine. Though the Homeric Greek's idea of divinity is defective, it is far from being wholly corrupt. Corrupting forces were at work and were to continue to operate till the relative purity of the concept of god-nature grew nearly debased. The corrupting forces are noted in Homer's opening of Olympus to an *"omnium gatherum"* of gods who cut a sorry theologic figure. To say nothing of the naturistic gods like Poseidon, certain other divinities held freehold of Olympian palaces because of their readiness to justify the acts of illicit human passion. Hera borrows a specious dignity from the mythical marriage with Zeus, but in herself she is the deification of the passions of jealousy and suspicion. Ares and Aphrodite, stripped of poetic vesture, are personifications of the deadly sins of anger and lust.

Pagans almost universally see divinity through the spectacles of anthropomorphism and mythology. Anthropomor-

---

[3] *Iliad,* Bk. V, ll. 874 sqq.

phism, or the fancy that gods have human forms, thoughts, and desires, is rooted in the limitations of our mode of cognition. For every idea we have of God is derived from our direct knowledge of creatures and must be analogous and imperfect. Precise philosophic thought or the light of supernatural revelation is needed to render our ideas of God even relatively clear. How powerful, then, the tendency to humanize the gods in a mentality such as that of the Homeric Greek, which on the one hand was innocent of refined philosophic thought and on the other lacked rapport with any revelation capable of affording a catharsis and clarification of the idea of divinity! Abhorrent, too, to a mentality which, even in the epic dawn of its self-expression is seen to be enamored of concreteness and crystal clarity, would be a divinity conceived under the amorphous and only vaguely personal notion of *mana* or "power." If the gods were to be acknowledged by this intellectually independent race, they must be made intelligible and adaptable to human needs. The bent of the Greek mind was rationalistic rather than mystic.

The gods, in consequence, move and speak on the Ilian stage in a consistently anthropomorphic character. Immortal, but not really eternal, they are begotten and beget. Conforming to the prejudices of worshipers esteeming noble lineage, the Olympians are built up into a sublimated peerage tracing back to Ocean and Old Time. Their official residence is the slope of Mount Olympus in Thessaly, though, by way of concession to ancient local cults, particular gods may maintain villas in other sacred regions of Hellas. Within Olympian palace walls the daily routine of anthropomorphic life occupies the immortals. They tread their golden halls engaged in anxious converse on the latest news from Troyland, they lave in ambrosial baths, they banquet and seek repose when Sleep enfolds them. Demigods minister to them, steeds stand by ready to be yoked to jeweled chariots when the god may be minded to go journeying, or to take the field against some human hero whose valor is disturbing the balance of power between Acheans and Trojans.

Zeus' own palace towers above the rest upon the very pinnacle of Olympus, where the Cloud-gatherer lives with Hera in a union which, already in Homer's day, political and religious expediency had chosen to hold up as the prototype of the sacredness of the marriage bond. Zeus summons all to his council-hall to debate the affairs of the war and listens to discussions, not always parliamentary nor temperate. Against his determined will there is no appeal, though even after he has spoken it, cliques of certain gods and goddesses scheme how they may by subterfuge gain the object he has denied them. For just such ethical failings as we see in courtiers or members of a family, anthropomorphism complacently attributes to the Olympian court and family. Worse yet are the ethical failings implied in Hera's jealousy, shrewishness, and mendacity; in Ares' berserk blood lust; in the treachery which mars even the relatively noble characters of Apollo and Athene.

Taking all in all, we must admit that the Olympians are distinguished from mortals rather by a superiority of physical attributes than by moral perfection. "As a god will" is a familiar Homeric phrase, but one that exalts the preternatural or magical power, not the attributes of goodness and wisdom. It is an apt phrase which the poet uses to explain the pictures he paints of a god flashing through the air or invisibly striking off a hero's armor in battle. By greater speed and cleverness of operation does the anthropomorphic divinity surpass the man in whose image he is imagined. A naïve attempt to unravel these tangled concepts of divine and human natures is noted in the Homeric reason for the Olympian's possession of an undying life. Through the god's veins flows a fluid called *ichor* which, though it flows forth on occasion, as when Diomede wounds Aphrodite and Ares, yet constitutes a principle of immortal life, as blood does of mortal life. Just as

Fig. 25. The Poet Homer

In his epics he crystallized Greek religious tradition. His poetic anthropomorphism determined for future ages the form and character of the gods.

blood-cells depend for health and multiplication on food and drink, so ichor-cells find their specific support in a balanced diet of ambrosia and nectar. It is even implied that, had some new Prometheus succeeded in stealing the chemical formulas of the divine comestibles, he could have secured for mortals a synthetic immortality.

Though the statement that Homer made the gods of Greece contains an exaggeration, there is truth in it. His gods are not pure creations of poetic fancy, but are the gods who emerged from the union of Mycenean and Hellenic cults under the complex influence of genuine religious reverence and spurious mythologic story. Yet he did effect an important alteration. He harnessed the extravagant stream of Mycenean-Hellenic beliefs, forcing it into a sharp-cut channel, suitable for the work of the epic poems. Since the gods had to turn the turbines which controlled the machinery of the Trojan war, they had to be circumscribed, concrete, and rationalized forces; they had to exhibit the sensible qualities of shape, color, and activity demanded of actors in a drama. An inevitable emphasis of anthropomorphism resulted. What before was vaguely apprehended under no concrete form, but for that very reason more conducive to religious reverence for the "Overpower," was now presented to readers and hearers of *Iliad* and *Odyssey* as a crisply finite figure, contending with men on a plane of equality for the petty prizes which men ambition.

The work of a second-rate poet who thus denatured the gods would have effected little in the line of changing the religious thought of his countrymen. The stupendous genius of a Homer, however, appearing just when the Greek race was emerging, fixed the concept of divinity for the unfolding mind of Hellas. He became the nation's schoolmaster, whose poetic pantheon was accepted as the basis for orthodox theology. The religious gain from his teaching consisted in precision of the objects of worship and in unification into a close-knit family of a variety of gods. The loss and wound he inflicted on essential religion consisted both in the fact that he committed Greek thought to the acceptance of a theology intrinsically contradictory, and in the fact that his gods, with exceptions already noted, are seriously deficient in moral attributes. Philosophy never did or could accept these divinities, and, after a feeble cry of protest, contented itself with the axiom: "of the nature of the gods we can know nothing." Hence failed one of the natural means which should operate toward preserving and purifying religion.

The living religion of the people, of course, took its tone from the character of Homeric Olympians. What presumptuous votary will seek for a higher norm of conduct than that lived out by his god in the myths? And for what human sin could the believer not find prototype and warrant in Homer's Hera, Poseidon, Aphrodite, and Ares? Both intellectually and morally, Homeric theology sows the seeds of the religious decadence which stirred the zeal of the Apostle Paul. There was need for him to preach to the Greeks "the God they knew not, who dwelleth not in temples, nor needeth anything, but who giveth to all life and breath and everything."

As anthropomorphism gave the gods a tangible form, so mythology gave them a history. To understand this simple statement, we must drill down and lay bare a few fundamental ideas. For an inconsiderate identification of the term "myth" with the term "fiction" underlies our thinking on the beautiful stories which delight equally the child reader of *Tanglewood Tales* and the student of classical literature. Theseus and the Minotaur, the sojourn of Persephone in Hades, the siege of Ilion, all these are narratives which we are apt to deem as fictitious as Jim Hawkins and John Silver, the life of Little Dorrit in the Fleet, or the storming of Front de Boeuf's castle. Stories of the former class are thus misjudged, since in reality they are parented by objective truth as well as by the storyteller's imagination. Though not strictly a narrative of fact, the myth has fact for its starting point, and so stands midway between pure history and pure romance. To illustrate graphically:

Writing	Basis	Acceptance	Class
Four Gospels.	Fact just as narrated.	As pure history.	History.
Labors of Heracles.	Fact and romantic fancy.	As pure history.	Myth.
Nicholas Nickleby.	Romantic fancy	As romantic fancy.	Fiction.

Though the fact which founds the myth may be of various kind, yet two comprehensive classes of these facts have been recognized. Heracles and Theseus, for instance, were probably historical heroes, while Troy was certainly an ancient city. The myths, then, centering around these names appear as embellished history. If a myth be traceable to a historic fact, person, or event, it is called an euhemeristic-myth, borrowing the name from the philosopher Euhemerus who in the fourth century B.C. theorized that all the gods were once human heroes whose exploits had been magnified by mythographers.

The second class of facts on which myths are based embraces beliefs and cult practices. Projecting our historical vision into the dim past of religion, we see votaries worshiping the powers of physical nature as well as certain gods already more sharply personified and iconized; engaged besides in a variety of ritualistic practices. These were the gods their fathers worshiped, these the practices understood to be efficacious in securing the gods' favor. Yet devotion, to a degree, and speculation, to a much greater degree, always seek a reason for cult beyond the mere traditional and incurious acceptance. Even in natural religion man desires a knowledge which will enable him to "give a reason to any inquirer for the faith which is in him." Mythographers undertake for an unphilosophic and untheologic age the task of the philosopher and theologian, forming stories which will justify the popular faith. The natural power of the life-giving sun becomes personal in the story of a god driving his flaming chariot from east to west in the firmament. The spirit of the new vegetation in the spring becomes the daughter of the vegetation goddess: the daughter is stolen by Dis and carried beneath the earth; her rescue and reappearance are the coming of spring. At Gortyn in Greece an immemorial cult centered about a plane-tree. Mythology traced the cult to the belief that under this tree Zeus and Europa celebrated their nuptials. And so on with many other myths, though even the most downright of critics speak in modest terms of the amount of positive and certain exegesis of myths which research warrants. If a myth has arisen in the way indicated, namely, as an explanation of a belief or a cult practice, it is called an etiological myth.

Mythology, to sum up, is reason's attempt to give plausibility to the object of religious belief. Where the believer cannot find — as the Christian can and does find — preambles for his faith in reason and history, he seeks them instinctively in the caricature of reason and history furnished by the mythological story. Religion refuses to rest in the emotions of cult alone. In the half-truths of their myths, though a half portion of truth is obviously too generous a measure to accredit them with, Greek believers found a partial and temporary stay for their intellectual hunger. But mythology proved after all of the same stuff as anthropomorphism. Its texture was too unsubstantial to withstand the thrust of philosophy's lance. Besides, the attribution to the gods of morally discreditable biographies by mythology offered the sanction of religion for licentious conduct.

The sense of dependence, never absent from the practice of religion, withstood the trial of humanized gods and fairy-tale apologetics. Prayer to a god whose midriff may be pierced by a human spear; vows and sacrifices to an Olympian oligarchy whose private lives merit the frown of even human censorship; these and similar anomalies throw our thoughts back to fundamental considerations. The pure element of religion is not to be confused with derivatives such as mythology and superstition. It is the invisible element or soul from which all religious self-expression proceeds. To that soul we must accord the primacy in appraising the genuine value of any particular cult. Within the Homeric man's soul there pulsated a religion of relative correctness and purity, which winged arrows of prayer through the haze of anthropomorphic mythology to the heart of a divinity who sat on a higher throne than Olympus. The injured priest, Chryses, though far away from the shrine where he ministers to Phoebus Apollo, is certain of the god's attention to his plea:

> Hear me, god of the silver bow, that standest over Chryse and holy Killa, and rulest Tenedos with might, O Smintheus! If ever I built a temple gracious in thy eyes, or if ever I burnt to thee fat flesh of thighs of bulls or goats, fulfill thou my desire; let the Danaans pay by thine arrows for my tears.[4]

Not even the vocalization of prayer was essential, for Ajax instructs his men:

> Pray ye the while to Kronos' son king Zeus, in silence to yourselves.[5]

And, running in second place on the last lap of a foot race,

> Odysseus prayed in his soul to bright-eyed Athene: "Hearken, goddess, come thou a good helper to my feet."[6]

All the Acheans pray to Zeus and expect him to bring to woe the guilty man in the trial by ordeal between Paris and Menelaus. Odysseus, sore in doubt, asks confidently for a preter-

[4] *Iliad,* I, ll. 37–42.
[5] *Iliad,* VII, ll. 195–196.
[6] *Iliad,* XXIII, ll. 768–770.

natural portent to show him his way (*Iliad,* III, ll. 320–323; *Odyssey,* XX, ll. 98–101). Prayer which realizes the omnipresence, omniscience, and omnipotence of the divinity, and which appeals with childlike trust to that divinity for help in spirituals and temporals is a positive religious factor of high rating. It is the brightest feature in the subjective religion of early Greece, just as the attributes of Zeus constitute the noblest feature in the objective religion of that period.

Though direct invocation of the gods still held this comparatively high level, a superstitious formalism had already invaded the field of ritual observance. Here is recognized a presage of the legalistic externalism that was later to canker the Greek soul. The belief in gods who surpassed men in physical strength, knowledge, and craftiness, but who were quite capable of feeling slights, cherishing grudges, and playing favorites, was not a belief calculated to let the votary's head rest on an easy pillow. To keep the gods in good humor was, therefore, an objective of first importance. Odysseus cautions his son Telemachus:

> Easy it is for the gods who hold the high heavens either to exalt a mortal man or do him ill.[7]

The gods wanted their due share of fatlings, fine flour, and rich wine before they would leave their younger mortal brothers in secure possession of these blessings. Failing the libation and the sacrifice — and these at the recurrence of every season, every crisis, every fresh undertaking — the god was understood to be prepared to put the remiss votary "on the spot," unless speedy reparation were forthcoming. The idea expanded till it assumed the magnitude of a vast and long-tentacled supernatural "racket," which exacted a heavy toll in temporals and a more grievous one in the spirit of genuine religious reverence. Sacrifice should be the sublimest form of man's service of the divinity, but anthropomorphic reasoning

[7] *Odyssey,* XVI, ll. 211, 212.

was cheapening it into an insurance-policy premium guaranteeing against interference from the powers above.

The Olympians saw to it, moreover, that mortals did not attain overmuch prosperity, lest occasion be given for the conceit that mortal life was as desirable as the "easy" life on Olympus. Jealousy was really the motive here, not the worthy purpose of securing man against the dangers of pride. Achilles, all too glorious a hero to escape Olympian envy, must die of the arrow winged from the bow of the effeminate Paris. Too great a fame had accrued to Odysseus by reason of the stratagem he devised to end the Ilian war; hence he alone of all the princes was denied a speedy and happy return home. For, explains Menelaus:

> The deity himself envied him these things, who has prevented him alone, wretched one, from return.[8]

Boasting in good fortune, as Ajax found to his cost, was sure to invite retribution from divine jealousy. Rather one had to take one's gifts and fortune pragmatically for what they might be. Thanksgiving to the gods is an emotion which the Greek realized very imperfectly. By avoiding boasting and by being bounteous, in hecatomb and libation, a mortal favored by good fortune might hope to avoid the green-eyed jealousy which ever watched from Olympian heights. To Hector Zeus bears testimony:

> Nowise failed he in the gifts I loved. Never did my altar lack seemly feast, drink-offering and the steam of sacrifice, even the honor that falleth to our due.[9]

Nevertheless, though Hector was "dearest to the gods of all mortals that are in Ilios," they could not save their darling from the fate that dogs his steps throughout the poem. This introduces the last point to be treated in Homeric religion. "Lot," "portion," "destiny," "Moira" are terms which settle

---

[8] *Odyssey,* IV, ll. 181.

[9] *Iliad,* XXIV, ll. 69–70.

a vast number of problems and discussions in the minds and in the assemblies of Homeric gods and heroes. Not even recourse to a god in prayer and sacrifice avails to alter what is allotted. Stranger yet is the attitude of Zeus toward what is allotted. For, though his desires be for an outcome precisely opposite, he does not act to change what is allotted. "He does not act" is a phrase deliberately chosen, for "he cannot act" would be a phrase not quite warranted by the evidence in the poems. Whether this Moira is to be understood as the established order of events already fixed by Zeus' own decrees, which order he does not choose to alter, or whether on the contrary Moira is a power impersonal, distinct from and above Zeus: these are questions which must remain unanswered, at least for the Homeric age. The answer offered by the scholar Walter Leaf is as adequate as the evidence permits:

> If we ask how Zeus himself is bound by fate, we come only upon a rough form of the general problem of free-will and determinism, such as certainly would have been unintelligible in an age which had not yet thought out even the relation of cause and effect.[10]

---

[10] *Companion to Homeric Studies,* p. 162.

CHAPTER « 21

HESIOD THE THEOLOGIAN

THE religious scene that Homer paints in *Iliad* and *Odyssey* is a faithful, if poetically shaded, picture of Greek cult of the ninth and tenth centuries. Faith here, even in a chimeric polytheism and a mythology filled with bedtime-story motifs, is simple; relations with the anthropomorphic rulers of human destiny, cordial and familiar; religious emotions quite as spontaneous as the rest of the pleasingly unstudied Homeric emotions. But within a century the fresh-hued poetry of the picture begins to be sicklied o'er with the pale cast of thought. For just as in literature criticism ever limps in the footsteps of swift-running creative genius; so didacticism shuffled along to the work of codifying and systematizing the cult of the new-born Greek race. It was a work that bore an analogy to the construction of a scientific theology, consisting as it did in theorizing on divine and human origins and in linking man's conduct with his destiny and with the will of the Olympians. In this quasi-theologic movement the name of the didactic poet Hesiod stands out, though it would be an error to fancy him the sole operative in the same. Rather did he take up and develop currents of religious inquiry familiar to his predecessors and contemporaries.

Note in our table that gods of major rank are marked in larger type, also, that the table presents only the part of Hesiod's Theogony which traces the origin of the Kronidae who established themselves as lords of Olympus; finally that Hephaestus is rated as a child of Zeus and Hera, according to the more generally accepted Mythology, though Hesiod himself ascribes the origin of the lame god to parthenogenesis from Hera.

Hesiod's genealogy of the gods is here presented in outline:

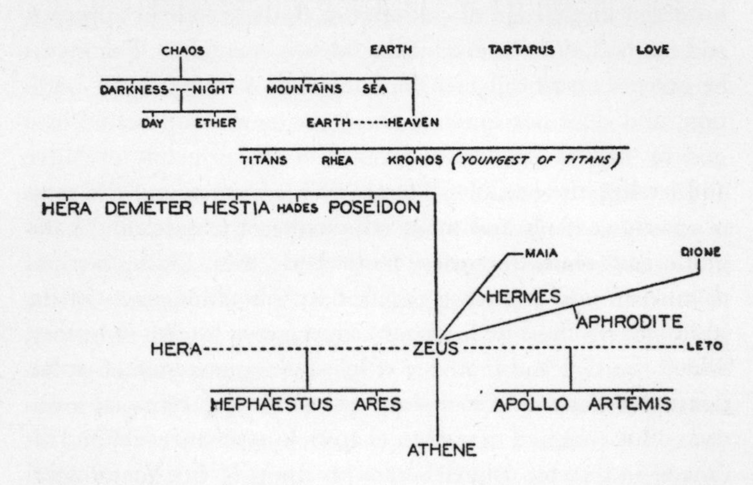

With every name in the above table is found joined in the Hesiodic poem a mythical biography of considerable complexity. For his other gods, whom we have not tabulated, and for the god-born monsters, such as Gorgons, he likewise offers abundant biographical detail. It is not hard, then, to surmise how vast an amount of cultural facts he is engaged in synthesizing. For, according to the principles studied in the last chapter, every myth is the function — to borrow a term from Trigonometry — of a belief or cult-practice. In other words, the intense and curious complexity which characterizes this mythology of the late ninth century clearly indicates how many had been the polytheistic generations which preceded and how far afield they had wandered from primitive and purer religion.

That Hesiod could have satisfied the scholarly curiosity of a present-day historian of religions as to the local origin and significance of the myths he narrates, or even as to such simpler points as to what tribe primarily worshiped Hephaestus and what manner of god they conceived him to be, is not likely. He gives so little information of this kind, that it is legitimate to infer that he possessed comparatively meager historical knowledge of cult-origins. Rather, both in approach and method, does he exhibit the fideistic mentality. The myths he accepts uncritically on the authority of immemorial tradition, and does not question the right to worship vested in a god by title of immemorial cult. On the principle of "Live and let live" he occupies himself with systematizing the mass of incoherent cult and myth indicated in the preceding paragraph. Bits of myth-tapestry he sews together, adding sections of his own weaving when required by the homogeneity of the ideal pattern he has in mind. Thus grew his Myth-history, which the Greek accepted as a species of proto-code of orthodoxy. Religious reverence — as well as the superstitious solicitude we mentioned in the last chapter to assure to every god his "share" — directed the elaborate precision of his genealogical tables. For it was necessary, and even peculiarly necessary, if we recall that the Greek was as jealous of distinguished lineage as are Massachusetts Puritans or French aristocrats, that every god be able to verify his kinship to the divine race. Hesiod, in fact, shows himself an adept in the art of ingenious and fanciful accommodation which enables present-day genealogical investigators to secure ancestral "somebodies" for the *nouveau riche.*

A question which presents itself in connection with the genealogy of the divine race is whether there is implied in this genealogy a dependence upon one deity of all the rest. This dependence might be that of creation, emanation, or separate hypostatization of divine attributes. Obviously it is an anachronism to seek in the Hesiodic age crystal-clear concepts of such eminently philosophic notions. The question is merely whether Hesiod, popularly or unphilosophically, recognized the gods as coming into being from the substance of Gaia or Ouranos, of being made by the power of old Kronos, or of being mere personifications of perfections which were united in their fullness in Zeus.

Supposing an affirmative answer to this question, and further, supposing that Hesiod but voices the *lex credendi* of Greek believers, we should be able to note a remarkable testimony to monotheism. For considerable error in concepts of secondary moment would fail to alter the striking nature of the central concept of a substance and person essentially divine. Unhappily for the cause of the eager apologete of monotheism, Hesiod's theology must be criticized as definitely polytheistic. Zeus, to be sure, enjoys a *relative* transcendence among the gods, as we have seen him to enjoy in the Homeric poems, but the transcendence is not *absolute. The other gods are of the same nature.* There is not much of a limp in the well-known comparison of the Olympian court with the royal court in any one of the Greek states. Both Zeus and the Greek king enjoyed a degree of authority, but the concept that Zeus was of different stuff than the other gods was as foreign to Greek thought as any suspicion that the king was not a man just as the nobles were who did him homage.

The genealogies are, however, an adumbration of better things. From the depths of the dense forest of mythology in which he found himself, the pious Hesiod was incapable of taking a step consciously in the direction of a clearer ground of truer religious concepts. He contributed, however, to the clarification by the very fact that he synthesized cult. The lushness of growth in the mythologies was checked because his quasidictionary of the myths became the official version. An indefinite expansion of the pantheon was stopped because similarly his genealogies were accepted as about the last word on divine peerage (even though certain quite important divinities later immigrated into Greece and were acknowledged). He left, then, the Greek belief in the mold of tangible categories which the keen Greek mind was before long to submit to the test of rational criticism. The philosophers, in

Fig. 26. The Throne of Zeus

The "father of gods and men" was thought to dwell on the summit of Mount Olympus in Thessaly, while his divine family grouped their palaces on its slopes.

other words, were supplied by Hesiod with the ore from which they might smelt out the metal of a natural theology and cast away the useless residue of absurdities and chimeras.

The origin of men is likewise detailed by our didactic poet. The lines from his *Works and Days* are so important a document not only for our present theme, but for the history of religions in general that they merit quotation in full:

> First of all the Olympian gods made "The Golden Race of Men." These men lived when Kronos was king in heaven. They fared like the gods themselves, always making merry, and untroubled by toil or care, for the teeming earth bore of its own accord an abundance of all good things, and there was no old age. Even death itself, when it came at last, stole upon these men like a pleasant slumber. When this race passed away, Zeus made them the good spirits that live above the earth and are the invisible guardians and helpers of mortal men.
>
> Then the Olympians made a second race, the men of the Silver Age. These were far inferior to the Golden Race, for they remained little children for a hundred years, and when they finally reached maturity they straightway perished by their own folly, for they slew each other and refused to worship the immortal gods, as men ought to do. Therefore Zeus was wroth and put them away. But even these men were honored, for they were made the good spirits that live below the earth.
>
> Then Zeus made another and a third race, the men of the Brazen Age. They were sprung from the ash-trees, and were strong and terrible, eating no corn, lovers of war and violence, knowing nought of pity. Their weapons and houses were of bronze and they wrought in bronze. There was no iron. These men, too, fell by the works of their own hands, and fared to Hades, nameless and unhonored. Mighty they were, but dark death laid hold of them, and they left the bright light of the sun.
>
> Then Zeus made a fourth race, better and more just. These were the heroes of the elder days, such as fought at Troy and at Thebes. We call them the demigods. And when they perished, Zeus gave them a life and an abiding place at the ends of the earth. There they dwell in careless ease in the Isles of the Blest, hard by the deep-eddying stream of Ocean, and twice a year the earth bears them fair fruit.

Would that I had not been allotted to the fifth period, but might have died earlier or else have been born later! For this is the Age of Iron. There shall be no surcease from labor and sorrow by day or by night, and the gods will lay bitter burdens upon us. But even yet, not all will be bad. This race shall Zeus destroy, when men are born with hoary hair, when fathers strive with sons and sons with fathers, guest with host and friend with friend; when brothers cease to be dear, when goodness, justice and piety are no longer regarded. . . . Then Aidos and Nemesis, whose fair bodies are clothed in pure white raiment, shall depart to heaven, and men shall find no succor in their grievous calamity.[1]

Jesus said something similar

The folklore of civilized and uncivilized races has many variations of the story of the ages of men. The general framework of the legend is obviously the tenure of the earth by successive races of distinctly different degrees of temporal felicity, culture, and virtue. The scale is retrogressive, rather notably to the discomfiture of evolutionistic theorizing. For the conviction of peoples, as interpretable from their folklore, is that they fell from a better state instead of climbing up from a worse.

The Hesiodic version of the story is now known by scholars to be a transcription from immemorial Greek folklore, but scholars likewise note a liberty taken by the poet with the original. The interpolation of "a fourth race, better and more just," between the rowdy Brazen Age and his own, breaks the orthodox downgrade of man's history. Undoubtedly we have here an obliging adaptation by Hesiod of his theology on human origins to the growing hero-cult. Realizing that his contemporaries already classed as "Demigods" the Cadmaeans who fought at Thebes, and the Achaean and Trojan men of might, he could not include these supermen schematically either in the savage Brazen Age or in his own age. To meet the impasse, he introduces a strange upcurve in the folklore account of man's descent from a better state.

[1] *Hesiod's Works and Days,* II, pp. 109–201.

We must restrict observations on the intriguing theme of the Ages of Men to considerations strictly apposite to the subject of this chapter. With the exception of the Golden Age, which began "when Kronos was king in heaven," the ages are contemporaneous with the hegemony of Zeus among the gods. Excluding the cryptic phrases which state that *the Olympian gods* made the first two races (which statements include Zeus as, at least, one of the agents), we note Zeus to be the one who *"made"* the successive races of men and who brought them to their happy or less happy terms. Creation in the philosophic sense cannot be read into the word *"make,"* both because of the intense difficulty experienced even by later scientific philosophy in groping for this concept of how things were made from nothing, and because Hesiod himself tells us of what material the men of the Brazen Age were fashioned. However, a sufficiently high degree of dependence on Zeus is retained in the ideas of him as maker, destroyer, and apportioner of the future lot of men. It is a dependence of a moral kind, not merely a fatalistic subjection to a blind destiny; for Zeus is wroth at men's contentiousness and impiety, which he punishes accordingly, while noble conduct he is pleased with and rewards. A final remark on Hesiod's Ages is that the poet concludes his outline history of man with an apocalyptic vision of the *hora novissima* when, amid portents which remind us of certain details in the genuine prophecy of the end of the world, Zeus will bring dire calamity on the human race and finally destroy it utterly.

The last of the paragraphs cited from the *Works and Days* may stand as a theme song for the whole of this poem. For the poem is a Jeremiad on conditions in the Greece of that day. A period of economic distress grips Hellas as it emerges into the light of authentic history. Overbearing nobles had capitalized the traditional distinction between men who could trace their lineage back to the great of olden days and men who pertained to the *laos* or "herd" (the half-contemptible term which even Homer employs to designate commoners). Nobles appropriated all the land worth having, and, as trade and industry developed, speedily acquired a monopoly through the capital which they alone were able to invest. Oppression of a despised laboring population followed as the first corollary of the system and a long and grievous depression, like to those of our day, followed as the second. Wholesale emigration partly relieved the pressure, while a nascent spirit of democracy screamed and struck out blindly at the arbitrary autocracy of the homeland. The demagogue stepped into the shoes of the deposed noble, but, lacking both high purpose and reconstructive ability, became the *aner turannos,* or tyrant, to perish by the assassin's sword.

Hesiod's depression remedies are work and frugality, justice between men, piety toward the gods. To reconcile men to the hard conditions and small remuneration of peasant labor, he weaves the threads of the old myths into patterns which exhibit toil first as an inscrutable predestination proceeding from the will of Zeus, and secondly as a punishment. Hesiod says Zeus firstly has placed this generation in the "Iron Age," in which the earth no more yields spontaneously the means for an easy life. Again, following out another cycle of myths, Hesiod pictures Zeus, offended at the impudence of the culture-hero, Prometheus, sending Pandora to let loose upon the race, inconsiderately befriended by Prometheus, the gadflies of toil and sorrow.

"Work, then, for you must," sermonizes Hesiod. "Work," he supplements in the strain of the Alsatian peasant farmer, "and cut expenses to the bone. Hire older farm-hands and servant-maids, who will not waste time keeping company and seeking amusements. Let not your wife be idle nor eat you out of house and home." Even birth control he seems to advocate in his injunction that only one son be raised, so that prosperity may be increased.

Perses, Hesiod's brother, had bribed the aristocratic judges of the Agora to make an iniquitous decision in the case of their common inheritance. Expanding on the theme, the poet diatribes both the venal legal justice of his time and the more fundamental woe of the dullness of the sense of justice in men's minds. Repeated exhortations to the practice of justice fill the pages of the *Works and Days*. As sanction he holds up the refurbished concept of the Homeric Zeus. He protects the city whose Agora reveres justice; he will dissipate ill-gotten gain; he will pursue the perjurer's offspring with nemesis; he will avenge a wrong done the guest, the fugitive, the orphan. Hosts of unseen watchmen hover invisibly along the ways of mortals, to bring swift report of misdeeds to Zeus and to his daughter Diké.

The rights of the gods are to be attended to, by prayer, libation, and sacrifice. Scarcely any new idea in this regard is found in Hesiod, save the insistence on the worship of the Olympians as a condition for securing from them a surcease of the evils of the day. However, there is noted in Hesiod a long stride in the direction of that superstitious formalism toward which Homeric religion was beginning to tend. A curious medley of superstitious practices is enjoined in various parts of the *Works and Days*. It is taboo to pare the finger nails during a sacrifice, to enter a shrine from the left or leave it from the right, to have any covering on the feet or to be clad in any but fresh garments while within the sacred precincts; and so on, through a rigmarole of taboos, both purely secular and connected with worship. Hesiod here supplied the first draft for a code of legalistic observances destined, under the influence of state supervision of cult, to grow into a burden of externalism not unlike the Pharisaical observances of later Old Testament days, and to have, moreover, an analogous effect in stifling real religion. But this consideration is leading us into the field of the next chapter.

CHAPTER « 22

APOLLO AND THE MYSTICS

THE iniquitous times lamented by Hesiod were happily destined to be a transition epoch between the simpler Homeric society and the organized justice of the Greek commonwealth. The *hora novissima* of the poet's apocalypse was not to strike. Instead, Hellas proved anew her clear-headedness and courage by thinking through her political and economic problems to an original and brilliant solution. She gave birth to legislative and executive leaders able to mold old tribal laws and sanctions into codes workable in the government of cities and close-knit states. She broadened the concept of family and clan loyalty into the concept of civic patriotism. She passed successfully through a crisis of threatened national dissolution, not truly into a national unity, but into a group of individually sovereign civil polities. Fidelity to traditions and a proud racial consciousness secured to the Hellenes a unity of spirit manifest no less in literature and art than in the common action the states were quick to take against any non-Hellenic intruder.

To weigh the effect of this political transformation on Greek religion is the purpose of the present chapter. That even in Homer's mind the sanction for the ordinances of human law was Zeus' headship of the human family, that Hesiod's passionate plea for justice evoked the same majestic censor of human justice — these are facts already demonstrated. The poets, of course, did not invent these principles, but rather stand as witnesses to a deep conviction in the minds of their contemporaries.

Early Greeks, in other words, had no concept of a purely secular constitution of society. They were a people who took kindly to civil authority on fundamentally correct ethical grounds. Yet in the transition age of which we treat — approximately 850 B.C. to 600 B.C. — the formers of states experienced a special difficulty in activating this potential submissiveness to law and order. Consciences found perplexing the transit from the obligations of a loose-jointed tribal existence to the minute duties of a dignified, well-ordered city life. For example, the distinction between murder and justifiable homicide, clear enough for peoples long inured to civic life, was vague to the emerging social-mindedness of the Argives. Similarly, the transference of the right of revenge to the civil authorities afforded a puzzling case of conscience to the kindred of a slain man. Furthermore, the codes of the great legislators, Lycurgus, Cleisthenes, Draco, and Solon, as well as those composed by lesser men must have seemed to a degree "commandments of men," since they were not as yet sanctioned by immemorial tradition. Lastly, it is scarcely to be supposed that any merely human prescriptions as to how the gods were to be served would be kindly received. The expanding ritual law, whose proto-code we noted in Hesiod, clamored for its due sanction.

There arose, as total result of the situation, the need for an easy and quick access to divine authority, to a revelation, in brief, or to a dogmatically infallible teacher. The figure of Zeus was remote, but not so was his son and the confidant of his counsels. For the belief of all the Greeks held that at Delphi in Phocis the spirit of Apollo emanated from the sacred cavern and answered questions. Statecraft proceeded to make wholesale use of this belief, for the good end, it is true, of amalgamating civil society and securing reverence for law and order, but by means which merit the appellation of chicanery. By an understanding with the priests who had charge of the Delphic temple, Apollo's voice was controlled.[1] Responses to doubts of conscience came forth ever in accordance with the legislation of the nascent states; ritual difficulties on how cult should be conducted, on what god was to be propitiated and by what means, were solved in accordance with the principles of the sacred codes which were developed, step by step, with the secular codes. Plato expresses in a neat phrase the contribution of Apollo to Hellenic legalism, in naming him the "ancestral exegete" — "exegete," because he furnished concrete interpretations of doctrine and law; "ancestral," because by Plato's day this function of the god had been exercised in favor of four centuries of Greek legislation.

In addition to a mass of casuistry dealing with sacred and profane law, Delphi gave forth official divine sanction to the very codes formulated by Lycurgus, Draco, Solon, and Cleisthenes, to omit the instances of earlier and less famous legislators. Whether Lycurgus is to be considered a historical person or a mythical figure, is beside the point: Sparta held as certain that his laws possessed Delphic sanction, Herodotus going so far as to state that they were specifically revealed at the shrine. Popular belief maintained that Apollo cooperated with Draco in his refinements on the distinction between murder and homicide; that the god supplied Solon with at least his ordinances on state-worship; that the Pythian priestess had obligingly received a revelation from the sacred cavern to give *post factum* approval to Cleisthenes' redistricting of the Athenian people.

An interesting analogy suggests itself, but one that must not be pressed beyond the limits set by the essential difference between a supernatural and a natural religion.

---

[1] Recent excavations at Delphi throw light on the machinery of Apolline prophecy. A Delphic priest was stationed in a subterranean cavern to prompt the prophetess upon the tripod.

In Israelitic Theocracy

The Law	*The Rulers*	*The Prophet*
Revealed by Jahve.	Administer and interpret the law as the approved representatives of Jahve.	is sent by Jahve to urge fidelity to the law, and to solve by directly divine interpretation disputed questions.

In Greek Polity

The Law	*The Rulers*	*The Prophet*
Asserted to have come from the god or to have received his approbation.	Accepted in a general sense as holding an administrative and interpretative commission from Zeus.	i.e., the Pythian prophetess inspired by Apollo, is asserted to give new laws, to approve the compositions of legislators, to interpret legislation.

The analogy may be regarded as a confirmatory argument for the apologetic thesis that pagan man needs revelation as a guiding light in religious matters. The keen Greek, realizing the moral impossibility of securing individual and social justice by appeal to principles of a purely natural ethic and theodicy, turned to the principle of supernatural enlightenment and sanction, which is eminently suited to supply a remedy to the corruption of nature. As individual first, then as a member of organized society, he had recourse to the supposed revelation of Delphi.

The beneficent influences of the aggrandizement of Apollinism on real religion were the moderation and reasonableness inculcated in cult-practices, the conservation of some of the better concepts of Homeric and Hesiodic religion, the good understanding secured between religion and civil society. The chief evil effect seems to be the stagnation of Zeus-cult, for Apollo became in practice the chief Greek god, though not such in theory. It need not be repeated that Zeus' attributes in the early Hellenic religion transcended any of its other elements. Akin to this loss to religion suffered from Apollinism, may be mentioned the ever-spreading formalism resulting from the continual leaning on the oracle for decisions, which *ipso facto* became a part of the legislation. The Pharisaic letter gradually obscured the spirit of worship. A third injury to religion was a species of what in later ages acquired the name of Caesaropapism. Greek priests seem never to have possessed a strikingly virile class-consciousness as the guardians of dogma and moral. The Apolline system put them definitely into the station of acquiescent "yes-men," at the service of the burly civil power. History has sung so many threnodies on this theme that it is unnecessary to dwell on the warping effect this subservience had upon religion. Finally, the flexiloquous prophecies dictated to the Delphic priestess by political expediency struck at the very heart of religious confidence in the honesty of the gods.

Two mighty rivals threatened for a time the ascendancy of Phoebus Apollo. The first led his disorderly train of Maenads and Satyrs over the Thracian mountains down into Apollo's territory. He claimed Zeus as his parent, and could point to Homer's recognition of him as a divinity. He was Dionysus. The second conducted a more staid procession of monastic theologians through the centers of Hellenic culture. He, too, claimed divine parentage, being born of the Muse Calliope, own daughter of Zeus. He was Orpheus.

Dionysus is recognizable by his attributes, by his cult, and by the mythology which was spun to fit into the Greek polytheism as one of Asia Minor's nature divinities. Gods of the earth, earthy, possessed the votaries of this land of dark magic and strange frenzies. They were nature-forces, such as the principle of vegetation and the procreative force, vaguely conceived as personal, but far removed from the sharply individualized deities created by Greek anthropomorphism.

Rather were they in the class of the *daimones,* who from the very amorphousness of their own proper shape were conceived as capable of incarnation in a variety of living forms. Cult took its tone from the want of logical definiteness in the divine form, and tended to an emotional mysticism. Not the reasoned, ordered, clearly finite service of a neatly understood god, but seizures, ecstasics, orgiastic ritual were the types of religious self-expression. There underlay ritual practices the supposition that the divinity could be brought to take possession of the votary and assimilate him into the divine substance. Theofagy, choric song and dance, the use of stimulants stand out among the ritual practices resorted to with a view to produce the emotional conviction that the desired transmutation of nature had taken place. Finally, Asia Minor is one of the fields where we find symbolized in belief and ritual the mystery of the changing seasons under the figure of a god dying and being reborn.

Dionysus was established on the Grecian mainland in pre-Homeric days, but we are able to trace the story of his coming thither from mythology. All early stories about him tell of his wanderings through Greece to establish his cult. His birthplace was Thebes in Boeotia, his parents Zeus and Semele, daughter of Cadmus — mythological accommodations meant to justify, on the one hand, his inclusion in the family of Greek Olympians and, on the other, the historical fact that Thebes was the immemorial center of his cult. Raised by the Nymphs, he reached maturity, to go campaigning for votaries. He canvassed Thrace, but the mythical king Lycourgos liked not the new brand of religion and drove the god into exile. In other countries, too, he met opposition from the authorities. Here, too, we can read through the translucent myth the historical fact that the disorderly Dionysiac practices were frowned on by the guardians of good order. The myth further tells of fearful revenge wreaked by Dionysus on those who refused to receive him and of the blessing of fertile vineyards conferred upon his well-wishers. Having conquered Greece, the myth continues, and established himself even at Delphi, he pursued his victorious course through the world, climaxing all by assisting the Olympian gods to defeat the giants and receiving as reward Olympian citizenship. Here, then, are still other spots where the etiological myth is translucent.

Another and independent myth-history connects Dionysus definitely with the "god dying and reborn" cycle, which, of course, is a symbolization of vegetation's death and renascence. According to this myth-history, seemingly a later composition than the one we give in full above, Hera was jealous of the new-born Dionysus and had him torn to pieces by Titans, but, after an interval in the lower world, Dionysus came to life again. Nor yet does even this exhaust the curious Dionysus-legend, but we must break the thread, since enough has been unraveled to serve the purpose of the present subject.

The Dionysiac movement is justly regarded as a chapter in the history of psychopathic religion, its delirious votaries as spiritual cousins of the Flagellants, the Adventists, the disciples of George Fox, the brethren and sisters of "Father Divine." The "reasonable service" commended to Christians by St. Paul does not flatter the desire for "religious experience" to which human sentiment, abetted by human pride, impels. Our senses clamor for stimulation even in so spiritual a pursuit as the service of God, while our conceit subconsciously nourishes the illusion that special divine favors are our due. To *feel* the object of faith is, therefore, very satisfying.

How the worshipers of Dionysus secured this feeling may be understood by following the steps of a typical orgy upon the wooded heights of Parnassus above Delphi.[2] Wine, the

---

[2] Obviously the description applies to Parnassan days antedating state regulation of the cult. The great antiquity of Delphic Dionysus-worship is unquestioned. The Delphic grave of the god, slain by Titans, was immemorial.

Fig. 27. Temple of Apollo at Delphi

Extensive excavation at Delphi in Phocis has confirmed what classic authors narrate of the city's glories. Earthquakes have destroyed the chasm from which Apollo was said to inspire the Sibyl, while raiders have carried off its vast treasures, but remains like the above still tell of the time when Delphi was a Hellenic and international shrine.

Fig. 28. Dionysus

Legend points to Asia Minor as the birthplace of his cult, but the Greeks gave him full divine citizenship. He shared with Apollo the sacred region of Delphi, where his orgiastic rites were celebrated on the slope of Mount Parnassus.

god's peculiar gift, puts the Maenads (a word significantly derived from *mainomai,* meaning "I am in a frenzy"), or female devotees, into congruous dispositions. Their streaming hair crowned with ivy or with serpents, brandishing torches and wands twined with vine branches, they rout through the forest. As physical and mental intoxication grows apace, they dance and shout madly to the music of drum and flute. They see themselves led by the god and accompanied by his familiars, the Satyrs, Sileni, and Centaurs. Woe to the rabbit, fawn, or even the child that crosses their path, for their mad eyes see in these living creatures an incarnation of Dionysus. They hasten to rend the unfortunate in pieces and, devouring it raw, consummate by this act of theofagy their assimilation with their god, and acquire imagined miraculous powers.

The legislators and practical politicians, who were succeeding so admirably in bringing religion into the service of the state, recognized the challenge to good order which lay in this un-Hellenic and uncontrolled ecstasy religion.[3] We may suppose from the mythological data detailed above an early period of attempted legal extirpation of the cult, but the definite solution was a syncretic one. Apollo was made to speak gently of his half-brother Dionysus. Oracles were forthcoming which commended the joyous character of the wine-god, exhorting men to the diligent culture of the vine and to gatherings in which, under the inspiration of the god's good gift, poetry and song might well up. So were Dionysiac festivals turned into one of the origins of lyric poetry and the drama. The practices of Maenadism were not harshly checked,

[3] Pseudo-mystic elements in Apollo's own cult are noted in the half-mythical histories of prophets, thaumaturgi, and cataleptics such as Abaris, Aristeas, and Epimenides. These, however, were solicitous servants of the Apolline spirit, who regulated their seizures and inspirations in accord with its principles of *meden agan,* moderation in all things, and statecraft. Even Pythagoras was popularly supposed to have attained such union with Apollo as to be endowed with miraculous power.

but the Maenads were made an official body of Dionysus servants, regulated by authorities. Indiscriminate enrollment in their ranks was forbidden. The orgiastic features of the ritual were replaced by practices which conformed to the Greek ideal of order and beauty. Where Dionysism began to take hold of some new population, as for example in some new colony, missionary Maenads were dispatched from Delphi to regulate the cult. At Delphi itself Apollo graciously shared with Dionysus, and the place remained a central shrine for both the cults. Even the liturgical year was shared, for during the winter months, when Phoebus was visiting his dear Hyperboreans, the dithyramb of Dionysus replaced the paean sung to Apollo. Archeology furnishes us with the commemoration in marble of this syncretism of two cults, whose fundamental spirits were naturally so contradictory, for on the pediment of the temple of Apollo at Delphi, we find sculptured on one side Apollo and the Muses, on the other Dionysus and his Maenads.

The claim to Hellenic citizenship in the case of Orpheus was undisputed, for he enjoyed the reputation of a culture-hero of the race. Mythologically acclaimed as the first to practice divination and expiatory rites, as the inventor of letters and master of the magic lyre, he occupied a place in Hellenic thought before Homer's day and long before the rise of the cult that goes by the name of Orphism. His reputed history need not detain us: child of a Thracian king and the Muse Calliope; lyre-player who could charm beasts and stones; one of the Argonauts; visitor in the regions of Hades, where he won by his music the right to bring back to earth his wife Eurydice; civilizer of Thrace, where, however, he met death at the hands of a band of Dionysiac Maenads.

It was professedly under the inspiration of this culture-hero that a number of men of no little genius, but whose names are for the most part unknown, taught and committed to writing a new synthesis of elements of Greek religion.[4] "Genius," we have said, because the work, unlike Pausanias' vast catalogue of cult-facts, selected practices and beliefs with high intelligence, combined them with fine coherence, purified and elevated grosser concepts, added, finally, much that must be considered the product of fresh and correct thought. The doctrine was propagated through the medium of the typically Hellenic *thiasus* or religious brotherhood. The Orphic *thiasus* or, more briefly, the Orphics may be characterized not ineptly as a group of monastic theologians, inasmuch as the organization's purposes were the study of the Orphic doctrine, the living out of the same in ascetical and ritualistic practices, the proselytizing of possible new members.

Orpheus held the position of prophet, not that of principal divinity, in the sect, for the orthodox fiction made the son of Calliope the primeval teacher of a religion which directed worship to quite another individual than himself, namely, to Dionysus Zagreus. A recasting of Homeric and Hesiodic mythology by tendentious Orphic writers supplied Dionysus Zagreus with the following extravagant and repulsive biography. Zeus and Rhea, metamorphized into serpents became the parents of the monstrous Persephone, a female being horned and with four eyes. Zeus, again in serpent form, by union with Persephone sired another horned divinity, Dionysus Zagreus, whom he committed to the warrior demigods the Curetes to be protected from the jealousy of Hera. Hera, however, sent the Titans who, after luring away the child, slew him and banqueted on his flesh. What was left Apollo buried at Delphi, except the heart which was carried by Athene to Zeus. Swallowing the heart, he gave birth to an-

[4] Onomacritus, an Athenian living toward the end of the sixth century, is to be regarded as a collator, rather than as an author, of Orphic doctrine. He forged many Orphic oracles and poems, claiming for these documents a great antiquity, but in respect to their doctrinal content he echoes ideas and principles already known and practiced in Orphic circles. His work was received gratefully, because the Orphic votaries desired antiquity and even authorship of Orpheus himself for their documents.

other Dionysus with whom he decreed to share his own glory and sovereignty. Zeus punished the murderous Titans by casting them into Tartarus and destroying them by fire. From their ashes sprang the first members of the human race.

The fantastic etiological story is pregnant with symbolism. The Orphics must bring their god into the traditional Homeric polytheism. He must be allied to the popular Dionysus cult. He must be revered by the Delphic Apollo and by the great city goddess Pallas Athene. He must derive his sovereignty from Father Zeus. He must, for mystical reasons, contribute of his own being to the composition of man's nature, while, for doctrinal reasons, man's nature must be shown to be composed of an evil principle as well. It is with this last-named Orphic concept of human nature as partly good and partly evil that we propose to deal in some detail, for so we trust to present with some approach to clearness the Orphic theology.

Observation of the vicissitudes of good and evil in the conduct and fortunes of men is a sufficient basis for the philosophic conviction of a double principle operative in his make-up. Human guilt as the cause of this penal state of internal strife is again a deduction of which philosophy is capable. Orphic philosophy laid this primal guilt at the door of the murdering progenitors of the human family, the Titans. Since the Titans had absorbed the divine substance of Dionysus into themselves by their cannibalism, their offspring, too, have in themselves a divine and good element. Man must, conclude the Orphics, expiate his ancestral guilt by his suffering in life and by the practice of such asceticism as the abstention from meat.

But asceticism would be unavailing were man to fail to reconsecrate himself to the principle of good which is the god Dionysus. Hence the need for the initiation, whose chief rite was a banquet on the raw flesh of a bull, which was understood to be the god-body inhabited by Dionysus. The immediate effect of the theofagy and the congruous ceremonies which accompanied it was, like the effect of similar rites in the pure Dionysism, to engender a psychopathic sense of assimilation into the nature of the god. The Orphics added to this emotional aspect of the proceeding the positive teaching that a real assimilation occurred in virtue of which the god would recognize the initiated votary as belonging to himself and so grant him a better lot in the future life. The future life loomed large in Orphic teaching and took on a definiteness of detail wanting in earlier Greek speculation. For the initiated who also observed the ascetical and purificatory practices that Orphism prescribed after initiation and who lived honestly, there was envisaged an enduring possession of joys, essentially the same as mortal joys, though sublimated. Initiation without the other requisites led to a period of purification by punishment in the other world, but final attainment of happiness. The uninitiated were to have no surcease of such trials as never-ending fetching of water in broken pitchers.

Time need not be spent in noting the religiously elevated features of the Orphic synthesis. The synthesis as a whole was destined to furnish an example of the insufficiency of merely natural religious teachers in the task of guiding the human race. The esoteric pride, which inspired the Orphics to despise the uninitiated, relegated the sect to the obscurity of isolated "lodges." Orphic speculation thus had but little effect upon the current of traditional religious thought which swept on the masses. Aversion to syncretic absorption with the Apolline tradition prevented the Orphic lodges from receiving state support. Finally, the lack of any authoritative voice worked the degeneration of the doctrine itself. For its ruder votaries mingled it with superstition and magic; its intellectual votaries entangled it in fine-spun speculations. Orphism passed as a religion, though later philosophers salvaged some of the treasure of its thought.

Eleusis furnished Greek religious desire with much that Orphism had to offer, but in a vaguer and less pure form. Eleusis is a town situated a few miles northwest of Athens. Here from time immemorial had been celebrated agrarian rites under the care of several noble families. Upon the agrarian cult there had been engrafted, at about the dawn of authentic history, a mystery element. In its simplest terms, this mystery element was an interpretation of the myth of the rape of Kore in terms of man's death and future state. For Dis was god of the dead, and it was obvious to symbolize death and residence in the Netherworld under the figure of Demeter's daughter snatched away by him. However, a better understanding of the matter will be secured by a brief outline of the ideas involved in every mystery-religion.

Etymologically derived from the word *musterion,* "secret," a mystery-religion may be defined as an esoteric cult, distinguished against cults open to all comers. A study of historical mystery-religions reveals the following characteristics. There is promised renewal or rebirth or passage to a new life, to effect which a negative condition is some purificatory rite, positive conditions being instruction in secret lore and rites supposedly productive of a union with the deity. Symbolism, such as sacred dramas and theofagy, is employed to make vivid the teaching and to stir up the emotions. The votary is generally in an emotional state bordering on hallucination, when he or she falls under conviction of being purified and received into the divine union. Finally, the genius of mystery-religions is to keep the object of faith vague and plastic rather than reasonable and reducible to precise terms.

Central feature of the shrine at Eleusis was the Telesterion or Hall of Mysteries. This was a square building, eighty feet to a side, with a roof supported by twenty-five columns and with a peristyle adjoining on the east. Interior arrangement conformed to the Greek idea of a theater. Beneath the building was excavated a room called the Hall of Initiations.

Erected before the first Persian invasion, the Telesterion was destroyed by the invaders in the early fifth century and rebuilt by Pericles. Another reconstruction took place in Roman times, to endure till Alaric the Goth overran Greece.

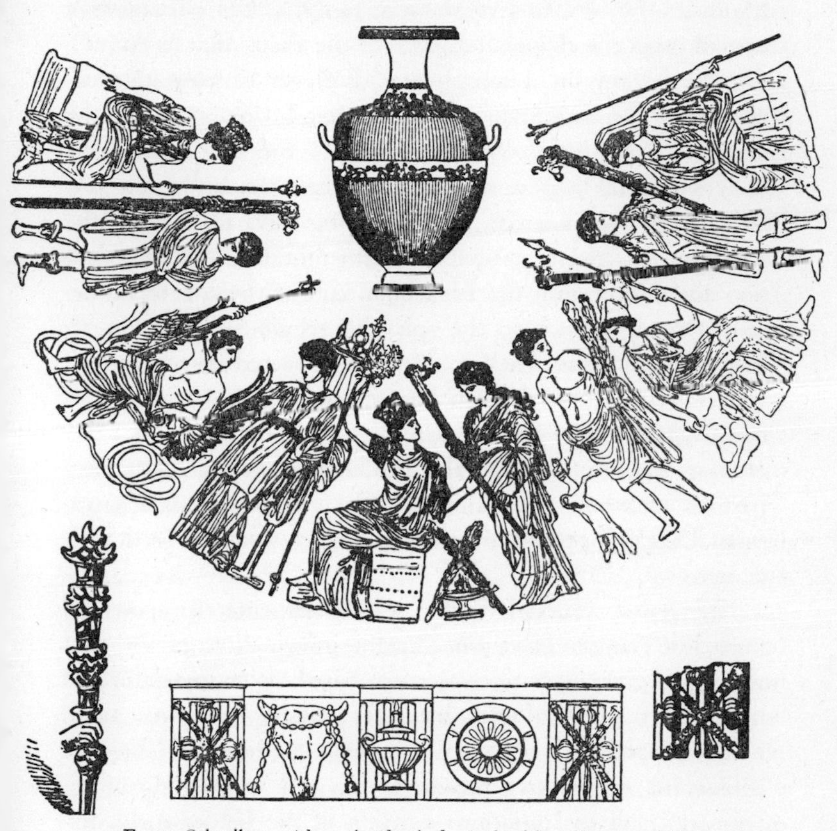

From Schreiber, *Atlas of Classical Antiquities*. By permission of the Macmillan Co.

Fig. 29. Divinities and Ministers of the Eleusinian Mysteries

The figures are painted on the neck of the vase shown at top. Divinities recognizable are Demeter seated in front, Core to her right, Athene seated and helmeted, Artemis and Aphrodite at either end of the line. Iacchus stands to the left of Demeter and converses with Triptolemus. The other figures are probably ministers who officiated in the mystic rites.

In the spring were solemnized the Little Mysteries, which consisted simply in a ritual bath taken by the candidates for initiation in the stream Ilissus, just outside of Athens. From September 13 to 20 preparations were made for the Great Mysteries. On the first of these days the sacred objects were carried from the chapel at Eleusis to the Eleusinion at Athens. On the second the Hierophant, "displayer of holy objects," addressed the candidates in the Painted Colonnade of the last-named building. On September 16 the candidates gave their sacrificial pigs a sea bath at Phalerum and took one themselves. And on the two following days took place the Epidauria, a festival probably commemorating the introduction and fusion with the Eleusinian cult of the cult of Asklepios. On September 19 the splendid religious procession reformed and carried back to Eleusis the sacred objects, which we conjecture to have been kept carefully veiled through all this pageantry from uninitiated eyes. For September 20 a day of fast was imposed on the candidates and at night they partook of what some commentators choose to call a sacramental meal, a repast on cakes and meal-water flavored with pennyroyal.

The repast concluded, the candidates entered upon the initiation proper. Here our certain information as to what was done gives way to conjecture based upon the nature of the cult, upon analogies in other mystery-religions, upon hints dropped by pagan writers, upon diatribes of Christian apologetes. A tentative reconstruction can be offered.

In the Hall of Initiations a vision of the Underworld, followed by one of Heaven, stirred up the candidates' emotions. These visions were doubtless fixed scenic effects, or acted dramas, or perhaps both. To attribute them to pure group hallucination in the imaginations of the candidates is impossible. The sacred objects were then unveiled before the eyes of those present. St. Hippolytus tells us that a sacred cornstalk, apt symbol of the ancient agrarian cult and of Demeter, was one of these objects: likely, antique statues of the three Eleusinian divinities were also unveiled. After this, in the Telesterion, was enacted a drama, most probably on a theme furnished by the Demeter-Kore-Dis myth. A sacred marriage was then symbolized, when the Hierophant and the priestess of Demeter retired from the view of the candidates, to return after an interval to the joyous proclamation of a herald: "Brima our lady has borne a sacred child, Brimos." This announcement marked the climax of the rites and the consummation of the initiation.

CHAPTER « 23

CULT AT THE DAWN OF THE GOLDEN AGE

AS THE sixth century passed into the fifth, great empire movements were stirring in Mediterranean lands. To the west Rome had expelled her kings and was trying her first essays in republican government. To the southwest Carthaginian galleys were extending the fierce semibarbarism of the Punic capital to new shores. The Jews, chastened by their exile, had returned to Judea and were rebuilding the Temple. More ominous than all this for the Greece we are studying was the awakening of Persia effected by the genius of Cyrus the Great. He and his immediate successors had girdled Hellas to the south and east with powerful satrapies and had sent punitive expeditions numbered by hundreds of thousands against the tribes lying to the north. The dawning fifth century would behold Greece clash with the giant in defense of the institutions she had developed during the five centuries of her national formation.

During this period of internal evolution, statesmen had done well their work of uniting religion to patriotism. Favored by the comparative geographical isolation of their country which tended to keep away foreign cult influences, rightly estimating how deeply rooted in the popular mind was the chauvinistic distinction between *Hellenes* and *Barbaroi,* always able to turn to Delphic Apollo as a court of last appeal, they had brought the citizenry to a mentality of obedient complaisance with the official forms of worship and belief, as well as of subservience to the civil law for the motive that the same enjoyed divine sanction.

Ancestral religious festivals, under state patronage, were celebrated with impressive pageantry of dramatic entertainment, brilliant procession, costly sacrifice. The care of officials was ever, as far as possible, to render these festivals Pan-Hellenic, not only by securing the attendance of delegates from all the Greek states, but by subsidizing needy citizens with money and food, that they might take part in the rejoicing and so feel their solidarity in the commonwealth. Art and athleticism, dear to the Greek spirit, likewise did their bit, under the same official patronage, toward the support of state religion by multiplying temples and icons, by affording splendid sport at the four great periodic festivals.

Biannually in the valley of Nemea in Argos occurred the Nemean Festival. Originally funeral games in honor of one of the heroes who fought against Thebes, the commemoration was transformed in historic times into a religious festival in honor of Zeus. From a local affair, it grew to be Pan-Hellenic and drew official ambassadors from various Greek states as well as crowds of pilgrims from all of them. In addition to religious sacrifices, there were gymnastic, equestrian, and musical contests. Victors received palm branches and garlands of wild celery. It was the prestige of victory which was coveted, not the intrinsic value of the prize.

The Olympian Festival was solemnized every fourth year at Elis, where was the temple of Zeus with Phidias' immortal statue. Besides religious observance, there were held games of almost every imaginable kind, participation in them being reserved for free men of pure Hellenic descent. Prizes were wreaths woven from the sacred wild olive which grew near Zeus' shrine. The carefully observed reckoning of the four-year Olympiad period has proved of immense value in determining Greek chronology.

Apollo was the god honored at the Pythian Festival held every four years in the plain beneath his oracular shrine at Delphi. Observances were religious, athletic, and musical. In the contests here some of the finest of Greek odes were first sung. The musical victor was crowned with a garland from the sacred bay tree and a palm branch was also given him: athletic victors received only the latter token. The Amphyctionic Council, which had charge of the Pythia, made the most of this occasion to assert its claim as a kind of Hellenic superstate.

Every fifth year Athens observed the Panathenea in honor of her tutelary Pallas. Musical contestants vied for a golden crown, athletes for a garland from the sacred olive tree and a vase of oil pressed from the fruit of the same. The high point of religious observance was a magnificent procession in which was borne the venerated *peplos* or robe of Athens' goddess. The frieze of the Parthenon depicts one such procession.

The specific gods in whose honor these official pageants flourished were the Homeric Olympians. Yet, it would be wrong to suppose that the state maintained an attitude of frowning intolerance toward gods who had slipped in by the back door and won popular favor, or toward the pre-Homeric daemons who had never developed into the full anthropomorphic nature. The mystery-religions, provided they observed the rule of moderation in all things, *meden agan,* were even encouraged by statesmen as a complement to the rather external civic cult, inasfar as they afforded an outlet for personal emotionalism. Furthermore, in rural districts woods and streams and caves were still, in popular belief, inhabited by immemorial nymphs and fauns and satyrs, whose benignant or capricious characters were a thing to be reckoned with in the conduct of human affairs.

No event can well be imagined more conducive to strengthening a close union of state and religion than the fifth-century struggle against Persia. From the first paralyzing despondency produced by the contemplation of an imminent contest with a hated and seemingly invincible power, Greece

Fig. 30. The Parthenon at Athens

During the Golden Age the state enlisted Greek genius and love of the beautiful in the service of religion. The resulting splendor of the cult of the time is suggested in the graceful lines of Athen's temple on the Acropolis.

Fig. 31. The Philosopher Plato

"He was acquainted with all the culture of his own and previous generations. — He aspired to construct a system of philosophy which should afford an explanation both of man himself and also of the universe in which he lives" (James Adam).

roused herself to invocation of her gods and consultation of her oracle. Though the gods themselves exhibited a mind sufficiently diffident as to the outcome, tiny land forces deployed in the path of the invading hosts, while skeleton fleets sailed forth to meet the Persian armada. Victory deliriously unexpected at Marathon, Salamis, Mycale, and Platea raised Greek patriotism and chauvinism to new highs. Their gods had gone forth against the gods of the stranger and vindicated their transcendency. Not merely was there the belief that the Olympians had responded invisibly to their votaries' impetration, but thick clustering myths grew up of epiphanies of Athene, Heracles, and other gods fighting in the ranks or aboard the triremes. In gratitude, the spoil was dedicated to the enrichment of the temples, which now were frequented with a new sense of confidence. The Greeks slain in the contest received from the state the official canonization of hero-cult. Glorification of the state—of the state the soundness of whose institutions had stood the acid test, of the state which was patron of cult and whose ordinances were sanctioned by the victorious gods—this was a corollary of the victory thesis all too obvious.

Homer and Hesiod had long been the religious schoolmasters of Greece. The Golden Age bore them in Pindar and the tragic poets able commentators and successors. Composing for recital or stage presentation at sacred festivals, Pindar and the tragedians were rather committed to the religious theme. Frankly accepting the traditional polytheistic mythology, they still made notable advances in its interpretation. "It is meet for a man," says Pindar in his *Olympian Odes,* I, 35, "to speak honorable things about the gods." Following this rule, the epinikean odes and the immortal trilogies ignore or dissent from all that is unworthy in the myths and in the characters of their divine actors. Ideal and noble attributes of the Olympians are emphasized—their omniscience, omnipotence, and truthfulness. An attempt is even made to soften the harsh doctrines of "the envy of the gods" and of "all-ruling fate." For it is suggested by Pindar that divine envy falls on those who indulge unrighteous joys, while Aeschylus implies that the gods envy only those mortals who have grown insolent in prosperity. Such exegesis clothes with a moral worthiness the stark ugliness of Homeric and Hesiodic doctrine. Struggling with the problem of reconciling Fate with the divine will, none of the poets we are discussing offer a clear solution, but there is a certain palliative in their suggestions that Moira is a rule observed by gods and men alike, that Moira is Zeus' coadjustor.

Unity of divine purpose, rather than monotheism, is the teaching of Pindar and the tragedians. This will is the will of Zeus, "king of kings all-seeing father, cause and accomplisher of all things." With his law and good pleasure the other gods are in agreement, but men by overweening pride sin in overstepping the bounds of right order in relation to gods and fellow men. Human guilt for sin is clear, at least for the first false step. That man perseveres in his evil course, the tragedians at least imply, is due to a madness cast upon him by heaven which blinds him to right and wrong. Properly analyzed, the trilogies do not present a picture of the innocent suffering unjustly and irremediably. Either there is an element of personal fault, or, failing this, there is always the prospect of the Hereafter and faith in Zeus forbids despair.

Both the essentially rationalizing bent of Greek religious thought and the subservience of cult to the state exercised deleterious influences on the dignity of Greek priesthood. The Greek, who did not generally sense an overwhelming majesty even in his gods, was not inclined to associate high sanctity and inviolability with the person of the priest. It was the work of politicians, who early molded the various independent civic units, to amalgamate the two powers which we call church and state. In return for state upkeep of temples and state subsidy of religious festivals, priests were content to submit to dictation in matters which properly belonged to sacerdotal competency. A species of ministry of cult, to borrow a phrase from modern state totalitarianism, directed doctrine, moral and ritual.

By inheritance, then, or election or purchase the priest acquired his title to a "benefice." The qualifications he need possess were neither many nor stringent. Physical integrity and innocence of graver external sins were generally required. Requirements in the line of chastity were recognized, but were far from uniform. For instance, certain priesthoods were open only to impuberes; others, only to priests and priestesses of such age that the passions would be cooled (Plato suggesting sixty years for the priest in his Utopia). Sometimes, chastity during the actual year of office was demanded; more rarely was strict celibacy a requirement. Greek instinct seems always to have been revolted by such excesses as the emasculation of Cybele's priests.

Since the council or other civic authority held real control of cult, intellectual requirements for priesthood were not high. Only in special cases, notably in the religio-medical cult of Asklepios, does any analogy to seminary training occur. The average priest did not need much intellectual equipment. For, as temple official, he had simply the duties of keeping the god's house in repair and duly adorned; he recited proper prayer-formulas for diverse acts of worship; he observed the traditional minutiae of sacrificial ritual.

Priestly privileges and emoluments were very diverse for diverse regions. Examples are the right to special places at the games and in the theater, freedom from taxation and from military conscription. State salaries for priests were rare. The priest was commonly entitled to claim for his own table a part of the animal offered in sacrifice, and often also to claim and sell the hide. Money fees from votaries who assisted at sacrifices were not uncommon. Some cults allowed their priests to take up collections in the public streets.

For reasons of emphasis we have chosen to paint the foregoing picture of fifth-century religion in relatively bright colors. Unfortunately, in simple fact, the color is more a pigment supplied by state externalism than the genuine glow of religious health. The shafts of criticism had been dinting and even piercing the mythologic panoply that clothed the popular faith before ever the fifth century opened. The thinking classes of all ages incline toward historical skepticism when presented with stories of the order of Jack the Giant Killer, and Beauty and the Beast. Offense was also taken by the judicious Greek at the impurities, levities, and superstitions associated with popular worship and justified by myths telling of immortals engaging in or instituting such practices. Against these intellectual attacks the Homeric tradition found in the priesthood no disinterested and able corps of defenders. Among the leisured and cultured classes, finally, there infiltrated a knowledge of non-Greek religions, with a consequent envisaging of the problem of where true religion objectively lay.

For the sake of clearness this struggle between the gods and the philosophers will be studied in a separate chapter. Here is appended a skeleton chronology of events and persons mentioned in the present chapter and to be mentioned in the next.

Chronology

538 Babylon taken by Cyrus the Great.
536 Cyrus permits Jews to return to Judea.
518 Darius Hystaspes confirms this edict.
457 Artaxerxes Longimanus' decree. (Beginning of Daniel's 70 weeks.)

509 Establishment of Roman Republic.
500 Hanno of Carthage explores and colonizes west coast of Africa.
480 First Carthaginian invasion of Sicily by Hamilcar Barca.

525 Egypt becomes Persian satrapy.
508 Darius' punitive expedition into Scythia and conquest of Thrace.
500 Ionian revolt against Persia supported by Greek states.
492 First Persian invasion of Greek mainland.
490 Second Persian invasion: Marathon.
481 Third Persian invasion: Thermopylae, Salamis.
479 Platea, Mycale.

522–443 Life of Pindar.
525–456 Life of Aeschylus.
495–406 Life of Sophocles.
459–431 Age of Pericles.
469–399 Life of Socrates.
428–347 Life of Plato.
384–322 Life of Aristotle: 342–339 Aristotle tutor of Alexander.

CHAPTER « 24

THE GODS AND THE PHILOSOPHERS

WITH the term "philosopher" we associate the accuracy of method and the fund of ideas which, after three millennia of labored research, are today the common treasure of thinkers. A "philosopher" of the first millennium B.C. would be busy, of course, at clearing away with clumsy tools the rank growth of folklore and popularly believed nonsense. If he succeeded, besides, in stripping off a few surface layers in the mine of truth, it is to be deemed a notable achievement. The results achieved, then, by earlier Hellenic philosophers, though mixed with errors and obscurities, are worthy of admiration.

The Pythagoreans borrowed from three great religious traditions already indicated. From Hesiodic taboos, which were conditions for ritual purity, they adopted a variety of rules for the *kosher* and the unclean. An important addition, however, was the reason they gave for their vegetarianism: namely, the doctrine of transmigration of souls, which made obnoxious the eating of animal flesh which had been perhaps the tenement of a wandering human spirit. For Orphic teaching they cherished such veneration that the Pythagorean *thiasoi* have been termed the militant order of Orphic religion. From Apollinism they derived an intense esteem for external law and order, which made them loyal to the forms of the state religion.

Pythagoras himself, mathematically obsessed, established as the First Principle of all things "Unity." Vague enough is the meaning he attached to Unity; but it is clear, on the one hand, that it is not a transcendent being and, on the other, that it is in some way the origin of perfections in all beings from popular gods down to tiniest gnats. Rejecting in theory the Homeric anthropomorphism, he taught that the true form of the gods is a mystery. For a like reason, he condemns the indecencies attributed by mythology to the immortals. Nor did he spare in his condemnation the excesses practised in worship. Yet so faithful a servant was he of the Apolline tradition that he insisted on obedience to the religious as well as the political ordinances of the civil power.

First, in their ranks, the immortal gods adore —
Thine oaths keep; next great heroes; then implore
Terrestrial demons, with due sacrifice.

In time of prayer and cleansing, meats denied
Abstain from; thy mind's reins let reason guide;
Then, stripped of flesh, up to free ether soar,
A deathless god, divine, mortal no more.

These study, practise these, and these affect;
To sacred virtue these thy steps direct:
Eternal Nature's fountain I attest,
Who the Tetractys on our souls impressed.

The above lines, selected from *The Golden Verses of Pythagoras,* summarize the solution of the religious problem arrived at by his sect. Their peculiar and vague concept of a mathematical First Principle is indicated in the Tetractys, which is the imprint of Unity on the fourfold human faculty of understanding, knowledge, opinion, and sense. Reason and Nature are man's only reliable guides to his goal in life, namely, Virtue. By asceticism and prayer he may expect to attain this earthly goal as well as the afterlife reward of Virtue, a deathless life. Yet, by a strange inconsistency, gods and *daimones* are to be accorded their due of adoration, though one inquires in vain of Pythagorean thinkers for a proof either of the existence of these supposed superbeings or of their claim to honor.

Reason's rushlight had revealed to Pythagoras the dim outlines of a First Principle that was none of the gods of polytheism. Yet another group of "lovers of wisdom," groping through the night of polytheism, discerned the same figure. In interpreting this First Principle, whose necessity they saw, the Ionians were misled by their preoccupation with physical science into the theory that all things must have come from a material cause. From fire all things proceeded, asserted Heraclitus; from water, said Thales. As a kind of divine all-substance, the Ionian First Cause lives and thinks and pantheistically pervades all being. Unprepared for a break with popular religion, the Ionians spoke of the Olympians as personifications of nature forces.

Protesting against the materialism to which the Ionians were committed, the great Eleatics, Xenophanes and Zeno, proclaimed a necessary distinction between the First Principle and the beings It produces and sustains. God must be unique, eternal, an immutable substance. Beware of reading into these terms the fine definition of meaning which Christian philosophy observes. The Eleatics had seen a great light, but were far from recognizing God as increate Being. Yet in the buzz of controversy about the old gods, their doctrine was a truly Copernican dictum. Negatively, the effect was speedy abandonment by intellectuals of literal belief in anthropomorphic superbeings who were certainly recognized as cut of the same cloth as the votaries who paid them homage. Positively, the profound, if vaguely grasped First Principle of the Eleatics became, like some newly found planet, the object of attentive reflection by other thinkers, till Aristotle discerned in it the necessary Existence prior to and productive of all contingent existences. As examples, on the one hand, of the destructive dynamite contained in Eleatic doctrine and, on the other, of its constructive force, the following citations from Xenophanes are offered:

1. If oxen and lions could paint, they would depict the gods with the bodies of oxen and lions.

2. If they are gods, how comes it that they die? And if they die, how are they gods? (In controversy on the mystery-religions which center about the death of Dionysus Zagreus and other gods.)

3. One God there is among gods and men the greatest, neither in body nor mind like mortals. . . . With the whole of Him He sees, He thinks, He hears. Without exertion, by energy of mind, He sways the universe.

Reason's triumph over mythology and her positive steps toward a reconstructed secular and religious science were followed by a period of decadence. The period is comparable to the period of decadence which came upon Scholasticism after the age of the great Schoolmen. Reasoning in the hands of the Sophists was made a plaything instead of an instrument for discriminating truth from error. A barren dialectic, whose boast was ability to prove the *pro* or the *con* of any proposition, replaced the inquiry into first causes. With this decadence we have present concern because of the religious corollary of Sophism. Anticipating by twenty-five hundred years the discovery of savants in the history of religions, the Sophists reasoned that, since religions varied in outward forms, therefore religion itself can be but a legalistic human institution. To counteract a primitive and natural state of disorderly "Might is Right," the gods were invented as bogies to terrify men into private decency and civic subservience.

Archelaus, the reputed teacher of Socrates, expressed this religious theory in thesis form. Since *fusis,* or nature, is simply unmoral, said he, all ordinances in regard to conduct come from *nomos* or positive human law. In the matter of man-made gods, Prodicus taught that gods were only personifications of natural forces and objects which man's experience had shown him to be useful. Agnosticism in theology ("of the gods I cannot say either that they do exist or that they do not exist"), and relativity in ethics (every man is individually his own judge in moral matters), were the *placita* of Protagoras.

Athens staged several prototypes of our twentieth-century Dayton "monkey trial" in an effort to check the rationalizing current of Sophist teaching. Far more effectively was advanced Greek thought turned into sober channels by the work of Socrates, Plato, and Aristotle.

Socrates was much less absorbed with the problems of theology than with those of ethics. He accepted Anaxagoras' "Mind" which pervades the universe, but gave greater definition to the idea. Man's mind he declared to be a ray from the world-mind or soul. In the same passage from Xenophon's *Memorabilia* (I, 4, 8), he develops arguments proving the supreme intelligence from the varied order in the world. However, his ethical speculations were the leading theme of the discourses which interested the youth of Athens and disquieted the city's rulers. He conceived morals as egocentric, not in the relativist sense of Protagoras, but in the sense that God spoke in the voice of conscience. Strangely, he taught that mere attention to this voice and intellectual analysis of its implications would make men moral. Such hearkening and reflection, according to him, constituted the elements of the "Know thyself" of the Delphic oracle. By them man oriented himself toward the Supreme Good, which we reasonably conclude to mean God.

It seems clear from the conclusions of critics who have patiently studied out the mind of Socrates as his pupil Plato presents it, that Socrates labored under the delusion that a moral philosopher would be automatically morally upright, and that ignorance was at least the chief element in sin. He did not envisage the possibility of a Professor of Ethics being a fine scoundrel, of the poor dullard on the two-obol bench in the theater pleasing God in his unscientific way, of the many finding the Supreme Good by simple uprightness and humility.

It is not curious that in a religious society strongly nationalized and leaning heavily on external authority the doctrine of individual conscience as the sole fount of moral obligation led to the charges of "corrupting youth and bringing strange gods into Athens." Socrates followed Anaxagoras and Protagoras into the shadow of state persecution, but escaped not so easily.

Plato and Aristotle, avoiding the dank morass of mythologic tradition and fighting free of the undertow of Sophism, advanced powerfully in the purer current of thought discovered by Zenophanes, Anaxagoras, and Socrates. Neither orthodox polytheist nor Sophist, they declared, could find the truth, for both merely cloaked a fearful ignorance beneath a vaunted knowledge. For the unphilosophic multitude Plato conceded that faith in the Homeric tradition was less blameworthy and less harmful. Yet even for these, belief in pornographic myths must debase standards of conduct.

The Golden Age had brought broadened horizons. Commerce and the reports of Grecian globe-trotters had brought into focus practically the whole Mediterranean panorama. Plato and Aristotle, too, by their own travels had grown acquainted with other peoples. From the same diversity of religions which had led the Sophists to argue that religion is man-made, the clearer minds of the two masters drew an argument for the existence of God. For, said they, men could not be universally in error in a conviction so important as their belief in their subjection to superior beings. How, then, did men come to center this belief on the members of so many and so diverse panthea? The answer of Plato and of Aristotle is the same—religious decadence. To cite Aristotle's analysis:

> A tradition, descending to us from the most remote antiquity, transmitted under the veil of fable, tells that the stars of heaven

are gods, but that the divine substance surrounds the whole of nature. Fable has added to this tradition, with a view to secure the enforcement of laws and to promote the common good. And so it comes that human or animal forms have been ascribed to the gods and that poetic imagination has run riot in the development of the anthropomorphic and theriomorphic theme. Yet, if we disengage from the tangle the one only principle that the primary substances are gods according to the earliest faith, we find that here we have a correct faith in the divinity. Philosophy has repeatedly recovered and repeatedly lost its hold upon these primitive realities, so that we find the faith of our ancestors in our own day a species of venerable ruin. From these ruins we can in a manner reconstruct what was the faith of our fathers and the tradition of earliest man.

The god in human form, then, is the fiction of statecraft and of romantic fancy, yet through the tangled web woven by these two influences human reason can still perceive a little of the light of truth. The truth, as Aristotle understands it in this quotation, is that the forces of nature, "primary substances" he calls them, are gods in an inferior sense, but that the true divine being surrounds and transcends all nature. However, the quotation is controversial rather than expository, so cannot be expected to present adequately the theology of the Stagirite or of his master Plato. An attempt will now be made to trace in outline their positive doctrine on the divine nature and on creation.

God, says Plato, began his work by putting order into chaotic matter, the principle of order being mathematical ideals of proportion. He could not render the order ideally perfect, for the ancient specter of Moira rose to hinder. God might persuade Moira — we may call this Necessity or Fate, for the concept is the same — to relinquish her rights in part, but the final work of putting order in chaos was only relatively perfect. Thus was formed the material Cosmic Body. It received motion and intelligence when God compounded the Cosmic Soul, half of which he infused into the outer firmament of the stars and half into the inner circle of sun, moon, planets, and earth. This Cosmic Soul was then appointed by God to be his vicegerent in the universe, while he himself retired into transcendent remoteness.

Sun, moon, planets, and fixed stars are gods, according to Plato. To them are aggregated the traditional gods of the Greek Pantheon. It would seem that the title to divinity for all was participation in the Cosmic Soul, but the point is not clear. To these demiurges or minor gods "the God" committed the task of forming animals and the bodies of men. For the "creation" of human souls Plato postulated the direct action of "the God," who compounded them, in number equal to the stars, of less pure elements than he had used to compound the Cosmic Soul. Before he sends a soul into its proper body, God instructs it in the laws of the universe and the laws of Fate.

Man's aim in life is to liberate himself from the tyranny of the body by conquering pleasure, pain, and fear. For these impede pure knowledge and contemplation of God. Plato calls the struggle *melete thanatou* or "preparation for death." The soul in its warfare may league itself with a secondary soul seated in the breast which is the principle of the irascible passions, but may expect only hostility from yet a third soul seated beneath the diaphragm which is the root of the sensual passions.

It seems that Plato really believed in the substantial part of the above mythico-philosophical reconstruction. His admission of the Homeric divinities as gods is quite certainly a sop thrown to popular piety and state jealousy. He believed, though, in the astral and planetary gods. It need not be remarked that neither to them nor to the Cosmic Soul did he attribute divinity in the transcendent sense. This "the god" alone possessed. Plato's "creation" is rather an ordering of matter already existing than a production of matter from nothing. Finally, the Platonic synthesis forcibly illustrates how feeble a candle is unaided reason for searching out man's origin and destiny. The mind needs the increate light of revelation to guide it.

The life of contemplation, Aristotle held, is superior to the life of action. Hence, the perfect God must lead a life of self-absorbed thought. So:

> In Him is life; for the activity of intelligence is life, and He is that activity. Thus His essential activity constitutes a perfect and blessed life. We speak of God, therefore, as a living being, perfect and eternal. For to Him is ascribed a life which is continual and eternal; or, we might rather say, He is life eternal.[1]

In repetitious phrase the Stagirite here is striving to clarify the idea of God as Pure Self-Originating and Self-Terminating Action, immanent and perfect.

Aristotle's stringent reasoning on causality made him realize vividly that God is the First Mover and Cause of all beings outside of Himself and of all actions which they perform. This sublime apprehension involved Aristotle in a difficulty which he never adequately solved. How was the eternal Self-Absorbed Thought to concern Itself with objects so inferior as man and the cosmos? Just how was the First Cause and Mover to effect and move the finite and contingent? The fact of such concern and causality, both originative and conservative, was clear to him. His attempts at defining the "how" were various, but all insufficient. He said, for instance, that there is something divine in man and in the world which moves them upward toward God. But the real difficulty is how God is to be moved downward toward the finite. Aristotle also stresses God's conservation of the world, but the question at issue is rather one of origination and co-operation. God, he further says, moves the world as the general moves the army, in whose intelligent discipline the general's mind is manifest; yet here we have only inconclusive metaphor.

---

[1] *Metaphysica,* 1072, b, 15.

PART FIVE
RELIGION OF THE ROMANS

CHAPTER « 25

A FORWARD GLANCE

ROMAN religion may be called a twin of the religion of the Greeks. Readers versed in classic lore well know to what extent the younger nation, Rome, took over the birthright of old Greece. Though it would be an exaggeration to characterize the former nation's literature, art, and social life as mere imitations of the achievements of Hellenic genius, the strong influence of Greek models and the fusion of Hellenic with Latin elements must be evident. In the matter of religion, the Italic twin, to return to the comparison employed above, grasped the Greek twin's heel with special insistence. Jacob-like, too, Rome secured the religious birthright of the Greek Esau, entering successively into the possession of the Homeric, the Apolline, and the mystic tradition, as well as of the destructive and constructive religious thought of Hellenic philosophy. Finally, though decline fell upon the city-states whose patronage had supported cult orthodoxy, the city on the Tiber took upon herself the responsibility of maintaining, on a world-wide basis, reverence for the traditional religious beliefs and forms.[1]

In addition to her office as tutelary of the Graeco-Roman tradition, Rome assumed the duties of foster parent to the *Sacra Peregrina*—a variety of Oriental cults practised at Rome which traced their origins to an immemorial antiquity. Thus was developed in imperial times a concentration, under the name of Roman Religion, of the chief errors and truths which man, in his sin-blinded quest of God, had evolved and to which he had clung.

---

[1] Cf. especially Fowler's *Religious Experience of the Roman People*, Chs. X, XI, XVI, XVII.

Conclusions diametrically opposed to each other are drawn from this fact respectively by Rationalistic historians of religions and by Catholic savants of the same science. By the former group it is asserted that Christianity borrowed its doctrinal structure from this conglomerate of religious beliefs, and patched together, from the myth-texture so abundant in the composite Roman religion, a suitable biography for the initiator of the Christian movement. For the Catholic historian the bringing to a focus in early imperial days of so many of the religions of antiquity stands as a Providential "preparation for the gospel." At Rome and in the provinces the Gospel message, namely, came into immediate contact with a fair cross section of the religious history of the children of Adam, a history of their painful groping after their God, of apprehending Him under myriad imperfect types, of ceaselessly longing for a clearer manifestation of Him and of His salvation.[2] To all this anxious questioning the Gospel message was the obvious God-sent answer, to which the men of good will, whether Roman or provincial, hearkened with joy. Furthermore, Greek philosophy had effected a clarification of concepts and a crystallization of terminology destined to be of immense service both to the Christian apologete in his presentation of the preambles of faith and to the systematic theologian in his expression of revealed doctrine.

Finally, Divine Providence had drawn up on the Roman battleground the united hosts of false religions, that so the triumph of Christ's truth might be the more striking and decisive. St. Peter's is built on ground where once was solemnized the characteristic rite of two of the ancient mystery-religions.[3] Before the Cathedral of Christendom rises an

---

[2] Cf. St. Paul's discourse to the Athenians, Acts 17:22–31.

[3] The *Taurobolium* or quasi-baptism of blood, a cult practice in the worship of Cybele and of Mithras. Numerous taurobolic altars were discovered during the excavations for St. Peter's, and from written sources we know that the Vatican Hill was peculiarly sacred to the rite of the Taurobolium.

obelisk, once sacred to the sun-god in Heliopolis. On its summit is a cross containing a relic of the True Cross, while its base bears the significant legend: *Christus vincit, Christus regnat, Christus imperat:* "Christ conquers, Christ reigns, Christ rules."

Having thus given some indication as to whither the present inquiry will lead us, we add a table which serves to summarize the foregoing remarks in a more concise and vivid form. Its purpose is to show: first, the progressive expansion of the Roman pantheon; second, the relative prominence of the various cults at different stages of history; third, the final triumph of Christianity.

TABLE OF RELIGIONS AS INTRODUCED AT ROME

Century	Religions
B.C. VIII, VII, VI	DI INDIGETES (gods *native* to Rome).
B.C. V, IV	DI INDIGETES. DI NOVENSIDES (*foreign* gods, adopted either *from Italy or from Greece*).
B.C. III, II, I	DI NOVENSIDES. DI INDIGETES DEIFIED ABSTRACTIONS (*desirable qualities or conditions* which have been invested with personality and made into gods; e.g., Pietas, Pax). SACRA PEREGRINA (*Oriental* cults at Rome).
A.D. I, II	DI NOVENSIDES. SACRA PEREGRINA. DI INDIGETES. DIVI (*emperors* who by decree of the Senate have been declared to be gods). DEIFIED ABSTRACTIONS. CHRISTIANITY.

A.D.	
III, IV	Sacra Peregrina.
	Christianity.
	Di Novensides.
	Di Indigetes.
	Divi.
	Deified Abstractions.
A.D.	
V	Christianity.*

* The table has been adapted in its method of presentation from that of Professor Gordon J. Laing, without, however, any substantial changes. We do not wholly agree with the position of relative importance accorded to Christianity in the last three divisions, but do not feel at liberty to alter in substance the professor's text. For the benefit of the uninitiate we are inserting an explanation of each new technical term as it appears for the first time on the list.

CHAPTER « 26

THE REIGN OF THE NUMINA

NO EPIC has preserved for us the record of earliest Roman society. An attempt to reconstruct the manners and thoughts of the Latin tribe which, about eight hundred years before our era, grazed flocks and planted fields around their rude hill town on the left bank of the Tiber is not as comparatively easy a task as the reconstruction of an early Greece from the Homeric and Hesiodic documents. A wealth of archeological data, furthermore, supplements and explains the Hellenic written documents, while from early Rome archeology has up to the present secured but meager and disconnected testimony.

In recapturing the vanished religion of primitive Rome, scholars have patiently followed out the clues offered by a few sacred lyrics and prayer formulas of unquestioned antiquity; by certain religious institutions maintained in the spirit of conservatism down into historic times; and finally, by indications which the Stone Calendars give of immemorial gods and festivals. Literature, it is true, is neither incurious nor silent on the religious theme, but it is literature born long after the somber Di Indigetes of the early city had resigned their thrones to the brilliant and popular anthropomorphic divinities immigrant from Hellas. The *Antiquitates Rerum Divinarum* of Varro is the work of a scholar of the first century B.C., whose title sufficiently indicates its purpose of tracing religious origins, but the author is driven to conjectures more or less plausible, in his reconstruction of the shadowy earliest period.[1] Ovid's *Fasti* was planned as a com-

[1] We know this work through the numerous citations of it in St. Augustine, the original being lost save for a few fragments.

mentary on the religious festivals of the Julian Calendar, and is valuable from a factual standpoint because of the poet's keen observation of the details of ritual. However, his exegesis of the more ancient festivals is governed rather by poetic fancy and poetic fondness for legends than by objective scholarship.[2] The conclusion is patent that, if even in these chief, though not sole, didactic tractates on Roman religion the primitive period is so badly known, little additional light can be expected from other literary sources.

In place, then, of splendidly complete written sources, contemporary with the earliest religious period, documents fragmentary and cryptic such as the following greet the investigator:

Enos lases iuvate!	Help us, ye Lares.
Neve luerve Marmar sins incurrere in pleores!	Let not blight and ruin, O Mars, haste upon the multitude.
Satur fu, fere Mars, limen sali, sta berber!	Be satiate, fierce Mars: leap the threshold, stay thy scourge.
Semunes alternei advocapit cunctos!	Summon ye in turn all the gods of sowing.
Enos Marmar iuvato!	Help us, O Mars.
Triumpe, Triumpe, Triumpe.[3]	Huzza! Huzza! Huzza!
	[Trans. by J. Wight Duff]

Mars pater, te precor quaesoque ut sies volens propitius mihi domo familiaeque nostrae, quoius rei ergo agrum terram fundumque meum suovetaurilia circumagi jussi, uti tu morbos visos invisosque, viduerta-	Father Mars, I beseech and implore thee to be propitious and gracious to me, my home and my household. To this end have I ordered that the sacred swine, sheep and ox be driven along the boundaries of my

[2] Only the first six months of the year are treated, the circumstances of the poet's exile, it would seem, preventing completion of the plan.

[3] From the Hymn of the Arval Brethren. These latter were the members of one of the eight early priesthoods, their special function being to secure divine protection for agricultural activities.

tem vastitudinemque, calamitates intemperiasque prohibessis defendas averruncesque; utique tu fruges, frumenta, vineta virgultaque grandire beneque evenire sinas, pastores pecuaque salva servassis duisque bonam salutem valetudinemque mihi domo familiaeque nostrae: harumce rerum ergo, fundi terrae agrique mei lustrandi lustrique faciendi ergo, sicuti dixi, macte hisce suovetaurilibus lactentibus immolandis esto.[4]

land and freehold. May thou, then, avert, forfend and keep away seen and unseen diseases, all barrenness, destruction, evil visitation and bad weather. Make my grain, my vines and my rushes flourish and come to harvest. Keep safe my herdsmen and my flocks. Grant health and well-being to me, my home and household. When I shall have beaten the bounds of my property with these sacred yearlings, accept the sacrifice of them and grant in return all the blessings which I have named.

Critics, on the principle of *lex orandi est lex credendi,* that as men pray so they believe, rightly attach the greatest importance to these and similar bits of the ancient liturgy. To illustrate merely cursorily, since we purpose shortly to treat the whole question of the character of the primitive *numina,* there appear in these few lines: Mars, as an agricultural divinity; the Lares and Semones, as spirits potent in the warding off of pestilence; the sacred victims proper to the Ambilustrium; and lastly an illustration of the scrupulous exactness demanded of the votary in his statement of the favor requested of the divinity.

Rome, it is certain, passed through the entire Republican Era without establishing any new priesthoods. This in itself is a singularly valuable clue in our investigation. Before commenting, however, we must here tabulate the eight ancient priestly colleges and their peculiar field of providence.[5]

---

[4] Prayer formula to be used at the lustration of the fields, quoted by Cato in *De Agri Cultura,* 141.

[5] Cf. article in *Hastings Encyclopaedia of Religion and Ethics* on *Priesthood* (Roman) by G. J. Laing.

Name *Characteristic Function*

Pontifices — Important duties as conservators of religious tradition, theologians, professors of sacred law, holders of great flaminates.
Augures — Intepretation of omens.
Fetiales — International relations, especially declaration of war.
Luperci — Lustration of the circuit of Palatine Hill.
Salii — Worship of Mars, especially during month of March.
Titii — Function obscure, probably the worship of the old Sabine king, Titus, Tatius.
Arvales — Divine propitiation to secure the success of agriculture.
Duoviri sacris faciundis[6] — Consultation of the *Sibylline Books* and execution of the directions they gave.

Knowledge of the antiquity of the priesthoods here named enables us to determine the age of many ritualistic acts in which these priests alone might engage. We are also aided in reconstructing the primitive Pantheon, inasfar as certain of these priests are found in earliest records inseparably associated with certain divinities. Examples are readily noted in the case of the mysterious rite of the Luperci, "beating the bounds" of the Palatine city, and of the devotion of the Salii to father Mars.

Upon the completion of his revision of the calendar, Julius Caesar, in the true spirit of the dictator, ordered the destruction of all the old calendars. The execution of the order effected the uniformity that he desired, but also did away with valuable records. The calendars were the work of the Collegium Pontificum, being composed by them with the primary purpose of reminding the people of the days consecrated to certain gods and to certain religious observances. They were, in fact, pagan parallels of one of our ecclesiastical calendars, which note the seasons of the ecclesiastical year, the fast and feast days, the saints' namesdays. In the Julian

[6] This priesthood is the latest in point of time of the old priesthoods, dating from the reign of the Tarquins. Its function of caring for the *Sibylline Books*, Greek in origin, indicates a transition from the period of Di Indigetes to that of Di Novensides.

revision of the calendar innumerable pontifical details are omitted. The ancient festival days are, indeed, indicated as such by the device of marking them in large capitals and it is precisely in these large-capitaled days that scholars have found their third chief source in reconstructing the character of earliest Roman religion.

The Julian Calendars that survive are cut on stone and have been found in Rome itself and in various municipalities of the Italian peninsula. Of the whole number of thirty, the one from Mattei is practically complete, four embrace a third of a year, while the rest are more or less fragmentary. Besides the scheme already noted of designating ancient festivals in large capitals, the calendars indicate the days when business might be transacted by the letters F and C (sc. *fastus* and *Comitiae*), and the days when business transactions were forbidden by the letter N (sc. *nefastus*).[7] Some explanatory cultural notes are added in various calendars. In the typical month here cited from Warde Fowler, explanatory notes from Latin authors are likewise added.

Julian Calendar for Month of December

MENSIS DECEMBER

Fasti Antiquissimi		*Additamenta ex Fastis*	*Additamenta ex Scriptoribus*
1 Kal.	N	1. Neptuno ad circ. Pietati max.	1. Fortunae muliebri (Dion.).
2	N		
3	N		3. Sacra Bonae Deae (Plut.).
4	C		
5 Non.	F		5. Faunalia Rustica (Horace).
6	F		
7	C		
8	C	8. Tiberino in insula.	
9	C		
10	C		

[7] EN *fastus* in midday hours. N. P. seems to mean *nefastus*.

Fasti Antiquissimi			*Additamenta ex Fastis*	*Additamenta ex Scriptoribus*
11	NP	AGONIA IN.		11. Septimontium (Varro).
12	EN		12. Conso in Aventino.	
13 Eid.	NP		13. Telluri et Cereri in Carinis.	
14	F			
15	NP	CONSUALIA		
16	C			
17	NP	SATURNALIA		
18	C			
19	NP	OPALIA		
20	C			
21	NP	DIVALIA		
22	C		22. Laribus permarinis in porticu Minucia.	
23	NP	LARENTALIA		
24	C			
25	C			
26	C			
27	C			
28	C			
29	F			

Three significant facts fix the date of these *Fasti Antiquissimi* well back in the earliest period whose characteristics we are endeavoring to recapture. The entry QUIRINALIA for February fifth indicates that the cult of Quirinus was a public cult. Now, it was not a public cult till the inclusion of the Quirinal Hill in the city limits, an event of the regal period. Again, the Etruscan triad of Jupiter, Juno, Minerva is unknown to the *Fasti Antiquissimi,* a fact that puts our date certainly prior to 509 B.C., the year of the dedication of the Capitoline temple to the triad. Finally, no reference occurs here to the worship of Diana, but Diana was certainly adopted during the regal period. "Argal," as the grave-digger in *Hamlet* argues closely, our *Fasti Antiquissimi* are festival days dating from the sixth or seventh century, and, since religious observances are slow of introduction, the inference is that the bulk of these feasts are of even greater antiquity. We have, then, in the large capitals of the Julian Calendar a body of cult facts about earliest Roman religion to add to the facts which emerge from a study of ancient prayers and ancient priesthoods.[8]

With the preceding brief indication of sources, we proceed to the reconstruction of the earliest period, following in all, save their occasionally rationalistic viewpoint, the reconstruction made by modern scholars.[9]

The first truly historical picture of Rome presented to our consideration is that of a people whose home life was close-knit and affectionate, who were just growing into race-consciousness, whose occupations were agriculture, stock raising, and war. The gods of this people were the tutelary spirits of the three activities here named: of family life, civic duty, and farming.

At the door of the home Janus, spirit of the doorpost, stood guard to keep out manifold evil influences lurking without and to secure a safe return from herd or field to the *paterfamilias*. Of strictly domestic worship the *paterfamilias* took charge. It was he who recited at the household shrine the minutely exact prayer formulas, such as we have seen, and made the simple offerings. It was he who at the Lemuria rose at dead of night to placate by reiterated incantations and an offering of black beans the *manes paterni* (spirits of their ancestors) who at this season were restlessly haunting the scenes of their past labors and joys. His own spiritual double or Genius, the paternal procreative power to which the family owed its origin and on which it depended for its well-being, was itself an object of domestic cult, reverenced along with the Lar familiaris or quasi-guardian angel of the quiet activities of the household.[10] The importance of the larder or

---

[8] The most readable book on the calendar is Fowler's *Roman Festivals*.

[9] Especially Bailey, Carter, Fowler, Halliday, Laing. Cf. Bibliography at end of book.

[10] That originally there was but one Lar to a household and that the Lares were not the spirits of ancestors, is shown by G. J. Laing in *Classical Philology*, XVI, pp. 124 sqq. On how the Lar came to be a household divinity cf. Fowler's *Religious Experience of the Roman People*, p. 78.

penus early led to the concept of *di penates* who protected the food supply. They were elected according to devotion from among divinities already recognized, much as one nowadays will choose patron saints. The hearth fire, both in its useful and its symbolic character, was divinized under the name of Vesta and received a cult destined to continue as one of the purest survivals through coming ages of decadence.

The Vestal virgins of Republican and Imperial days performed in behalf of the state the same sacred functions which the daughters of the family performed in behalf of the primitive household. These Vestals kept alight the sacred fire and guarded the *penus Vestae* in their house on the Capitoline where they lived under the *patria patestas* (a patriarchal power) of the Pontifex Maximus; they secured water not from the abundant aqueducts, but, like their ancient prototypes, from a sacred spring; each year they supervised a ceremonial sweeping of their temple precincts, the *aedes Vestae;* with their own hands they pounded in antique mortars the first ears of corn and baked the salt cakes, just as the daughters of the family, the *filiaefamilias,* had prepared of old like offerings for the daily sacrifice during the family meal.

Of other details of household religion the following may be noted. On Calends, Nones, and Ides the Lar familiaris received offerings. Ops, a divinity of the harvest, and Consus, who guarded the grain laid by for the winter, were honored and supplicated at the Opiconsivia and Opalia in August and the Consualia in December. Birth and death were surrounded by an anxious observantism. Fifteen spirits are named in the *Indigitamenta* of the *Pontifices*[11] as guardians of the stages of infant life from the period of birth to the toddling stage.

[11] The *Indigitamenta* may be popularly described as a sacred guidebook, giving the names of the divinities, their peculiar fields of providence, and the prayer formulas to be used in addressing them. Fowler has a quite invaluable discussion on the worth of the *Indigitamenta* as source material on p. 158 sqq. of *Religious Experience of the Roman People.*

Fig. 32. Sacrificial Animals of Early Rome

The boar, sheep, and bull were garlanded and led about the Roman farmer's land, then slain as a sacrifice to secure bounteous crops. The above relief adorns the speaking platform in the Roman Forum. In the left background are seen the columns of the Temple of Saturn.

Evil powers were believed to be lurking outside the house door to catch the newborn child, so three men proceeded to the threshold to strike it with an ax and a staff to frighten off the wild Silvanus, and to sweep away from it with a broom the remaining evil influences. It was not until the eighth day (ninth for girls), when a name was imposed and the magic *bulla* placed about the infant's neck, that fear of these envious sprites rested.

At life's conclusion, too, the primitive Roman felt the supernatural world draw singularly near. The heir of the family bent over a dying parent to catch the last breath. The corpse was laid out with feet toward the door and was carried out for burial at night, both observances seeming to instance a solicitude lest the evil influences vaguely associated with a dead body might find the way back into the house. After the cremation or inhumation, for both methods were used, the family purified themselves and the house, offering a sow in sacrifice. On the ninth day, after an offering made at the tomb and a family banquet, ritual uncleanness was conceived to have been removed.

What the early Romans thought of the condition of their dead is a mooted question. What to us is clear is their belief in personal survival, in the jealousy of the departed for continued remembrance by their former friends, in the haunting by the spirit of the tomb and of the scenes of its earthly pilgrimage. Such an interpretation of the Roman mind is necessitated by the facts of the Lemuria (May 9–13) and of the Parentalia (February 13–21), to mention merely the two more conspicuous pieces of evidence. The ritual of the Lemuria has been indicated above. On the occasion of the Parentalia the whole family repaired to the tomb, bearing offerings of food, of flowers, of blood of victims. They partook of a meal there with the spirits of their loved ones, spoke again the consecrated phrases *Salve, sancte parens* and *Vale, vale, vale,* petitioned the dead members of the family for all good gifts needed by the living members. There followed beneath the domestic roof a love feast from which all the misunderstandings and bickerings of the past year were banished. Frankly, we take these unquestioned facts of family cult as clear refutation of the postulate of many scholars[12] that individuality was believed to be swallowed up after death in a vague college of Di Manes. Certain it is that the family was directing its sepulchral observances to those precise individuals who had been known in life.

In concluding the sketch of family religion, it is apposite to comment on the solidarity of the Roman family group and on the depth of affection on which this solidarity was grounded. The solidarity of the family group contributed inestimably to the steady expansion of the Roman polity into a world empire, while family affection softened the sternness of national character. Cicero and his daughter Tullia, Aeneas and his father Anchises endure as literature's expression of these best of Roman traits.

Your Roman farmer peopled his agricultural and grazing land with *numina* even more abundantly than he did the interior of his *tugurium,* his humble hut. Pregnant cows had to be sacrificed to Tellus Mater on April 15 and the unborn calves torn from them were burned to secure the germination of the corn seed in the bosom of Mother Earth, while ten days later (so at least after the date had been definitely set by the Pontifices) a prophylactic offering of a sheep and a dog had to be tendered to Robigus, lest he send the dreaded red rust upon the growing crops.[13] Still in this month of anxious expectation for an agricultural population, the farmer took

[12] Cf., the analyses, to us unconclusive, of J. B. Carter on pp. 72 sqq. in *Religious Life of Ancient Rome,* and of W. R. Halliday on pp. 38 sqq. in *Lectures on the History of Roman Religion.*

[13] The *Litania Major* was fixed by the Church on the twenty-fifth day of April according to the policy of replacing the old pagan observances, which had such a hold on the people, by Christian rites. Cf. *Catholic Encyclopedia,* Art. "Litany."

care, on April 19, to propitiate the grain goddess Ceres. The character of the rites used on this occasion we are unable to reconstruct because Ceres was so soon (493 B.C.) to be assimilated to the Greek Demeter and worshiped *Graeco ritu.*

Of the ancient Parilia, however, on April 21, we have the most minute details. The festival was in honor of Pales, recognized as tutelary spirit of the flocks, but to whom the old prayer formula *sive mas sive femina,* "whether male or female," was applicable. Pales received a rustic worship that both Ovid and Virgil have delighted to narrate. The shepherd garlanded his fold and swept it clean. Hard by it he kindled a great fire. From the best that his simple stores could provide he then prepared a meal which he ate with his god. Four times over he said his prayer, voicing minutely his every fear and hope for the flock. Draughts of milk and hot wine followed, till the shepherd felt himself sufficiently warmed by his devotions and potations to undergo the last bit of ritual. For he had yet to drive his flock through the purifying bonfire aforesaid and leap through the same.[14]

The sacredness felt to be attached to boundaries found expression in the Compitalia and Terminalia, the one in early January, the other on February 23. The adaptability of the Lares as spirits of all work is illustrated by the belief, underlying the observance of the Compitalia, that it was they who guarded the intersection of the farmer's freehold with his neighbor's land.[15] Facing the intersection, and each man standing on his own land, they offered gifts and prayers to the Lares Compitales. Of like character was the cult of Terminus the spirit of the boundary stone, though there penetrated this latter cult a realization that the votary was dealing

---

[14] The description is taken from Ovid, *Fasti,* IV, v. 721 sqq. The day was also the traditional day of Romulus' founding of the city.

[15] The Lares were "place-spirits" and received specification of function according to this concept. For instance, in addition to Lar familiaris and Lares compitales, we have Lares viales (roads!), Lares permarini (sea!), Lares praestites (whole city!).

with a divinity of deeper mystery and more august majesty than were the elflike and friendly Lares. On either side of the doubly garlanded boundary stone the respective families grouped themselves, each before a fire that must be kindled by a brand from the family hearth. A daughter of the family tossed into the flames the various fruits of the earth and cakes of honey. A sacrifice of a ram and a pig followed, the blood being sprinkled on the boundary stone. The last feature of the observance of the Terminalia was a family banquet with rustic songs in honor of the god.[16]

Early cult facts point both to an agricultural and a martial function for the god Mars. Which function was first associated with him is a point of controversy between scholars, Mannhardt holding for the agricultural, Wissowa for the martial. Certain it is that the god is insistently invoked for blessing on the fields in the Arval hymn already cited and in the ancient prayer formula quoted by Cato. March, the month of reviving vegetation, had scarcely any religious observances save in his honor. Throughout the month his twelve priests, armed *cap-a-pié,* executed their dance in the city streets, symbolizing the conflict of spring with winter. Lest this interpretation seem farfetched we hasten to add that such martial proceedings against hostile Old Man Winter are not unusual among primitive peoples. On the fourteenth a man clad in winter attire was run out of town by the same Salii Palatini. Three other March observances are connected with Mars—the horse races (March 14), the purification of the shields of the Salii (March 19), and of the ritual trumpets (March 23). Of these it may be said that their occurrence in the month of the new vegetation is significant.

---

[16] Terminus may have originated from a separate hypostatization of an attribute of Jupiter. At any rate, there is a strong ethical connotation in the Terminus cult, namely, that the rights of property are under divine protection. Now, the Roman Jupiter no less than the Greek Zeus is the god who sanctions honest dealing. Cf. Fowler's *Roman Festivals,* pp. 326, 327.

Proceeding now through the year one meets Mars in the distinctively agricultural role of the god who originally was propitiated when the crops began to ripen. On May 29 the ancient sacred victims — bull, pig, and sheep — were garlanded and led about the boundaries of the ripening fields, then sacrificed with invocation of father Mars. In mid-October, when the season's crops were safely garnered, a thanksgiving festival was solemnized in the following highly curious manner. A chariot race being run on the Campus Martius, the victor gave his right-hand horse as a sacrificial victim to the god. Head and tail of the honored animal were amputated, the former member being hung on the wall of the king's house, the latter rushed posthaste to the same house that the fresh blood might drip upon the royal hearth. The use made of the congealed blood scraped up from the hearth, saved and used in the agricultural festivals of the Fordicidia and Parilia, indicates that the dominant idea of the rite of the October Horse was also agricultural. Add to this the fact already noted that the time of year points to the agricultural motif and another argument is at hand for identifying father Mars as a god of this ilk.

What happened in later times to this, his agricultural attribute, is plausibly explained on the theory that urgent wars impelled the people to seek aid from a god who had shown himself potent and propitious in another line and might be expected to aid against the enemy. The cult of Ceres, too, grew immensely after 493 B.C. and may be supposed to have overshadowed the agricultural attributes of Mars.

Uncritical legend and too critical scholarship have clouded the origins of Rome's civic institutions. Though, on the one hand, it be not necessary to do violence to our critical digestion by bolting the story of the Mars-born wolf-suckled twins, neither, on the other, is it reasonable to refuse to recognize a body of facts indicated by the three primary sources mentioned at the start of this chapter. Materially, then, during the early period of which we speak Rome was a city expanding from an original circuit of the Palatine Hill to city limits embracing the Quirinal, the Capitoline, the Esquiline, and the Caelian. The *ager Romanus* was similarly expanding along the left bank of the Tiber and southward under the exigence of growing population and the incidence of neighborly wars. Government was monarchical, though how many kings and what dynasties of them early Rome knew cannot be, and for our present purpose need not be, definitely stated. To these kings, and in all reasonable likelihood to the very Numa of tradition, the organization of the state cult is due. There is the wisdom of a wise legislator and potent executive only too clearly evidenced in the establishment of the great *collegia* of priests with their precise functions, in the shrewd molding of household and farm cults into a civic form. From home and field the central authority invited the gods of the people into the sacred Pomerium[17] and gave them honorable citizenship there. Pales, Ceres, Pomona, and the other farm divinities were assigned, every one, an attendant priest or Flamen devoted to the public exercise of worship. Vesta's fire was enshrined in an *aedes Vestae,* the only temple in the old time, and was tended by Vestal virgins chosen by the Pontifex Maximus. Mysterious Janus, spirit of the house door, was "indigitated" as spirit of the symbolic door of the city and given the mysterious Rex Sacrorum for attendant priest. The importance of Father Mars was recognized, as already indicated, by the terpsichorean efforts of his *collegium* of warrior priests as well as by the appointment of a Major Flamen. Another Major Flamen and two sacerdotal *collegia,* Augures

[17] The Pomerium meant the boundary of the city, primitively traced by the furrow of a plow. The connotation was distinctly religious, the land within being set aside for national gods, while divine newcomers had to be content with a cult outside the line. The distinction was enforced, as will be seen. There is a probability that the Pomerium was also understood to be a "magic circle" drawn to exclude malignant influences.

and Fetiales, ministered to the still more important Jupiter.[18] Under the wise direction of the supreme *collegium* of Pontifices the immemorial rites of family and farm religion were solemnized at public expense and *pro populo*.

The foregoing facts show an "establishment" comparable to the "establishment" of the Homeric tradition effected by the legislators of the Greek city state. Results, too, of the Roman experiment were not dissimilar. Decorum and commendable routine were secured for religious observances. Ideas of deity tended to become fixed. The extravagant and novel in religion became at the same time the illegal. Religion and patriotism entered on a nuptial contract destined to give birth to the ideal Roman whose *virtus* saw in civic duty and duty to the gods one indivisible motive.

Such were the spirits tutelary of home, farm, and city. Were they the original gods of the Roman people? They were the gods of that stock when it first emerged into history, but we cannot answer for the prior time. A few gods are known to have been common to Romans and to other Italic peoples, as Mars, for instance, was known to the Umbrians. Some cult institutions, too, are paralleled on the peninsula. The Fratres Arvales, for instance, are paralleled by the Umbrian Fratres Atiedii. However, evidence is so meager that even the most sanguine of theorizers avoid the problem of tracing Roman religious origins beyond the period of history we have just treated. One fact alone stands out clearly: the pan-Italic character of the "sky-god" Jupiter, but of this fact and its momentous bearing more will shortly be said.

A sense of the ubiquity of the world of spirits obviously characterized Roman religion of the earliest period. Back of this sense and originating it must be recognized the realization by a practical and unimaginative psychology of man's

---

[18] Jupiter, transcending the classification of functional *numina* hitherto dealt with, merits separate discussion.

dependence on mysterious natural forces — on the force that gave fertility to the field, for instance, on the force that made the ewe and the cow fecund, on the force that prospered the family, on the forces that controlled the good and evil fortunes of human experience. The beneficent operation of these forces was the objective of the Roman's concern. He conceived them as personal, of course, for prayer to an inexorably mechanical force would have appeared an absurdity to his downright way of thinking, while the sacrifice of his precious pigs and sheep to a force of this nature would have seemed madness. At the concept of personality and at the pragmatic performance of the duties of propitiation his theology was content to stop. With divine mythologies he was not concerned, and of native Italic mythology we have hardly a trace. Genealogies and iconic representation were equally foreign to his concept of worship. Indeed, his very sense of reverence prevented any attempt to represent his "*numina*" in storied or plastic art on the human model. Tellus was the earth force that vivified the seed, Ceres the force that grew in the grain, Janus the force that shut out evil invisibly as the door shut it out visibly. Goddesses touching the growing plant with potent wand and gods standing duty as janitors simply did not fit into Numinism. Since, too, the *numina* lived incorporated in the object or activity they protected, temples would have been an anomaly. The *aedes Vestae* was no more than a shelter necessitated to prevent the elements from extinguishing the sacred fire.

Potentialities for piety in Roman Numinism are obvious. The minutest of life's activities had to be consecrated. Sense of dependence on Over-Power, which is essential to religion, was strong. The sense of mystery which inhibits undue familiarity with the object of worship was vivid. The openness of the *numina* to impetration, finally, must be reckoned as a genuine, though clouded, element of religion and piety.

The most exalted religious concepts of the early Romans

centered about the cult of Jupiter. In his case the etymology of his name and the attributes the people worshiped in him are in agreement. The name, coming from the root *di* or *div* meaning "to shine, gleam," was originally Dious or Diovis. This original form survived in the name under which he was invoked as the god of good faith, Dius Fidius. A combination of Diovis with *pater,* philologists agree, produced Jupiter. Our name, then, signifies a god of light addressed reverently as father.

Seeking interpretation of philological data, we find Jupiter worshiped throughout the peninsula at the period of which we treat—among Faliscans, Oscans, Marsi, Picenians, Umbrians, Volscans. Everywhere his shrine is on the summit of a hill. Everywhere he is the light-giving god of heaven; to whom the *Ides* (the time of month when the light of sun by day and moon by night would be unbroken) were sacred; from whom all aerial and atmospheric phenomena came (Jupiter Fulgur, Jupiter Serenus, Jupiter Siccus, Jupiter Madidus); who was the holy one, the protector of truth and justice.

In Rome itself and its immediate environs he was worshiped on the Capitoline as Jupiter Feretrius, the cult title being likely derived from the idea that he was the one who struck with the lightning; on the Esquiline as Jupiter Fagutalis, for there was a grove of beech trees there; on the Viminal as Jupiter Viminalis; on the Caelian as Jupiter Caelius. An altar on the Campus Martius was dedicated to Jupiter Fulgur. Other Roman cults were those of Jupiter Liber, i.e., the bountiful, and Jupiter Elicius, explained by Livy and Ovid as a cult title referring to the god as the sender of rain.

Two facts must suffice to complete the sketch of Jupiter's attributes. His Flamen, who ranked first among the Flamines, emerges into history hedged about with the most minute taboos which made his life almost unbearable. Now, taboos are inevitably a sign of a naïve population's desire to recognize the sanctity of an office. Secondly, the Romans are remarkable for their sense of the sanctity of oaths. Now, both their private and official oaths were solemnized by an appeal to Jupiter as Dius Fidius. (*Mehercule!* was a later Greek importation and hardly rose above the dignity of a vulgar form of expletive.) The oath *Mediusfidius,* to be taken under the open sky, pledged a Roman on the highest honor he recognized. The Fetiales, in their declaration of grievance against other peoples, called Jupiter Lapis to witness and to sanction. In earliest historic times consuls took their oath of office at the altar of Jupiter on the Capitoline.

CHAPTER « 27

DIVINE NEWCOMERS AND ROMAN TOLERANCE

TO THE north of Rome stretched the more sophisticated Etruria. Not of the same stock as the Italic peoples, but immigrant to the peninsula, the Etruscans had contacted in their wanderings a variety of southern Mediterranean cultures. From these they borrowed a system of augury which seems to be Babylonian and a number of anthropomorphic gods who are clearly Hellenic. In the regal period they were busy indoctrinating their receptive-minded southern neighbors with reverence for such religious concepts.[1]

To the south of Rome lay Latium, a territory peopled by communities more akin in character and interests to the Romans than were the distinctly exotic Etruscans. In the traditions surviving from the prehistory of the regal days we justly read a story of how this kinship broke down the barriers of suspicious isolation separating the hill towns of Latium one from another. Hence the Latin League, the official "big, bad wolf" of whose defensive councils was no other than the ominous Etruscan power to the north of Tiber. Acquaintance with their Latin neighbors brought to the Romans acquaintance with their gods, while the very exigencies of league politics fostered religious syncretism.[2]

Beyond Etruria and beyond Latium the gaze of L. Junius Brutus and L. Tarquinius Collatinus, the first Consuls of Republican Rome, scarcely penetrated to the rest of the penin-

---

[1] Ch. I of Carter's *Religious Life of Ancient Rome* is excellent here.

[2] Cf. Livy, *Historia Romanorum*, Bk. I, chs. 7, 30, 38, 45, 52.

sular area. Trade relations and war, however, were soon to open Roman eyes to the whole of Italic culture, while the receptiveness already noted was to facilitate an expansion of the pantheon to admit the divinities of these other Italic peoples. They would be gods properly called Italic as well as Hellenic gods. For, especially in southern and eastern Italy, the Homeric tradition had long since been imported by Greek traders and colonists.[3]

The three hundred years of peninsular conquest, following on the Republic's birth, profoundly altered the spirit and form of Rome's indigenous religion. The period extends from the dedication of the Capitoline Temple, in 509, to the opening of the Second Punic War, in 219. In the main, the religious shift was in the direction of Greek anthropomorphism in theological concepts and toward the equally Greek fondness for artistic representation and splendid pageantry in cult. Strictly Italic influences contributed something to the transformation of the early religion, but such influences were largely kindred to the spirit of the old Numinism.

Livy tells us how the consuls of the first year of the Republic drew lots to determine which should dedicate the now completed Capitoline Temple, the honor falling to M. Horatius Fulvillus.[4] It was King Tarquinius Priscus, an Etruscan, who had vowed the temple and begun the foundations, so the legend goes, and his son Tarquinius Superbus who had finished the building shortly before he was exiled. Whatever may be the value of the legend, the cult itself was Graeco-Etruscan. For the triad Jupiter, Juno, and Minerva was an Etruscan adaptation of the familiar Greek triad of Zeus, Hera, and Athene. Greek, too, and not Roman in spirit were the very ideas of erecting a temple for the gods and of setting up images of them, for of such cult ideas the Numinism de-

[3] Centers of Greek culture near early Republican Rome were Cumae and Neapolis.

[4] Five consuls appear in the list for the first year, of whom two died in office and one was exiled.

scribed in the last chapter knew nothing. We can well imagine how the wondering Romans watched the removal of the simple shrines that occupied the Capitoline area to make way for what to them must have seemed a stupendous building project. Then, as the walls of the temple precinct rose and the massive masonry of the base was laid, awe must have grown for the divinity to be housed in the great structure. When, at last, the temple itself (crude though it might have seemed to a sophisticated Greek), with decorated frieze, columned portico and lofty steps, stood out against the luminous sky; when his own chief magistrate dedicated it; when he entered in and saw the fair cult statues, gorgeously robed and enthroned, each in its proper sanctuary, the Roman thrilled to a religious experience unfelt by his sires of the matter-of-fact, aniconic religious times.

The Capitoline Temple is rightly viewed as the memorial to the success of Etruscan religious propaganda.[5] That Rome was ready patiently to embrace the cult ideas there enshrined points to no small preparation of the native mind by the now exiled northern dynasts. It is tantalizing to our historical curiosity to be unable to trace in detail the stages of this propaganda; still, in the traditions carried down into historic times we can see dimly how the Etruscans played on the Roman mind. The elder Tarquin vowed a temple to the Graeco-Etruscan triad in the crisis of the Sabine War. The slave king, Servius Tullius, also an Etruscan, had multiple connections with a stranger goddess, Fortuna, and built her a temple across the Tiber at a short distance from the city. At his invitation Diana of Aricia, great goddess of the Latins, took up her abode in a shrine prepared for her on the Aventine. Tarquin the Proud was devoted to Greek Apollo and sent for oracles both to the god's Italian priestess, the Cumaean

[5] Standard tradition names the three Etruscan kings dealt with in this paragraph. We hold no bill for the defense of the threefold number, but hold, with the scholars frequently cited in these pages, the religious works here detailed to be recognizable as Etruscan.

Sibyl, and to the great prophetess at Delphi. The policy of the Etruscan kings, in fine, steadily looked toward shaking Rome out of her narrow isolation and bringing her into acquaintance with her Italic neighbors and, by consequence, with their religious culture.

Second in point of time, and bearing equally the stamp of Graeco-Etruscan influence, came the temple of Saturn. In the nuministic period he was a venerable spirit who prospered the sowing, but in his temple he retained little more than his old name and the date of his festival. In reality, it was the Greek Kronos whom Rome's Etruscan tutors had intruded. In place of his immemorial altar at the foot of the Capitoline, he now had a temple home, dedicated in 497, where he might be seen in iconic form holding Kronos' attribute of the scythe. His myth history grew oddly tangled by reason of the fusion of two divinities who were functionally different. Kronos, it will be recalled, was king during the Golden Age in Hesiod's account of the Ages of Man. Saturn was made out to have been king of Latium during a remote Golden Age of Italy. During his reign, he was said to have taught the art of agriculture to the people, a story seemingly thought out on the suggestion of Saturn's original function of an agricultural divinity. Under the influence of this festival, the Saturnalia, celebrated on December 17, came to stand for a memorial of this vanished Golden Age and the Romans made merry then, as they imagined men did in that carefree old time. The Saturnalia, it may be remarked in passing, has been seized upon by mad parallelists in the history of religions as the festival from which originated the Christmas rejoicing of the Church. Still more eccentric is Sir John Frazer's explanation of the origin of the doctrine of the divinity of Christ from one feature of the Saturnalia, namely, the King of the Saturnalia. This king, he tries to prove from a mass of perversely misinterpreted erudition, was the personification of a god to the revelers' mind and at the conclusion of the revels was scourged and crucified. Frazer's case may be read, if one have the patience, in *The Golden Bough.* Andrew Lang, in *Magic and Religion,* follows him point by point through his theory and fully refutes his position.

The whole religious policy of the Etrusco-Roman kings is illustrated in the continuous and finally successful efforts of Servius Tullius to have the Latin people unite with the Romans to erect a shrine of Diana at Rome itself. Recounting these details Livy adds that the inspiration came to Servius Tullius from the success of the politico-religious foundation of the temple of Ephesian Diana, *communiter a civitatibus Asiae factum,*[6] while Dionysius claims a more remote inspiration in the example of the Amphyctionic League. But no matter whence the inspiration was derived there arose on the Aventine, at a date close to the dates of the other temple foundations we have recently described, yet another temple. It was, in matter of historic fact, the common sanctuary of the nine members of the Latin League — Rome, Aricia, Tusculum, Tibur, Lanuvium, Larentum, Ardea, Suessa Pometia, Cora — of which the first named now exercised the functions of hegemon. Among these tribes, as indeed among Italic tribes generally, Diana held an immemorial position as a fertility goddess, both in the more universal sense and in the specific one of patroness of the fruitfulness of women. Modern excavation by its discoveries of extensive foundations and numerous votive offerings has confirmed what Ovid, Statius, and Propertius tell of the devotion centering at her temple on Lake Nemi.[7] Her Aventine temple, with all its political importance, never supplanted the Nemi temple in popular affection. In

[6] Livy, *op. cit.,* Bk. I, ch. 45.

[7] The priest at Nemi might hold office only by virtue of slaying his predecessor with a blow from a branch of the sacred tree. Virbius, a male divinity, probably with some function relative to childbirth, and Egeria, definitely a goddess of childbirth, were associated with Diana in the Nemi cult. The features of the cult of Diana of Nemi are the starting point for the Odysseus-like wanderings of Sir John Frazer's *Golden Bough.*

Rome the growing Greek vogue speedily identified Italic Diana with the huntress sister of Apollo both in myth biography and in artistic representation.

Homer's Olympian family was, in fact, rapidly moving into Rome with all the bag and baggage of the Homeric and Hesiodic tradition. Kronos, as we have seen, was accepted by an accommodation with Saturn; his offspring Zeus and Hera, disguised in the Etruscan triad; Zeus' brain-child Athene, under the name of Minerva, in the same triad; his children by Leto finally arrived to be welcomed in Cumaean Apollo and Aventine Artemis. Hermes Agoraios soon came up from Southern Italy with the Greek traders, to appropriate a Roman temple in 495 and the Roman name of Mercury. Venus, *numen* of Roman gardens, was before long to lose her character due to an identification with the disreputable Aphrodite. The identification of father Mars with Ares has been noted.

Similarly, the Greek heroic legend was engrafted on Rome's expanding religious tree through the importation of Heracles from Tibur and of the Dioscuri from Tusculum. In the busy cattle market the strong man of Hellenic lore received in earliest republican days a cultus at an open altar from whose environs the dogs and flies that infest cattle markets were said to be miraculously excluded. What was first a private devotion of immigrants from Tibur grew in public favor till, in 313, the state adopted the hero of the Twelve Labors, quieting theologic scruples if any by an identification of him with the Italic Semo Sancus. Castor and Polydeuces, patron deities of near-by Tusculum, and probably for this very reason long familiar to the Roman mind, received their first temple in the city[8] in 484, though it had been vowed as early as 496 by the

[8] Dedicated by the son of the Postumius here mentioned, at the spot where legend places the Roman apparition of Castor and Pollux, the temple underwent frequent restorations probably due to the wealth of the equestrian order. The last restoration occurred under Tiberius, of which three magnificent columns still stand. On the Dioscuri, Cf. Livy, *op. cit.* Bk. II, chs. 19, 20, 42.

Fig. 33. The Sibyl of Cumae

Michelangelo painted this likeness of Apollo's oracular priestess in the Sistine Chapel. Even in the period of the kings Rome sought her guidance in crises, while in the sixth century B.C. a collection of her responses was enshrined in the Capitoline Temple. These were the *Sibylline Books* so sedulously consulted in later centuries.

Fig. 34. The Deified Abstract Victory

The worship of abstract qualities frequently developed from cult titles of the old gods. Thus Jupiter was worshiped under the title of Jupiter the Conqueror. Later the cult title was separated from the god and Victory personified into a new divinity.

Dictator Postumius in the heat of the onset at Lake Regillus. The story goes—a type story told long before of various battles in Greece—that the Heavenly Twins on their white steeds rode the tide of battle in the Roman ranks and later were seen watering their mounts at the spring of Juturna in the Roman Forum. Through authentic republican history the Dioscuri rank as patrons of the equestrian order and of chariot races. Both the cult of Heracles and that of the Dioscuri became connected with the sanctity of oaths, as attest the well-known invocations *Mehercule, Mecastor, Ecastor, Edepol.*

In 496 a famine occurred to complicate a condition of the body politic already distressing because of clashing interests of patricians and plebeians, and of jealous hostility of neighboring peoples. A consultation of the *Sibylline Books* brought the usual response flavored with Greek propaganda. *Placate Demeter, Dionysus et Kore.* Thereon, the same Postumius who that same year vowed a temple to the Dioscuri made a like vow in favor of the new Greek triad. It was the triad worshiped in the Eleusinian Mysteries, but it would be a misapprehension to set the formal introduction of "mystery religions" at Rome at so early a date as the beginning of the fifth century.[9] Instead, the three divinities adopted the names of Ceres, Liber, and Libera, recognized *numina* of the old system, with functions relative to the grain supply. The popular gratitude for the speedy cessation of the famine is attested by the prompt erection of the promised temple and its dedication in 493. From this date the temple, situated at the foot of the Aventine at the west end of the Circus Maximus and, therefore, in the center of plebeian life, grew to be the rallying ground for plebeian politics. For it was naturally the plebeians who were specially interested in the grain supply which these three "celestial patrons of the full dinner pail" had in charge. The Plebeian Aediles, officers created for the first time at a

[9] At a later date there was instituted the Sacrum Anniversarium Cereris, a midsummer festival along the lines of the mystery religions. Greek priestesses had charge, matrons alone might attend, and they fasting.

date coincident with the temple's dedication, cared for the grain supply and were called Aediles of Ceres. In the temple basement were preserved the records of the plebeian officials. April 19, the anniversary of the dedication, the people made a great holiday and held games, called the Ludi Cereales, on this day and on several preceding days.

With the dedication, in 431, of a temple to Apollo as god of health, the surprising immigration of Di Novensides was checked. It was not till 293 that the fashion revived with the coming of another god of healing, Aesculapius, to open his temple hospital on the Island of the Tiber. We have only conjecture to guide us in seeking an explanation of this long period of religious conservatism following so sharply upon the quest for strange cults which marks the first republican century. The early republic, as yet inexperienced and for the present striving rather uncertainly to orient its policies, naturally tried religious as well as political experiments which offered solutions for domestic and "international" problems.[10] When civic institutions tended to stabilization (though a definite balance of power between patricians and plebeians was not struck till later), and when uniform success in arms minimized the external peril, the city's relative security was attributed both by political interpretation and by popular devotion to the might of Rome's gods. The conservative spirit reasserted itself in things religious. As a matter of fact, Greek divinities *who were recognized as such* had not been admitted in the fifth-century expansion of the pantheon to an equal footing with the old Di Indigetes, nor even with deities of genuine Italic origin. Against Hellenic newcomers the sacred Pomerium stood as a rampart, and only outside this spiritual boundary might they raise their temples. Their cult was not in charge of any of the old Roman priesthoods, but

[10] As instances of these experiments may be adduced the *commune Latinorum Dianae templum* on the Aventine, and the *aedes Cereris* (Liberi, Liberae), in the plebeian quarter.

was committed to a newly organized priesthood, the *Duoviri Sacris Faciundis.*[11]

Despite the conservative reaction, Greek cult ideas which had so overlaid the structure of the old Numinism had come to stay. There was much more appeal to sense and imagination in the brilliant Hellenic newcomers than in the somber *numina.* The child heart of the Roman votary proved responsive to the attraction of graceful cult statue and fair temple, of intriguing mythology and spectacular rite.

The distinction between the divine and the human had been safeguarded in the earlier religion by the concept of the *numina* as invisible forces energizing the objects and activities on which human life depended. The concept may be regarded as an approach to the correct one of the good God from whom man must expect all benefits. The *numina,* moreover, were kindly and benevolent, provided the *jus divinum,* the divine right to prayer and sacrifice, was faithfully observed. The mystery, finally, that enveloped these potent personal forces was only enhanced by the lack of iconic representation. Sense of dependence and of mystery, however, was weakened when the *numen* became so far disassociated from the object or activity he patronized as to dwell in human form in a temple cell. Religious ideas had to change, the gods had to grow disastrously humanized.

What icon and temple began, was completed by the mythologic story. Not only might the god be seen, but his all too human history was published. Scholars are in agreement nowadays on the fact that Roman Numinism recognized no parallels among the gods to man and wife, parent and child. But in the imported Greek Anthropomorphism divine geneal-

[11] As is obvious from all that has been said, many Greek gods slipped in unrecognized because of identification with Roman gods. The cases of Heracles and the Dioscuri are special, for they were known to be Greek divinities, yet received temples within the Pomerium. The reason is that these gods were so immemorial in Tibur and Tusculum respectively that the Romans regarded them as equivalently Italic.

ogies constituted a fundamental doctrine. The Hesiodic tradition demanded that every god have definite relationship to the Olympian peerage, and a highly complex mythology had furnished every god with the necessary credentials long before the immigration of Greek divinities into Italy and Rome. How the gods were thus reduced to human level is all too obvious: they became, at best, a sublimated royal family, and reverence for them declined. Their individual biographies, as retailed in orthodox mythology, exhibited them as petulant, envious, revengeful, and lustful. Professor Nilssen, in his *Religion of the Greeks,* no less tersely than justly characterizes the divinity attributed to Homer's Anthropomorphics as a superiority, not of moral, but of physical perfection. The moral spinelessness of the Olympians is reflected in the moral levity and skepticism of the typical Greek. For how can a worshiper be expected to rise above the moral standard that satisfies his god? Now, in the very century which witnessed the importation of the Olympians into Rome, Zenophanes was bitingly declaring in Greece: "Homer and Hesiod have attributed to the gods all that men hold to be infamous."[12] Honor, justice, and decency, it is true, marked the typical Roman for some centuries even after the Hellenization of theological concepts, but this fact is probably attributable to the relative incorruption of household religion and to the lack of means for luxurious living in Rome prior to the Second Punic War. The substitution, however, for the old Numinism of the Greek system with its immoral connotations was the *prima mali labes,* the first step in the downward path, and the sequel will show on Roman soil the same moral breaking up and the same obscene indignity of cult which Greece had known.

External religious forms underwent striking changes. Before, these had been simple and unstudied expressions of reli-

[12] From fragments of Greek poetical and philosophical writings, edited by H. Diels.

gious reverence; under Greek influence, they now assumed the artificial character of the showy pageant. Rome, too, as the Greek states had done, held religious games at public expense to afford a thrill to the people, and changed for this purpose the character of some of her most venerable festivals.[13] At the behest of the Grecizing *Duoviri Sacris Faciundis* the Supplicatio was introduced, and in time of peril the people gathered at the temple of Greek Apollo outside the city, prayed on bended knee,[14] and then marched into the city, men, women, and children bearing Apollo's laurel branches. At every shrine they again knelt to implore aid. Here, as Professor Halliday remarks, an emotional reaction in the people seems to have been the proximate end of the ritual, an end hardly sought in the matter-of-fact observances of old Numinism. Still at the behest of the *Duoviri Sacris Faciundis* was introduced, probably for the first time in 399, a practice that to earliest Rome would have seemed blasphemous, if indeed it could have been at all understood. Tables and couches were prepared in one of the temples and a banquet laid forth. The guests had to be carried in, for they were the wooden images of six of the Olympians — Apollo and Latona, Hercules and Diana, Neptune and Mercury. The triumph of Anthropomorphism over Numinism is fitly symbolized in this banquet of the gods.[15]

The startling spectacle of the Lectisternium, as this rite was

---

[13] Instances which may be noted are the Saturnalia, already treated; the Ludi Romani, on which cf. Fowler's *Roman Festivals,* pp. 216 sqq.; the Ludi Florales, on which cf. the same, pp. 95 sqq.; the Ludi Apollinares, on which cf. the same, pp. 179, 180.

[14] Supplicatio derives from *sub-plico,* meaning to "bend the knee." This attitude at prayer was not originally Roman (the Roman stood) but Oriental; the Greeks adopted it from Oriental worship. The Supplicatio was also solemnized in thanksgiving, e.g., for a victory.

[15] Five Lectisternia are recorded in the period treated. The Lectisternia of 217 show us the Di Consentes (the Gods in Council, an adaptation of Homer's council on Olympus): Jupiter-Juno, Neptune-Minerva, Mars-Venus, Vulcan-Vesta, Mercury-Ceres, Apollo-Diana. Other foreign infiltrations in this period are noted in the growing official consultation of Etruscan haruspices and in human sacrifices (in 226 of a Gallic man and woman, in 216 of a Greek man and woman).

termed, inspires an inquiry into the religious psychology of image worship. We mean, of course, image worship among idolaters.[16] Now, idolatry is a species of the genus superstition, superstition being one of the vices contrary to the virtue of religion. Numa Pompilius, the legislator of Nuministic days, was superstitious when he worshiped and enjoined the worship of the unseen *numina,* but specifically he was an idolater. In his worship of natural forces, such as the power that energizes the growing grain, he was offering to the creature the cult due to God alone. He rated among "the vain men in whom there is not the knowledge of God: and who by these good things that are seen, could not understand him that is, neither by attending to the works have acknowledged who was the workman: but have imagined either the fire, or the wind, or the swift air, or the great water, or the sun and moon, to be the gods that rule the world. With whose beauty if they being delighted, took them to be gods, let them know how much the Lord of them is more beautiful than they: for the first author of beauty made all these things. Or if they admired their power and their effects, let them understand by them, that he that made them is mightier than they."[17]

Yet the Holy Spirit partially condones the theological error of Numinism, for the votaries of the *numina* "are less to be blamed. For they perhaps err, seeking God and desirous to find him. For being conversant among the works, they search: and they are persuaded that the things are good which are seen."[18] Strictest censure, however, is leveled by the inspired writer against the worship of images, whether the image were conceived as possessing divine power in itself or as a mere representation of some worshiped creature.[19] By way

[16] On the cultus of sacred images in the Church, read Otten, *Institutiones Dogmaticae,* III, pp. 195–200, pp. 441–459.

[17] The Book of Wisdom, 13: 1–4.

[18] *Ibid.,* 6, 7.

[19] *Ibid.,* 10–19 and 14: 1, 14, 15.

of causes for the fashioning of idols the sacred text assigns human desire to represent a departed friend or a powerful ruler, human delight in curious and beautiful images, human inclination toward making the object of worship concretely accessible, finally the influence of governments which for political reasons enjoined the worship of definite idols.[20] The Book of Wisdom then dwells on the savage and obscene cult-practices and the corruption of morals which are the consequence of idol worship: and on the fostering of idols by the demons.

St. Thomas' analysis of idolatry[21] is a paraphrase, in scholastic terms, of these two striking chapters from Holy Writ. Our Religion of the Romans, up to the point which we have reached, has appeared true to the type of idolatrous religions indicated in the same chapters. Numinism, it has just now been pointed out, is the form least severely reprehended, in which man mistakes the powers of visible nature for divine powers. The Di Novensides are the true idols whom Scripture censures in unmeasured degree. They may not be considered as innocent iconic representations of nature forces, but they are rather images of the anthropomorphic Olympians, beings a little stronger and cleverer than men and a great deal more depraved morally than men dare to be if they expect to be tolerated by their fellows. They allure the affections of the worshiper from more spiritual concepts of divinity both by removing the mystery surrounding the unseen *numen* and by pleasing the senses through curious and graceful representation.

Lastly, by no means to be overlooked in Roman religion such as we have studied it, is the factor which St. Thomas names the "*causa consummativa idololatriae quae fuit ex parte daemonum, qui se colendos hominibus errantibus exhibuerunt,*

[20] *Ibid.*, 13: 17–19; 14: 15–21.
[21] *Summa Theol.*, II–II, Q. XCIV, a. 4.

in idolis dando responsa, et aliqua quae videbantur hominibus mirabilia faciendo,"[22] the clinching cause, which consists in the interplay of evil spirits, manifesting themselves to the worshipers in the responses given by them and in the marvels they work. For instance, though we need not accept as historically certain all the prodigies narrated in Roman cult-history, we can reasonably recognize a definite amount of *mira diabolica,* i.e., preternatural manifestations. Again, the findings of the haruspices and the Sibylline responses cannot be explained wholly as political hoodwinkery, but were surely directed to a certain degree by diabolical conjecture.

The period between 500 and 200 saw the development of another set of ideas of divinity which must be distinguished both from the nuministic and the anthropomorphic. Moral qualities which men admired, such as Fides, Spes, Honos, Virtus; and conditions which they desired, such as Concordia, Pax, Salus, became objects of cult. Temples were built and sacrifices offered to them. A few examples, before venturing an interpretation. In 367, on occasion of an adjustment of differences between capitalists and plebeians, the dictator Camillus dedicated a temple to Concordia in the Forum. In 294, after a great victory over the Samnites and Etruscans, a temple was erected to Victoria. In the middle of the First Punic War, the people vowed a temple to Spes. These are early and definite examples, but indications are not wanting of even earlier cult of the like abstractions. In the later Republic the introduction of new abstractions grew into a fad, while during the Empire court flattery multiplied the abstractions yet further to extol Providentia Augusti, Clementia Imperatoris, and so on.

Are we, then, to recognize here a host of new divinities or merely a form of poetic personification, such as students of Victorian Literature will recall from the poets of that era?

---

[22] *Ibid.,* a. 4.

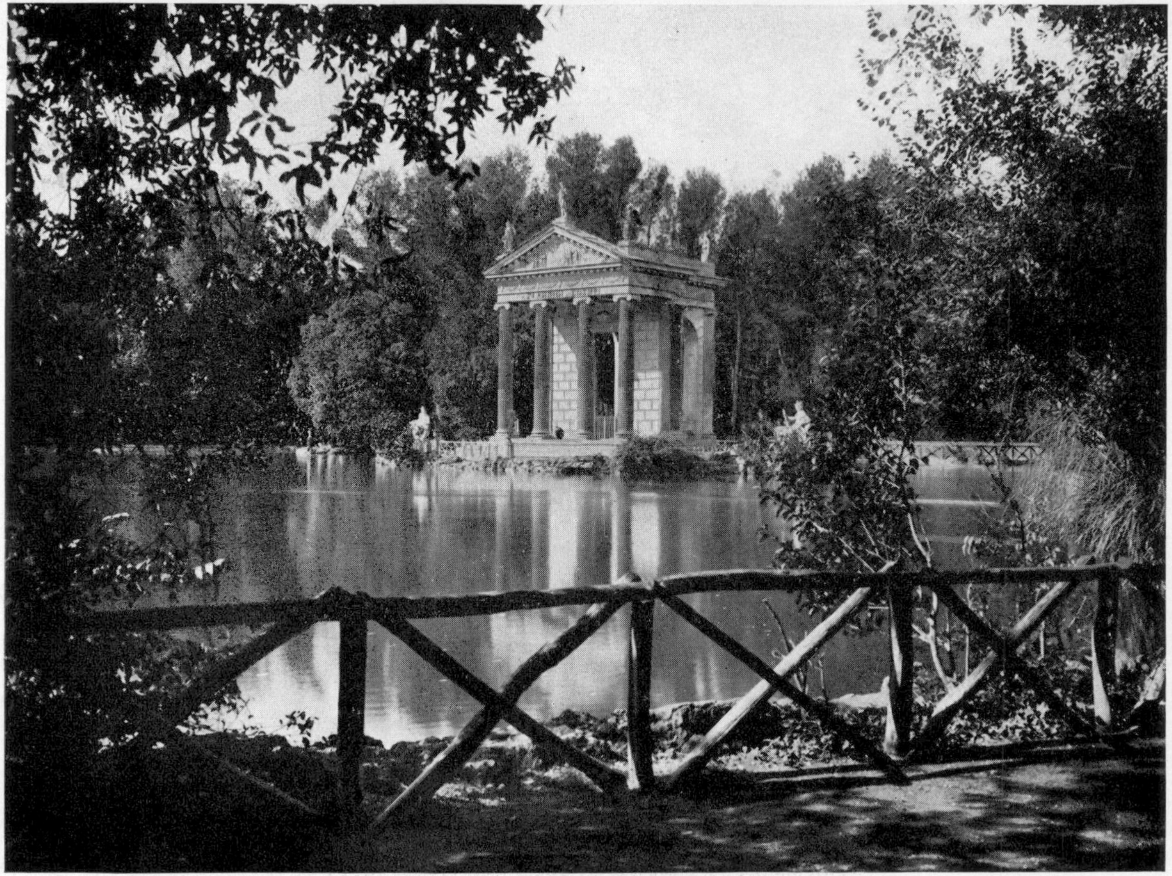

Fig. 35. Façade of Temple of Aesculapius

This ... of the newer temples of healing built and patronized by aristocrats when the famed

We follow in general the solution offered by Professor Axtell.[23] Nuministic influences inclined Roman psychology to the conception of divinity as abstract power. Philosophic abstraction later helped on this psychological bent. Finally, certain of the Deified Abstractions are known to be derived from separation and hypostatization of attributes of old gods. Thus Fides, Libertas, Victoria are derived from Dius Fidius, Jupiter Liber, Jupiter Victor; similarly Honos and Virtus are separate hypostatization of attributes of Mars.

In 293, probably on occasion of one of the recurrent plagues that harried her early history, Rome sought aid from a healing-god, as she had before sought Apollo under his attribute of god of healing. An embassy was sent to Epidaurus in Argolis, where the chief shrine of Aesculapius was situated. The priests there willingly agreed to the founding of an Aesculapius-cult in a center of so much importance as Rome, and accordingly dispatched one of their number to act as founder. It was indispensable that he take with him one of the temple snakes, the symbol of Aesculapius, and supposedly endowed with some efficacy in the cures desired. Legend tells how the snake disembarked to pay homage to the father of Aesculapius, Apollo, at a shrine in one of the ports the ship made; nor could it be coaxed away till it had satisfied its devotion, when of its own accord it returned to the ship. Ascending the Tiber, the ship was preparing to dock, when the sacred snake again asserted itself by sliding overboard, heading for the Isola Tiberina and disappearing in the reeds. An omen was seen in this and the temple hospital of Aesculapius was built on the island. From that date, through more than twenty-two centuries, the island has been consecrated to healing, the temple of Aesculapius giving way in Christian times to the hospital under the patronage of St. Bartholomew.

The extraordinary popularity of the cult of Aesculapius

---

[23] Axtell, *Deified Abstractions* (Doctorate Thesis), Chicago University, 1925.

through Roman and Greek history was surely based on belief in the actuality of cures effected in the Aesculapia. Innumerable thank offerings have been excavated by archeologists, and even if there is no inscription on the votive object, its form is eloquent, for every conceivable member of the human body was modeled and the model hung up in thanksgiving for a reputed cure. It may be taken for certain that several of the priests who ministered in an Aesculapian temple were skilled physicians, and thus we have a partial explanation of cures without postulating the preternatural. Further data for an explanation may be drawn from a study of the routine procedure followed when a suppliant came seeking a cure. He was examined both medically and with regard to his moral dispositions. This latter proceeding was in fulfillment of the motto inscribed over the temple door: "None but the pure shall enter here." If the examinations proved satisfactory to the priests and if the suppliant manifested faith in the god, a preliminary laving followed and he was received into the temple. Here he slept and was visited and touched by the priests during sleep. The god was said to send him a dream to indicate the method of treatment to be followed. These dreams, of course, had to be interpreted by the priests, and the interpretation would follow the indications discovered during the examination aforesaid. It is certain that definite medication was employed in addition to the psychic remedies of suggestion and of religious faith in the power of Aesculapius. If cured, the suppliant contributed to the temple treasury and hung up in gratitude a votive ear, foot, or whatever the nature of the cure demanded.

CHAPTER « 28

RELIGIOUS PSYCHOLOGY OF THE HANNIBALIC WAR

LIVY introduces his fascinating narrative of the Second Punic War by a picture of Hamilcar Barca leading his son Hannibal to the altar at Carthage, that the boy may vow enmity to the Roman name. The historian closes his narrative by telling how the Fetiales with the symbols of their office — the bundles of sacred herbs plucked by the city magistrate from within the citadel, the flint stones sacred to Jupiter Fulgur — repair to Africa to solemnize peace with Hannibal's conquered nation. The whole narrative, told in Books XXI–XXX, is a precious historical classic, but no less valuable as a document of religious psychology.

The peril that from 219 to 202 put Rome's civil polity and religious soul to the test appears of unprecedented magnitude for two chief reasons. By 216 the Republic's effective fighting force had been nearly swept away before the tactical genius of Hannibal at the Ticinus, Lake Trasimene, and Cannae. For Fabius there remained no feasible policy but to prowl with the thinned ranks of his army through the mountains, always threaten but always decline battle, and so distract the Carthaginian from any attack on the city. The anguish of the citizenry was to find no substantial assurance against sack by a barbarous army till Nero's brilliant stroke at the Metaurus, in 207, broke the Punic power in the peninsula. Second, added to this strictly domestic anxiety, was Rome's knowledge that still other of her commanders were striving, in a doubtful war, to protect her interests at sea, in Sicily, in Gaul, in Spain,

TABULAR OUTLINE OF HANNIBALIC WAR

Year	Livy	Progress of War	Religious Events
239	Bk. XXI, ch. 1	Hamilcar Barca takes command in Spain.	Vow of nine-year-old Hannibal, to fight against Romans as soon as his age allowed.
219	XXI, 22	After subjugation of Spain, Hannibal proceeds to Alps, to enter Italy.	In dream Hannibal sees celestial youth sent by Jupiter to lead him to the conquest and devastation of Italy.
218	XXI, 46	Battles of the Ticinus and Trebbia; Romans twice defeated.	Prodigies begin to be reported, wolf running amuck in Roman camp and swarm of bees settling in tree near tent of general. Expiation by sacrifices.
217	XXI, 62, 63 XXII, 1, 3	The Consul Flaminius disastrously defeated at Lake Trasimene.	Flaminius, fearing augurs will be bribed to find omens against him, secretly leaves to take command, omitting the sacred rites to Jupiter Optimus Maximus on the Capitoline and to Jupiter Latinus on the Alban Mount. He is recalled to perform them. Prodigies: two-week-old baby cries *Io Triumphe,* fowls change into men, ox climbs to third floor of house, sun and moon fight, Flaminius falls from horse, his standard cannot be pulled up. *Sibylline Books* enjoin, as expiations, sacrifices, gifts to gods, lectisternia.
217	XXII, 9, 10, 29	Q. Fabius, the Dictator, tantalizes Hannibal by delay and saves army of Minucius from Hannibal's ambush.	*Sibylline Books* direct: "Fulfill vow made to Mars at start of war: hold games for Jupiter: build temples to Venus Erycina and Mens: have a Lectisternium for Di Consentes: vow to sacrifice a Ver Sacrum if state is preserved five years." All this is done.
216	XXII, 33, 36, 37, 42	Hiero of Syracuse renews friendship with Rome. African campaign fails. At Cannae Romans defeated with loss of 80,000 men.	Another temple to Concord in acknowledgment of quelling of mutiny among troops. A rain of stones, statues sweat blood. Golden statue of Victoria, gift of Hiero, placed in temple of Jupiter Optimus Maximus. The sacred chickens refuse to eat when omens are sought before Cannae.

216	XXII, 56, 57	Hannibal joined by many of Rome's Italian allies. Sicily harassed by Carthaginians.	Sacrum Anniversarium Cereris not held due to grief of mothers and wives. Two Vestals break vow of virginity; one is buried alive, while other is a suicide; the seducer scourged to death. Embassy sent to Delphi on occasion of this prodigy. *Sibylline Books* also consulted, at whose direction a Greek man and woman, and a Gallic man and woman are buried alive as sacrifices. (Probably, says Fowler, as sacrifices to Tellus and the Manes.)
215–213	XXIII, 11 30, 31 XXIV, 24, 44	Marcellus' valor and Hannibal's failure to push his advantage keep the enemy away from city.	Delphic Oracle advises checking of religious hysteria. Prodigies: temples struck by lightning, rains of blood and stones, cow bears colt, ox talks, woman turns into man, legions and ships are seen where none are. Expiation of these by Novendiale Sacrum, Supplicatio, sacrifices.
212	XXV, 2, 7, 12, 16, 23, 24	Rome conscripts boys under seventeen. Hannibal defeats one Roman army, Mago another. The two Scipios commanding in Spain are slain. Hannibal takes Tarentum; Marcellus, Syracuse.	Senate puts stop to strange rites and excessive manifestations of religious emotion in public and orders *carmina vaticina,* prophetic songs, handed in to praetor. One *carmen vaticinum* by a certain Marcius is found to contain a prophecy (*post eventum*) of the defeat at Cannae; another by the same man directs institution of games for Apollo as a means to expel Hannibal. The second *vaticinum* gaining credence from the first, Ludi Apollinares are instituted after the *Sibylline Books* have given approval. More prodigies and their expiation.
211–210	XXVI, 19, 23	Capua falls into hands of Romans. P. Cornelius Scipio goes as proconsul to Spain.	Praises of P. Cornelius Scipio as man of *virtus prisca* and a devotee of the gods. Legend of his miraculous birth from a god and a human mother. Prodigies: *mula peperit,* rivers run blood, lightning strikes. Expiation of these.

TABULAR OUTLINE OF HANNIBALIC WAR (*Continued*)

Year	Livy	Progress of War	Religious Events
209	XXVII, 4, 11	Fulvius Flaccus defeated at Herdonea. Marcellus encounters Hannibal in several battles, none decisive. In Spain young Scipio takes New Carthage and defeats Hasdrubal.	Temple of Jupiter struck and almost unroofed by lightning. Various monstrous births: pig with human face, boy with elephant's head, a hermaphrodite. Rain of milk, statues sweating blood, birds abandoning grove of Diana. Expiation by day of prayer. Supplicatio, sacrifices.
208	XXVII, 23, 25, 26	Hasdrubal dispatched to aid Hannibal in Italy. Marcellus ambushed by Hannibal in Apulia and slain, the other consul dying later of wounds.	Temples struck by lightning. Mice gnaw gold in temple of Jupiter. Water of lake turns to blood. Marcellus detained at Rome till a curious dispute about the legality of building a temple he has vowed to two gods (Honos and Virtus) is settled. Just before he falls into the fatal ambush, dire prodigies are noticed in the entrails of the sacrificial victims.
207	XXVII, 36, 37, 51	C. Claudius Nero by daring maneuver outwits Hasdrubal, sent to help his brother Hannibal, slays the former and annihilates his army. The turning point of the war. Hannibal on the defensive in southernmost Italy.	Jovis Epulum and religious games in city. Prodigies: hermaphrodite child born, developed like four-year-old, is put in box by advice of haruspices and drowned in sea. Chorus of Roman maidens on occasion of this prodigy goes through city singing religious hymn and executing religious dance. After Hasdrubal's defeat at the Metaurus all the temples are thronged with grateful citizenry.

206–205	XXVIII, 10, 11	The young Scipio continues successes in Spain, and with aid of African king Massinissa drives Carthaginians from Spain. Roman troops and Greek Allies successful in Greece against Philip. Scipio is elected consul and takes charge of war in Sicily.	Prodigies: snakes falling in temple; two-headed pig and hermaphrodite lamb; altar sweats. The Vestal fire goes out and the negligent Vestal is scourged by the Pontifex Maximus. Supplicatio *ad Aedem Vestae.*
204–203	XXIX, 10, 11, 14, 27	Laelius and Massinissa carry on successful campaign in Africa and latter returns with booty and request for Scipio's transfer to Africa. Scipio departs for Africa.	Temple to Virtus dedicated. In *Sibylline Books* is found oracle promising expulsion of Hannibal if the sacred stone of Cybele be brought to Rome from Pessinus in Galatia. An embassy goes to Delphi first and is instructed to secure the stone through King Attalus of Pergamum. He gives it to them. It is received, according to oracular direction, by the "best man in Rome" (Scipio Nasica) with great solemnity and joy, put in temple of Victory. Solemn prayer and sacrifice of P. Cornelius Scipio.
202	XXX, 2, 17, 38, 40	Scipio, Laelius, and Massinissa by their successes force Hannibal's return to Africa where he is overwhelmed by superior forces at Zama. Triumph of Scipio at Rome.	Religious games in fulfillment of vow. Prodigies: ground sinks, crows eat gold, fires in heavens, inundations. Expiation by sacrifices and Supplicatio. The Fetiales are dispatched with their sacred flint stones and bundles of sacred herbs to conclude peace in Carthage.

in Greece. It was a true "world war," and the conditions of peace the vanquished might anticipate were slavery or galling tribute.

The religious facts of the Hannibalic War presented in tabular form on pages 284–287, show at a glance the evidence upon which the comments and interpretation of this chapter are based.

The curious form of superstition, consisting of belief in prodigies, occupies a prominence in our religio-historical table which first calls for analysis. Some of the prodigies, being trivial natural accidents, may be dismissed with Livy's comment: *Adeo minimis etiam rebus prava religio inserit deos,*[1] "So even into trifles a base religion injects the gods." In the importance attached, for example, to Flaminius' clumsy toppling from his horse before Lake Trasimene and to the sacred chickens' disinclination for food before Cannae, we need see nothing but the *prava religio* fostered in Roman psychology by the humbuggery of the augural system borrowed from Etruria and developed for several centuries.

A second class of prodigies embraces unusual, but still quite natural, phenomena in which the superstitious mind was inclined, *a fortiori,* to recognize the miraculous. Nowadays were a Fascist peasant to report to Mussolini a rain of blood in his southern Italic field, another a rain of stones near Vesuvius, and a third the increase of his livestock by the birth of a five-legged colt, there would be no consultation of sacred books about the events. Instead, the scientific professors of the University of Rome would inform the first narrator that the sirocco occasionally blows up clouds of red sand from the Sahara; would mention to the second that showers of pebbles are a form of self-expression in which Vesuvius at times indulges; would give the third Ripley's address.[2]

---

[1] Livy, *op. cit.,* XXVII, 23. Cf. XXII, 2: *"Minoribus etiam dictu prodigiis fides."*

[2] Cf. Fowler's *Religious Experience of the Roman People,* Lecture XIV, p. 316.

To the third class of prodigies, represented by such tales as those of the fowl metamorphosed into a human form and of the cow that bore the colt, one is justified in applying the historian's cool remark: "Many prodigies took place, or (as happens when minds are stirred by religious emotions) were proclaimed and rashly believed."[3]

The explanations just now offered evidently reduce the prodigies to the plane of the purely natural. It is not intended, however, to leave out of consideration St. Thomas' alternative of a diabolic intervention, already referred to in the preceding chapter.[4] Where ignorance, excessive credulity, or augural trickery needed reinforcement, it is plausible to admit diabolical meddling in the affair of fostering the cult of false gods. For, after all, "All the gods of the gentiles are demons"[5] and their cult a thing dear to demons' hearts. Especially subject to suspicion of diabolical origin are prodigies occurring in the temples or manifested even by the very cult-statues, as when Juno was seen to sweat and Mars to shake his spear. The Sibylline oracles ordering the four human sacrifices and the importation of Cybele might be numbered among the *responsa diabolica* mentioned by St. Thomas, because of the cruel injustice of the rite and of the revolting indecencies connected with the worship of Cybele.

Expiation, or appeasement of the gods after the occurrence of prodigies, was attended to, at first, in a spirit of sobriety and reverence by traditional prayers and sacrifices. But, with the growth of religious hysteria, consequent on the agonizing uncertainty of the war, expiation tended to become unusual and extravagant, a climax being reached when the four unfortunate foreigners were buried alive. A return to sobriety was initiated by the politic warning brought from Delphi against excessive *religio,* for thereafter the Pontifices reverted

[3] Livy, *op. cit.,* XXI, 62.

[4] *Summa Theol.,* II–II, Q. XCIV, a. 4.

[5] Ps. 95:5.

to the simpler and more truly religious modes of expiation, prayers and the immolation of animals.

When Venus Erycina and Mens,[6] in 215, were lodged in their own temples on the Capitoline, the Di Novensides had won their three-centuries-old fight to pass the sacred Pomerium. The Greek mode had prevailed. Evidences of Greek ascendancy crowd the historian's page. Consultation of the *Sibylline Books* had grown to be the normal recourse when religious doubts arose, while almost as usual in the matter of expiations was the Greek Supplicatio. Lectisternia, too, are of frequent occurrence, most noteworthy being that of 217 in which twelve strongly Hellenized divinities[7] reclined at the banquet board. The Greek city-states, when they brought religion into the service of civic patriotism, had subsidized brilliant religious pageants. Rome, under the guidance of the Grecizing *Decem Viri Sacris Faciundis* had recourse to a like externalism to solace its sorely tried citizenry, instituting the Ludi Apollinares and training the twenty-seven maidens for their choric presentation of Livius Andronicus' sacred hymn. Finally, it is significant that the same men had a hand even in the vow of the distinctly Roman *Ver Sacrum*.

That *religio* rose to the height of hysteria among the people is evident from a glance at our table of religious events, as well as from the analysis of prodigy-mongering already given. The gods who had been maintained on such a footing of honorable citizenship, and who during three centuries of peninsular conquest had aggrandized their darling city, now seemed indifferent to the annihilation of whole consular

---

[6] Mens was a deification of intelligence and prudence, the temple being perhaps rendered apropos at this period because of the rashness of certain of Rome's generals. The temple to Venus Erycina was definitely recognized to be erected to the Greek Aphrodite worshiped on Mt. Eryx in Sicily. Cf. Laing in *Classical Journal,* VI, pp. 51–64, for nexus between Venus Erycina and the Aeneas legend.

[7] They were all Olympians and were called collectively Di Consentes, or the council of the gods. In the Lectisternium they were paired off as follows: Jupitor-Juno, Neptune-Minerva, Mars-Venus, Apollo-Diana, Vulcan-Vesta, Mercury-Ceres.

armies and to the occupation of Italy by Public Enemy Number One. Had the smoke of holocausts ceased to ascend to their nostrils and the phrasing of old prayer formulas to their ears? New rites and even new gods were invoked to secure the speedy action and palpable results which hysterical minds, impatient under trial, endeavor to force from Providence. "Superstitious observances," says Livy, "and these mostly from abroad, gained such ground among the people in general that it seemed as if either mankind or the deities had undergone a sudden change. And now the customed rites were disused not only in private and within doors, but even in the public streets, the forum and the capitol. These were frequented by crowds of women sacrificing and offering prayers to their gods, in modes hitherto unknown in Rome."[8] The *mulierum turba,* "crowd of women," emphasized by the writer is shrewdly commented on by Warde Fowler[9] as an indication that the salutary restraint of the *patria potestas* upon mobile feminine religiosity had been removed by the death of so many *patresfamiliarum,* heads of families, on the bloody fields of the war. *Sacrificuli* and *vates,* sacrificers and would-be prophets, came in with the miserable *omnium gatherum* of fugitives herded into the city by Hannibal's raids, and these religious practitioners made up for the loss of their former clientele "out in the sticks" of Italy by captivating the superstitious minds of Roman women. In the fall of 213 and the spring of 212 the Senate, through the Praetor Urbanus M. Atilius, took strong but judicious action against popular religious hysteria,[10] though we cannot absolve even the highest authority from the charge of loss of poise in matters religious. It was with full approval of Senate and Pontifices that absurd prodigies were taken so seriously, that human sacrifice was resorted to, that the Cybele-stone and the indecencies of its cult were imported.

---

[8] *Op. cit.,* XXV, 1. Baker's translation.

[9] *Rel. Exper. of Rom. People,* Lecture XIV, pp. 324, 325.

[10] Cf., table given above under these dates.

But brighter aspects of Roman character are also revealed through the war clouds to cheer the lover of old Rome. A solicitude to secure the *Pax Deorum,* peace with the gods, by prayerful and sacrificial expiation, attest a serious and vivid sense of dependence. Gratitude to the gods for the salvation bestowed burst out spontaneously after Metaurus and Zama. A fine spirit of discipline among her troops and of pliability to direction among her stay-at-homes evidence the firm fortitude, which, rather than the more brilliant but more mobile qualities of the Greeks, stands out as Rome's moral distinction. A testimony to the soundness of her social structure may be noted in her ability to produce a Fabius, a Marcellus, a Scipio —men who exhibited in the period of crisis the requisite leadership, common sense, and sober genius.

CHAPTER « 29

PROGRESS OF RELIGIOUS EXHAUSTION (200 B.C. to 31 B.C.)

WE NEED not seek testimony beyond our own experience to check up on the statement that postwar days, even in a victorious country, may bring a profound alteration in a people's temperament and views. We can conjecture from Livy's estimates of casualties, as well as from the fact that in 212 conscription of boys under seventeen was begun, how disastrously the blood of the pure Roman stock was drained. Again, in the same year, the historian informs us, the city was crowded with a refugee population from all parts of the peninsula. Not only, then, was the psychological problem of postwar reconstruction the simple one of restoring balance to distraught Roman minds, but also the more complex one of adapting the politico-religious constitution to the religious and moral standards of a hybrid citizenry. It seems that it did not occur to any of the legislators to solve the problem by sterilization of non-Romans, as the Nazi professor suggested for the Afro-Aryan children of the Ruhr district. What made religious reconstruction yet more difficult was that officials had compromised the dignity of the religious motive and diminished the respect due it by the wholesale use they had made of it for purely political ends during the stress of the war.[1]

[1] Instances are found in the smoothly politic *harmonia praestabilita* of the Sibylline responses and in the use of novel and spectacular rites as a kind of paregoric for the anguish of the popular mind.

Within the year that witnessed the Fetiales solemnizing peace at Carthage, the Roman Senate oiled up the machinery of government and cult to popularize a renewal of war with Philip V of Macedon. The peace struck with him in 205 had been understood by both parties as a mere armistice, and Philip in fact ignored the terms by continuing aggression against Rome's Grecian allies. To protect through them the city's Adriatic interests and with an eye cast hopefully toward desirable territory lying to the east, the Patres Conscripti settled on immediate war. A war-weary and reluctant citizenry were then rendered duly war-minded by the bugaboo of another Pyrrhus or another Hannibal rampant in Italy, as well as by the assurance that P. Sulpicius, the consul, had immediate certainty from the gods of a victorious campaign and that the haruspices had read in the entrails of the sacrificial victims omens of triumph and territorial expansion. The victory, gained three years later when Flaminius won the field of Cynoscephalae, led to Roman sovereignty in Hellas, but to Rome's own hellenization in art, literature, and philosophy. One of Philip's allies, an Antiochus and father of the Antiochus against whom the Maccabees rebelled, carried on against Rome after Cynoscephalae. In 188 he surrendered all his territory in Asia Minor west of the Taurus Range, a fact whose religious significance for the Romans was portentous. For Asia Minor at the time was a land of dark magic and strange frenzy, just as in early Christian days it was to prove so fertile a hotbed of bizarre heresies. Its conglomerate population, from 188 incorporated into Rome's expanding empire or in close rapport with her soldiers and merchants, was initiate in the Orient's mystery-religions. Isis, Mithras, and Cappadocian Mâ were ready to follow Cybele to the Tiber.

While eastern conquest was thus opening a channel for the entrance of Sacra Peregrina, the astonished urban magistrates were witnessing, in the Aventine quarter, a practical demonstration of oriental cultual orgy. From somewhere in

Greece a vagrant priest had come to Etruria and thence slipped into the midst of the city's postwar population. His character and methods excite the indignation of the patriotic Livy. *Graecus ignobilis,* he calls him, with nothing to confer that might profit body or soul, but a hierophant of occult and nocturnal rites.[2] The god he ministered to was Bacchus, but not the respectable divine citizen whom the Romans for three centuries had known in the Ceres-Liber-Libera triad. Rather was he the god of the Maenads who on the wooded slopes of Parnassus above Delphi sought absorption of their own personality into the divine spirit by stimulating nerves and imagination with wine, raw meat, mad shouts, and the riot of disorderly cult-dances.[3] Livy, indicating only briefly and contemptuously the dogmatic (so to speak) and cultual content of the religion introduced by his Greek *sacrificulus,* gives his attention to the gross crimes for which it was made a cloak. Of these, murder, inebriation, and pretty well all the categories of the external sexual vices were sanctioned in the initiate and even required of him under peril of himself falling a victim to the suspicious rage of his fellow-votaries. A strict *disciplina secreti* [oath of secrecy] among initiates, as well as the fact that Rome's new population was, to a degree, unknown by authorities, concurred for a time to maintain the Bacchanalia in the rank of tolerated private devotions. The secret finally transpired, whether in the highly romantic way recounted by Livy or otherwise hardly matters, and, with the able consul Postumius bringing to bear against them all the fine machinery of government, the Bacchanalia bolted from the Roman stage as rapidly as they had appeared. Death was the penalty for initiates who had perpetrated crimes in the Aventine conventicles, imprisonment for those who had merely pledged themselves to commit the immoral indecencies of the cult. It is

---

[2] *Op. cit.,* XXXIX, 8.

[3] For the Bacchanalian cult and "theology," one may consult the chapter entitled "Apollo and the Mystics."

altogether interesting to note that a limited tolerance was yet conceded to Bacchanalia. The decree of the Senatus Consultum allows recourse to the Roman praetor, in case anyone deems this rite necessary for himself because of religious reasons. The praetor is then to refer the petition to the Senate. If it is approved by that body, the one requesting the permission may perform the rite in a small group of not more than five persons and under other limitations.[4]

Just as the investigation of the Aventine doings had been conducted by the civil officers, so this final decree adjusting the status of the worship of Dionysus savors of police regulation rather than of any pontifical judgment upon the theological tenability of Dionysism. One might be tempted to read into the Senatus Consultum De Bacchanalibus a recognition of the principle of freedom of conscience, but the document seems motivated by no principle higher than determination to preserve civic order by suppressing orgiastic public exhibitions. Private observance of Bacchic rites, free of murder and *stupra,* of course, was regarded by the magistrates with a shrug of the official shoulders.

The lasciviousness uncovered by the Bacchanal flurry of 186 as well as the luxury that poured in from the conquests on the eastern front found a harsh censor in the Elder Cato. Personally, he was a compendium of the moral and intellectual qualities which the literature of the Augustan Age has extolled as those of the ideal Roman. Frugal and hard working from the novitiate of his peasant early youth, brave and resourceful in the field as he proved in Spain and at Thermopylae, an orator and lawyer whose words could win over both patrician and

[4] The decree reads: "Ne qua Bacchanalia Romae, neve in Italia essent. Si quis tale sacrum solenne et necessarium duceret, nec sine religione et piaculo se id omittere posse, apud praetorem urbanum profiteretur, praetor senatum consuleret. Si ei permissum esset, cum in senatu centum non minus essent, ita id sacrum faceret, dum ne plus quinque sacrificio interessent, neu qua pecunia communis, neu quis magister sacrorum, aut sacerdos esset." The archaic form of this decree can be found in *Andrew's Dictionary.*

Fig. 36. A Dionysiac Maenad

A votary of the orgiastic cult of Bacchus is shown here in one of her milder moments. The excesses of the Bacchanals in 186 B.C. were sternly repressed by the still virile government of the Republic.

plebeian mind, he entered at fifty on a long term of office as autocratic guardian of Roman morals. Luxury he attacked by prohibitive taxes on the articles that ministered to it. Private immorality he ferreted out and prosecuted with his compelling eloquence. Senators even were expelled ignominiously for falling short, though it were in a small matter, of the propriety due their office. Great names did not halt him, for he humiliated a Flaminius and a Scipio. His influence can justly be said to have been a barrier which held back for decades the final debacle of Roman religion and the corruption of Roman morals.

Cato, despite the handicaps of a youth spent in farm labor and in the camps, acquired education and culture superior to those of the average second-century Roman man of affairs. He seems to have known Greek and was acquainted with Pythagorean philosophy. However, the ideal of character that he set for himself and for the Romans excluded speculative philosophy and, in general, the intellectual and esthetical culture of Hellenism. His ideal embraced the rugged simplicity of private life which he had admired in the illustrious Manius Curius, and the practical talent for state enterprises which he had noted in Fabius Maximus, under whom he had served at Tarentum. He urged, then, the claims of the old indigenous Roman religion as against the growing pretensions of the Greek mode, ridiculed and repressed *ex officio* the soft living of the nobles, and had the brilliant Carneades packed off to the groves of Athens' Academy lest the Roman youth lose their martial character in eagerness for Greek speculation.

The embassy which Carneades made the occasion for his philosophic propaganda arrived in 155, but even before this date the Greek philosophic schools, with characteristic proselytizing zeal, had tried the Roman mission. It was in 204 that Cato himself brought Ennius to the city from Calabria. Ennius was a writer who under the patronage of Scipio Africanus, familiarized the cultured class with Pythagorean ideas on the soul, as well as with Euhemerus' theory that the gods of polytheism were originally merely great men whom mythographers had transmuted into divine beings. While this propaganda proceeded unchecked, the Senate suppressed another bit of Pythagorean proselytizing as a religious innovation. It was on the occasion when, in 181, the spurious *Books of Numa* were dug up on the Janiculum. The unknown forger thought to secure credence for his Pythagorean tracts as the work of the venerated ancient legislator by enclosing them in a leaden coffin inscribed with Numa's name. When the writings finally fell into the hands of authorities, the absurd apocrypha were condemned as teaching strange religion and burned. It is tempting to conjecture that the spirit of Cato animated the condemnation for heresy, as also the banishment of two Epicurean philosophers, in 171, but the conjecture can rest merely on the general fact that he was Censor during these years.

The seeds of Stoic doctrine were sown more thoroughly among the city's intellectual circles, and, besides, were in themselves more likely to germinate in the downright mentality of the Roman than were the teachings of Pythagoras or Epicurus. The Pythagorean's elusive mathematical concept of divinity failed to square with the concept of the gods as active powers, while the contemplative illusion of metempsychosis would hardly fasten upon a man convinced of the unalterableness of his personality by the constant calls upon him to assert the same in the exercise of military and civic duty. For analogous reasons the Romans, at least in the latter days of the Republic, were unprepared for Epicurean doctrine. The *ataraxia* proposed by the great Greek master as the goal of human effort was as chimeric an ideal for the hectic days of Rome's expansion into a world power as, let us say, for the restlessly active temperament of present-day America. Epicurus again, made room in his Atomism for the gods of polytheism, yet allowed them no concern nor contact with mortal affairs. Now, for the Romans such an arrangement could mean only the virtual disfranchisement of the divine citizens whose rights and duties were a real element in the politico-religious constitution. Quite in contrast with the tenets of Pythagoras and Epicurus, the principles of the Stoa entered the cultured circle of second-century Rome rather neatly in phase with the western people's native character and religious development.

The effective engrafting of Stoic principles began, as Warde Fowler[5] shows, in the close friendship that arose between an eminent Stoic philosopher, Panaetius, and Scipio Africanus Minor. The "Scipionic circle"—the name given to the group of better educated men of affairs drawn together under the leadership of the latter—found in Stoicism not precisely an intellectual apologetic for traditional Roman cult and ethic, but rather a system for reinterpreting Roman religion in intellectual terms. The key for the reinterpretation was the Stoic concept of Reason, universal, divine, pantheistic, pervading all nature. This one Reason manifests itself variously in various natural forces; hence the old Roman numen might be interpreted as one of these manifestations. Ceres, for instance, might be taken for the manifestation of divine Reason in the laws governing the growth of crops. The pantheistic principle thus applied a gloss of reasonableness to the pantheon. From the concept of universal Reason, further, the moral aspect of religion derived sanction. For man, recognizing himself, more specifically his reason, as part of the divinity, is bound to seek self-realization through a life according to reason. Here was the deep sense of duty of the disciplined Roman sublimated in motive and incorporated into a philosophic synthesis.

Such speculations, it is true, were but sand ropes, incapable alike of holding together the cracking idols of polytheism's temples and of binding the wild beast of passion in the temple

---

[5] *Religious Experience of the Roman People*, pp. 362 sqq.

of man's heart. It is necessary to indicate the above adaptation of Stoicism to Roman ideas of deity and duty, for this precise type of pagan virtue — concreted in a Scipio, a Seneca, a Marcus Aurelius — is not infrequently urged to show that the ancient world could have gotten on without the moral regeneration effected by Christianity. The argument ignores the relative fewness of these paragons of philosophic virtue, as well as the fact that the opinions and lives of pagan philosophers exercised a negligible influence as leaven among the masses.

The acquisition of rich new territory made the prizes of public life much more numerous and more attractive than in the days when Rome's power extended merely through the peninsula. A proconsulate now in one of the newly organized provinces opened the way for speedy self-enrichment, and this even without the commission of acts officially censurable as malfeasance in office. We need not dwell on the details of the violently agitated politics of the last century of the Republic — from Cato's feud with Scipio Africanus through the Gracchi disturbances down to Sulla and Marius, Caesar and Pompey, but it is clear that this was no atmosphere favorable to the due fostering of national religion. The priesthoods and the Flaminates were not remunerative offices: they might be accepted by prominent men with a view to gain prestige and further political ambitions, but the incumbents neither had technical knowledge of religious laws nor bothered much about cult functions. Augurs are reported to have been in the habit of winking knowingly when they met by way of comment on the clever use they were making of good and bad omens to help friends and hinder rivals. Several of the priestly colleges became wholly disorganized because of lack of interest, while for seventy-five years no one could be found to accept the Flaminate of Jupiter, because this office was traditionally so holy as to inhabilitate the incumbent for civil and commercial life.

Deserting the temples, as the religio-civic bonds that drew them thither were allowed to fall slack by authority, the people lost rapport with the old gods. What is more, they beheld these same gods ridiculed on the public stage, as Plautus and others Latinized the irreverent Greek comedy.[6] The people's natural religiousness found, however, new modes of expression in the pseudo-mystic cults, whose entrance into Rome has already been noted. The *sacrificuli* and *vates,* who draw Livy's fire, no doubt increased in number as new elements of population came into the city after every new foreign conquest, and found proselytizing in favor of their strange rites easy among a religious but religiously bewildered citizenry. Bacchic initiations were tolerated, as has been shown. Cybele reigned serenely in her temple on the Palatine with her own hierarchy of priests, her own festivals and public games. Isis-cult in Rome dates from the second century, it would seem, though, it was Sulla's devotion to her that led to the erection of her first public shrine in the early first century. Soldiers returning from the First Mithridatic War brought from Comona in Pontus Mâ with her wild and sanguinary ritual. For Mithraism at Rome there is no certain evidence till imperial days, though Roman contacts with it go back as far as Pompey's war with Cilician pirates.

---

[6] Cf. Fowler, *op. cit.,* pp. 350 sqq.

CHAPTER « 30

REFORMS OF AUGUSTUS

THE need for reform in religion, morals, and government had impressed the better minds of the last half century of the Republic. The reform was envisaged quite uniformly as a restoration of old institutions and standards, not as a revolution bringing in new ideas. The Sullan Constitution addressed the reform problem in its governmental aspects, while Varro's *Antiquitates Rerum Divinarum* and Virgil's *Aeneid* may be regarded as literary pleas for a renascence of the vanished *religio* and the *virtus prisca et pietas* respectively. Another Cato carried on in the uncompromising spirit of his great-grandfather. Cicero's vacillating temperament nullified his efficiency as political and religious savior, though his intellectual and idealistic equipment qualified him for that function. Julius Caesar cherished comprehensive and brilliant plans for reorganization of the Roman constitution to fit the conditions created by imperial expansion, but the fatal Ides of March ended his too brief period of supreme authority. It was only after Octavian, the legal and spiritual heir of the great Julius, had ridden through another civil storm to supreme power that Caesar's plans were realized. Upon the religious aspects of the Augustan Reforms the present chapter will touch.

Two symbolic actions early revealed the religious intentions of Rome's new master. In 32, as one of the Fetiales, he revived the immemorial rite of declaring war when he cast a spear into a plot of ground situated near the temple of Bellona and belonging to an Egyptian. For it was against Egypt's queen Cleopatra and her paramour Antony that he was taking up arms. Returning from Egypt two years later, he made a feature of his three days of triumph yet another immemorial rite of the city's old religion, closing the doors of Janus' temple in token of the restoration of peace. Exercising the undisputed supremacy which was now his after Actium, he initiated the reforms, which we here catalogue.

Particular Reform	Religious Significance
1. Augustus himself fills office of Flamen Dialis, there having been no incumbent for seventy-five years. Is also Pontifex Maximus.	Fostering of respect for early religion, as well as for Emperor's person.
2. He increases the privileges of the Vestals and builds a temple of Vesta on the Palatine to replace the ancient one in Forum.	Rebuilding of collapsed Roman family life: idea of Emperor as *paterfamilias* of State.
3. Restores credit of old priesthoods (e.g., Sodales Titii and Fratres Arvales) by influencing the ablest and noblest to hold the same.	Building of prestige for old religion and insuring of due performance of rites.
4. Revives the Lupercalia.	Same: also encouragement of family life.
5. Repairs all decaying temples, eighty-two in all.	Dignity of public cult.
6. Revises *Sibylline Books.*	Boost for Apollinism.
7. Builds great temple of Apollo on the Palatine.	Same.
8. Holds the Ludi Saeculares in 17 B.C.	Great pageant symbolizing Rome's rebirth.
9. Dedicates temple to Divus Julius, whom the Senate had declared a god.	Familiarizing of people with Oriental concept of divine right of Emperors: beginning of cult of Divi.
10. Builds temple of Mars Ultor to commemorate the vengeance taken on Julius Caesar's murderers.	About the same as preceding.

11. In every one of Rome's fourteen regions (wards) were a number of *vici* (precincts). In every precinct he had a shrine erected to Lares Compitales and the Genius of Augustus: the figure of his Genius stood between the figures of the two Lares.

Augustus the *paterfamilias* of State: an astute permission of limited cult even of living Emperor.[1]

Three distinct aims are discernible on a careful examination of the above measures. The first is revivalistic, consisting in a rehabilitation of Rome's traditional religion[2] both in its externals and in the inner *religio* of the people. Secondly, Apollo-cult is to be accorded a position of importance quite novel to Roman religious experience. Finally, the person of the Emperor is to be clothed with a divinity akin to, and modeled on, the divinity of certain oriental monarchs. It begins to be clear, then, that the term "reformer" applied to Augustus includes both restorer of the old and innovator. In fact, what strikes us is the genius displayed in the symmetrical combination of these new parts with the columns and stones of the old temple of Roman religion which he restored.

A politic fusion of old and new were the measures catalogued in the first and second places above. By the assumption of the greatest of the Flaminates and of the headship of the pontifical college, he established in himself a plenitude of spiritual power, added to his authority as supreme civil lord, thus preparing the way for the introduction of the idea that the Emperor was something more than a human person. Discreetly revolutionary, also, must be judged the new temple of Vesta built on the Palatine next to the Domus Augusti. He was to be the *paterfamilias* of the state and signified his intention no less by this juxtaposition of the state hearth and his

[1] The tabular view of the Augustan Reforms here presented is based upon Professor G. J. Laing's excellent analysis.

[2] The Nuministic religion as modified by Greek Anthropomorphism is meant.

Fig. 37. Augustus as Pontifex Maximus

Though desirous to place himself at the head of the state religion, Augustus waited patiently till the death of Lepidus in 13 B.C. He then assumed the office and brought to bear all the prestige of the crown to revive the piety of earlier days.

own residence than by exercising the *patria potestas,* as Pontifex Maximus, over the Vestals.

Horace, lamenting the collapse of religion and morals, sings:

Delicta majorum immeritus lues,	Ye Romans, ye, though guiltless, shall
Romane, donec templa refeceris	Dread expiation make for all
Aedesque labentes Deorum, et	The laws your sires have broke,
Foeda nigro simulacra fumo.[3]	Till ye repair with loving pains
	The gods' dilapidated fanes,
	Their statues grimed with smoke.

Augustus, in the account he wrote of his own achievements, takes special pride in having remedied the conditions which formed the theme of Horace's jeremiad.[4] Eighty-two temples he restored, a work which in some cases involved the building of practically a new structure. A rebirth of the old piety was, of necessity, the result, for the temples were once more attractive and capable of arousing what the Roman understood by devotion. As a supplement to temple restoration, the Emperor fostered a liturgical movement, both by reviving old festivals, such as the Lupercalia, and by filling up the ranks of the long neglected old priesthoods. The new incumbents understood very well that Augustus expected of them the due performance of the traditional rites under penalty of imperial displeasure. In the descriptions of Ovid's *Fasti* we have sufficient evidence that the sacred observances of the Julian Calendar were scrupulously attended to by the rejuvenated priesthoods.

On the promontory at Actium stood a temple of Apollo. Under his protection Caesar Octavian placed his fleet, and legend has it that the god of the silver bow was seen fighting on the conqueror's flagship. In gratitude Octavian, now Augustus, and secure in his position as Emperor, erected on the Palatine a temple surpassing all the city's divine residences in

---

[3] Book III, Ode VI. Trans. by Theodore Martin.

[4] Inscription on bronze tablet set up before his mausoleum, a copy of which has been found at Angora.

richness of equipment. He seems to have planned to exalt Apollo in Rome at the expense of Jupiter, much as he had been exalted in Greece at the expense of Zeus. Apollo, of course, was no stranger in Rome, for perhaps as early as the regal period he was honored as the god who spoke through the oracles of the *Sibylline Books.* In 431, as a god of health, he was lodged in a temple built in the Prata Flaminia near the city, and thereafter references to him as "Apollo of health" and "Apollo the physician" are usual. When in 212 Hannibal and Mago had in turn crushed Roman armies, a certain Marcius palmed off on the frightened people an oracle ordering the establishment of Apolline games. Delphi's Pythian games were the obvious prototype, but the Romans departed from the Greek model by making dramatic representations the central feature.

From the time when Tarquin the Proud introduced the *Sibylline Books,* two priests, called *Duoviri Sacris Faciundis,* were commissioned to interpret the oracles of that curious compilation. In the course of centuries, the functions of this priestly college were expanded to include all the cult of the Di Novensides, till press of work necessitated increasing the original number of two to fifteen. Of these Augustus appointed himself the head. Under his direction they expurgated the *Sibylline Books* of the centuries' accretion of interpolations and restored, as far as possible, the original text. The finished work was enshrined in Apollo's fine Palatine home instead of in the Capitoline temple which had always housed the Sibyl's utterances. Here was but one instance among a number of Augustus' policy of transferring ancient cult privileges from father Jove to his mythological son.

Augustus desired that the popular imagination see his reform policy, of which the religious reforms were but a part, as a New Deal. To this end he chose to play upon the immemorial superstition that the gods at the conclusion of definite cycles of years (*saecula*) periodically renewed the face of the earth. The superstition, as it reached Rome through Greek and Etruscan channels, computed the *saeculum* at about 110 years. Now, the Romans in 349 (?), 249, and 146 had held in the Campus Martius sacrifices and games, whose origin and meaning were pretty well lost in a maze of myth. The fifteen priests, constituting his new priestly college, were accordingly ordered to sell to the people the idea that the year 17 B.C. was both the year of the periodic divine renovation and the year which called for the Roman observances just noted. The fifteen wise men found a Sibylline oracle which declared that Ludi Saeculares had been first celebrated at Rome in 456 and every 110 years thereafter, so that the year 17 was the close of the fated cycle.

All the religious ideals of the Augustan Reform found expression during the three days of the Ludi Saeculares. To each of the Di Indigetes was offered the traditional victim, Augustus himself as Pater Patriae slaying the white bull of Jupiter. To these hoary *numina,* who had nurtured the fine strength of the old Roman character, supplication was made for the new generation symbolized in the chorus of *virgines lectae puerique casti* who sang Horace's *Carmen Saeculare.* The Emperor himself was prudently and gracefully insinuated into prayers and ceremonies as something more than man. To Apollo, as might be expected from what preceding paragraphs have explained, was accorded chief honor. His Palatine temple was the real focal point of the celebration, while care was taken to make it clear in the sacred ode that Phoebus was definitely elected as tutelary of the new Rome.

Augustus' Reforms were homeopathic in the sense that he purposed to restore a natural religion to health by a skillful prescription of finer elements of natural religion. His goal as well as many of his means were admirable. But it was no natural religion that was destined to revivify Rome. The remedy that Providence supplied was the allopathic one of a supernatural religion.

CHAPTER « 31

WORSHIP OF DEIFIED EMPERORS

CAESAR-WORSHIP, which the preceding chapter revealed newly planted in the herbarium of Roman religious ideas, was an exotic of Graeco-Oriental antecedents. In Greece it was ordinary for founders of cities and not unusual for famous generals to receive after death a religious cult expressed in prayer and sacrifice. They were understood to have been transfigured into a state of immortal felicity and to have acquired efficacious protective power in favor of their devout clients. Olympians they were not, according to the proper concept, though — and this especially after Euhemerus' theory gained ground — the distinction between god and hero not infrequently grew obscure.

Among the Persians, whose ideas of the divine attributes remained notably correct, there still arose a worship of Cyrus akin to the worship of the Greek heroes. "Magi were on duty at his tomb at Pasargadae and every day offerings of meal and wine were made and a sheep was sacrificed; once a year a horse was offered."[1] What is, however, of more direct importance for our present subject is the honor paid by the Persians to the spiritual double of their living king. Every man had his spiritual double or *fravashi,* not an individual guardian spirit, but *perhaps* a being imagined during the intellectual effort to express adequately the duality of soul and body. For the king's *fravashi* a special table was laid at banquets, and before this shadowy being the guests made obeisance as before the king himself. The Romans, it will be remembered, had a concept of

[1] Taylor, *The Divinity of the Roman Emperor,* p. 3, Appendix I.

man's spiritual double, namely, Genius, so that ideas connected with the *fravashi* were adapted, as we shall see, without too violent a shock to sensitive ears along the Tiber.

Egypt's contribution to the religion of king-worship was yet more explicit. In their language the king's Genius or *fravashi* was his *ka,* and modern Egyptology has uncovered detailed evidence of divine honors paid to the royal *ka.*[2] A theory of divine origins, moreover, similar to Euhemerism prevailed in hieratical theology, according to which the major Egyptian gods had once been kings of that country. In the living king the god Horus was reincarnate. The living king was officially "the son of all the gods and goddesses," but in a special manner of the sun-god Ra, to whose shrine at Heliopolis a new king had to repair to secure a declaration of his divine legitimacy. A suggestion that a living king was not regarded as a full-fledged god is contained in the facts that in cult he was always joined with Osiris, Horus, or other gods and that, instead of having his own temple, he dwelt in his iconic representation with the various state-gods in their temples.[3]

Alexander the Great, by inheritance ruler of Greece and by conquest ruler of the empires of Darius and of the Pharaohs, centralized in his own person all the foregoing titles to man-deity. Founding or renaming for himself numerous cities, he received according to the Greek manner a cult of hero-founder. Through directed decree of the commonwealths of the Greek mainland he was proclaimed a son of Zeus and seems to have received confirmation in this dignity from the oracle of Zeus Ammon. Taking over the prerogatives of the Persian kings, he insisted on none of them so punctiliously as on the one connected with the worship of the *fravashi,* and

---

[2] *Ibid.,* pp. 5, 6.

[3] The statues of Pharaohs regularly bear the attributes of the god incarnate in them. Cleopatra was an incarnation of Isis, hence appears with the cystrum of that goddess in her hand and crowned with the sun's disk between the horns of a cow.

this against the opposition of his Macedonian and Greek courtiers. Without opposition he was accepted by the compliant Egyptians as a new Osiris, his final divine name thus becoming Dionysus Osiris (for Dionysus he was by his Hellenic apotheosis). The Seleucid and Ptolemaic dynasts, successors of Alexander to the Syrian and Egyptian kingdoms respectively, kept alive these ideas of divine honors due to their own persons till time's wheel brought around Roman legions, to snatch off the halo of the oriental divine kingship for the adornment of western rulers.

The field of Cynoscephalae may be regarded as marking the commencement of Rome's toying with the idea of man-deity. This victory together with Flamininus' subsequent complete expulsion of Philip from Greece gained for the Roman commander the deep gratitude of the Hellenic cities. Besides the titles of *Soter* and *Euergetes,* the Asiatic Greeks bestowed upon him honors specifically divine by associating his name in religious hymns with the names of Zeus and Heracles. At Smyrna as early as 195 B.C. a *templum Urbis Romae* was erected[4] in which the general was associated in cult with this new deification of the magnanimous western city. A little later, when the former territory of the Syrian king Antiochus III was organized into Roman provinces, the officials sent out to administer them naturally were regarded by the inhabitants in the same light as had been the former Seleucid lords of the land. In general there is little evidence to show that officials of Republican days took the profered divine honors seriously: they rather looked upon them as mere forms, but as forms which made the populace more tractable to authority. Cicero's later opposition to the deification of Julius Caesar was foreshadowed by his downright refusal to allow the province of Asia to build a temple to himself and the proconsul Quintus Cicero, and again by his boast that he had ac-

[4] Tacitus, *Annales,* Liber IV, c. 56. Alabanda in Caria built one in 170 B.C.

cepted no shrines nor statues to himself when proconsul of Cilicia.[5]

Julius Caesar, like Flamininus, claimed divine descent through Aeneas, for the Aeneas legend passed on the blood of the god-born hero through the gens Julia. Like Flamininus, too, he was acquainted with the divine honors which Greek and Asiatic cities bestowed, having been a wide-awake observer when soldiering as a youth in Asia Minor. His first taste of something akin to divine honors may have been during his tenure of the office of Pontifex Maximus. For in holding this dignity he was legally the successor to the sacred character and power of the semidivine kings of early Rome.

Whether or not dreams of reviving in his own person the sacerdotal kingship came to him on the occasion of his pontificate, it is certain that the idea of securing his own official apotheosis grew rapidly in his mind as he rode to supreme power in the spectacular cavalcade of events of the years 49 to 45. Alexander's career of conquest was not more brilliant than Caesar's victorious progress during that period. Sweeping down from the theater of his successful wars with Gaul, German, and Briton into Italy, which he mastered within sixty days, he crossed to Spain to receive the submission of Pompey's western army; pursued his enemy to Greece and overcame him at Pharsalus; took Alexandria and conquered Egypt; sailed for Asia Minor to crush the king of Pontus; returned to the southern Mediterranean to defeat Cato and Sextus Pompey; finished the four-year job of world conquest at Munda in Spain against the two sons of Pompey.

That success really unbalanced Caesar to such an extent as to generate hallucinations that he was more than man, can hardly be maintained. Most probably his genius, prospecting a world empire, perceived that the new emperor would have to conform to the Oriental doctrine of divine kingship. Alexander, who was his model, had calmly demanded the worship

[5] *Epp. ad Quintum Fratrem* I, 1, 26, *et ad Atticum* V, 21.

accorded to the Great King and the Pharaoh whom he had supplanted. When in Egypt, the Macedonian had journeyed to the desert oracle to have Jupiter Ammon recognize him as his son. The Roman was not ready for that step, but during his amorous sojourn there in the toils of Cleopatra he shrewdly observed divine kingship in practice in the veneration paid his paramour and the worship offered to the images of dead Pharaohs. On his return to Rome, his unparalleled triumph and the circus games in his honor exalted his mind and convinced him that the time was propitious for insisting on his own apotheosis. The coolness with which he went about it furnishes another argument that it was the politician and not the hallucinate at work. To Rome's Venus, but under the invocation of Genetrix as ancestress of the Gens Julia, he erected a temple and planned another to Rome's Mars whom he also claimed as his forebear. His was to be a Roman deification, not one effected by the importation of strange gods and theology. An artful series of "must" decrees was presented to the Senate. The Patres Conscripti decreed him one honor after another till in the year 44 they hailed him as *Divus,* or The Divine. The fatal Ides intervened to delay the execution of the decree.

Events after his death, however, led to the decree being executed as the enthusiastic will of the people instead of as the enforced will of a dictator. His generous last testament was read to the people and won them — an effect enhanced by Antony's funeral oration. They wanted to enshrine Caesar's ashes in the Capitoline Temple. The spot in the Forum where his body was cremated became a shrine, and under the influence of his veterans and the demagogue Amatius sacrifices were offered there. At his funeral games a great comet appearing in the sky was popularly interpreted as the spirit of Caesar in heaven. In the year 42 Octavian Caesar felt himself strong enough politically to insist on the execution of

Fig. 38. Temple of the Deified Antoninus Pius and Faustina

The stroller in the Villa Borghese is reminded by the inscription on the above façade how the immemorial king-worship of the Orient passed into the Western World.

the deification decree of 44. He at once began the erection of the temple to Divus Julius.

In the light of the characters and careers of the majority of the first-century Caesars, it is not surprising that of the first eleven Emperors only Augustus, Claudius, Vespasian, and Titus were deified. But after the first century, when the people had grown accustomed to the new form and the intellectual class could even regard it with satirical tolerance, it became *de more* for the Senate to pass a deification decree immediately on the death of an Emperor, no matter how rascally he might have lived. Certain women of the imperial family were also deified — Augustus' wife Livia, Caligula's sister Drusilla, and so on — but these were never important in cult and never had separate temples. The multiplication of Emperor-temples was checked, for obvious reasons of economy and religious decency, by the erection of the Temple of the Deified Emperors, whose ruins still remain on the Palatine. A statue of each new Divus was set up in it. The last of the Emperors of the West, Romulus Augustulus, was honored with his own temple, which stands today almost intact in the Forum as a memorial to pagan Rome's adoption of the Orient's divine kingship.

Sodalitates, a species of new priesthood, were founded to attend to the cult of the Divi. Thus there were the Sodales Augustales for the deified Augustus, the Sodales Flaviales for Vespasian. The Sodalitates were patrician bodies, membership in which gave social standing akin to Knighthood in the Order of the Garter or of the Bath. That belief in the godhead of their dead rulers became a vital element in the people's religion, would be hard to show. What kept Emperor-worship an official article of faith was the patronage of living Emperors, who felt their own dignity and authority enhanced by the fiction that they sprang from a divine line and would themselves one day be deified.

CHAPTER « 32

ORIENTAL CULTS AT ROME

IN THE Chapter on the Hannibalic War Rome's adoption of the Great Mother of Pessinus, first of the Sacra Peregrina, has been narrated. She entered the city in no iconic form, but merely in the shape of the black stone which the Roman matrons carried in turn in the procession from the ship to the Capitoline temple. Later on the newcomer was given a temple of her own with a marble cult-statue, while still later there was erected a silver statue into whose face had been worked the original black stone. (Just how to visualize this last-mentioned detail, or even whether we may believe the very fact, must remain uncertain from the confused classical reference.) In iconic art Cybele, for so the Magna Mater was named, is given a scepter and a crown modeled on a city's battlements. To these her attributes of city guardian and sovereign are frequently added the cornucopia, which her votaries probably purloined for her from Ops or Demeter, and the paten which she extends to suggest to her worshipers that they make their offerings. Attis, her associate in the myth, is represented as an effeminate youth in shepherd's garb and peaked Phrygian cap, who sits upon a bull or reclines beneath a pine tree.

The Cybele-Attis myth is a lush growth. Following the fairly typical account of Arnobius, we find the Great Mother one of the creatures made by Deucalion and Pyrrha. A monstrous hermaphrodite Agdistis is procreated by Zeus and emasculated by Dionysus. From the blood of the hermaphrodite grows a pomegranate tree, from whose fruit the daughter of the river-god Sangarius becomes pregnant and gives birth to Attis. The object of the love of both Agdistis and the Great

Mother, he is nevertheless betrothed to King Midas' daughter. To the nuptials Agdistis and the Great Mother come as uninvited guests, whereat Attis, driven to frenzy, emasculates himself and dies. Agdistis buries the body at Pessinus in Galatia and Zeus grants the body incorruption.

Agdistis seems to be a fertility principle; the daughter of the river-god typifies the fertilizing power of water. Offspring of Agdistis' blood and the maiden is Attis, or the spring vegetation. The love of Attis for the Magna Mater or "mother of all life" symbolizes the luxuriant growth of vegetation during summer. But Attis is parched by this midsummer ardor and dies, as the vegetation dies at summer's end. His burial is the winter season and his incorruption, the hope of the coming spring. This is the interpretation given by Rapp in Roscher's *Lexicon* and it fits well into the details of both the myth and the cult.

The Great Mother, a Phrygian nature goddess of universal function, was adopted as early as the sixth century by the Greeks, who identified her with Cretan Rhea. Her Metroon at Athens was decorated by Phidias and made the depository of the public records. With this Greek popularity in mind, we are not surprised that the Grecizing *Sibylline Books,* under the circumstances detailed in preceding pages, ordered her introduction into Rome. There her history falls naturally into two periods. Under the Republic she was regarded as a powerful protecting deity of fertility, the promoter of success in arms, and so on, and, although the foreign priests who attended to her cult doubtless knew the full significance of the religion of Cybele and Attis, it seems clear that Roman votaries failed to recognize the difference between it and the traditional Greco-Roman cults of, say, Venus, Apollo, or Juno. Under the Empire the full meaning of this oriental mystery-religion was grasped and its whole striking ritual enacted, while the old prohibition against Romans serving as *galli* grew obsolete. The writers of Rome's Golden Age bear witness to the prominence of the cult, though Varro and Lucretius scorn and ridicule its observances. Augustus rebuilt the temple of Magna Mater, destroyed by fire in 3 B.C., while imperial patronage of the strange Phrygian worship continued almost uninterruptedly up to the triumph of Christianity. In the sunshine of this favor the ritual expanded until the city, which had for centuries witnessed the decorous liturgy of Pontifices and Vestals, beheld in its streets all the indecencies of a typical Phrygian religious orgy.

Priests of Cybele were called *galli,* probably from the River Gallus flowing near Pessinus. Their chief was the *Archigallus* or *sacerdos maximus.* There were also priestesses, and two inscriptions at Rome testify to a *sacerdos maxima.* The *galli* were eunuchs, and to this unnatural castration more than to any other reason is traceable the prohibition against Romans being priests of Cybele. Minor officials of the cult were named from the functions they performed: *dendrofori* who carried Attis' sacred pine tree; *canofori* who bore reeds to commemorate Cybele's search for Attis among the reed thickets; *cernofori* who carried boxes containing the sacred cult-symbols; *hymnologi, tympanistriae, cymbalistriae,* whose functions in the noisy ritual are patent; *aeditui* or temple porters. At first the Pontifices supervised the cult, but later the Quindecim Viri Sacris Faciundis took over this office.

The Spring Festival was not celebrated at Rome till the time of Claudius, though it was immemorial in Phrygia. It began on the Ides of March when the *Archigallus* attended by a priestess and the *canofori* sacrificed in the mountains near Rome a six-year-old bull for the fertility of the fields. One form of the legend tells of Cybele finding Attis concealed in a reed thicket and the rite just noted is supposed to be a clumsy adaptation of a Phrygian rite dramatizing this feature of the legend. On March 22 the *dendrofori* carried a pine tree, trunk wound with strips of wool and branches adorned with violets, into the temple. The tree stands for the pine tree beneath which Attis mutilated himself and died, but also for the dead body of Attis which was wrapped in wool and from which violets grew. March 24 was Dies Sanguini. The *galli* fasted, danced wildly, wagged their heads in an insane fashion, and at the height of their simulated grief for Attis slashed their arms with knives. March 25 was the Hilaria, a day of complete abandonment to rejoicing and was generally accompanied by unrestrained license. The Hilaria, occurring on the first day when daylight exceeded darkness in the new year, symbolizes the conquest of winter by spring. The day's connection with the myth is likely found in Zeus' grant of incorruption to Attis' body. It may be noted that there is no resurrection of Attis from the dead, so that the prop falls from under the theory of a parallelism to Christian history. March 26 was the Requictio, a concession doubtless to jittery nerves strained by the rites of the foregoing days. March 27 marked the close of the Spring Festival with the Lavatio. The statue of Cybele was escorted in a procession of the greatest magnificence to the banks of the Almo a short distance from Rome, where it and the sacred utensils and instruments were laved. The votaries then restored their darling goddess to her temple and gave themselves up once more to rejoicing.

The Taurobolium, a rite probably borrowed from the cult of Persian Anahita, appears late in Roman Cybele cult. On the testimony of a recently discovered inscription we may set the date at about A.D. 150. The Vatican Hill became the favorite locale for the rite. The votary descended into a pit over which was laid a stout lattice. A bull was then enticed on to the lattice and slaughtered, the votary thus receiving a blood bath and emerging an object of superstitious veneration to his fellows. Inscriptions attest that the rite might be undergone by proxy, as also to the fact that a ram was sometimes used instead of a bull (in which case the rite went by the name of

Criobolium). The taurobolic altar which the happy votary invariably set up after his gory bath attested that he was *renatus in aeternum* or *renatus in XX annos*.

Originally, that is to say in early Mediterranean days, Cybele cult was doubtless, like its many parallels, a form of naturistic religion in which the forces which bring about the changes of the seasons were worshiped. When the etiological myth arose, there came in additional ideas, such as sympathy for Cybele and for Attis and lust-worship typified in their amours. A third category of ideas was then introduced into the cult, deriving in the first instance from the Eleusinian Mysteries, but much reinforced, we are inclined to judge, by infiltrations from Christian teaching. This third category developed a conviction that initiation into Cybelic mysteries mystically incorporated the initiate with the divinity and was a pledge of a happy lot in the Afterlife. In the Roman exercise of the Cybele and Attis cult it is safe to say that the second and third class of ideas quite predominated over the naturistic features. The Taurobolium may be said with certainty to have had for its imagined effect the rendering of the votary an object of complacence to the divinity, but it would be going beyond the available evidence to interpret it as a rite conferring remission of sins and rebirth to righteousness. It is not improbable, however, that some votaries who knew something of the Gospel Message may have believed that the Taurobolium possessed efficacy akin to the efficacy of Christian Baptism.

In the passage of the Egyptian triad of Isis, Osiris, Horus into Greco-Roman religion, the names of the last two were modified. From the words Osor for Osiris, and Hapi or Apis for the bull sacred to him, was formed the word Hosorapis, then Oserapis, finally Serapis. From the Egyptian Har-po-krat, i.e., "Horus-the-child," the Greeks formed Harpocrates. Thus the triad worshiped at Rome was Isis, Serapis, Harpocrates.

Isis was originally a cow-headed goddess, one of the theriomorphic divinities so perplexing in early Egyptian religion.

In Rome she was represented by a woman's figure, while the cow idea was preserved both by accepting a cow as her usual symbol and by crowning Isis statues with a cow's horns. Between the horns was placed a disk to represent the sun. In her hand was the cistrum or rattle which was an indispensable noise-making instrument in her ritual. Other attributes too numerous to mention were later added to her representations as she grew in popularity and absorbed the functions of other divinities. Serapis is found crowned either with the double crown of Upper and Lower Egypt or with the corn measure symbolic of his power as lord of the Netherworld. One hand held the symbol of life, a kind of sawed-off shepherd's crook; the other the scourge with which he punished the wicked. As in the case of Isis, he later absorbed functions of other gods and is pictured with their attributes. Harpocrates, as we have previously said, is commonly shown as a little boy, unclothed, holding a finger on his lips.

Since in previous pages the Osiris myth and its interpretation have been discussed, it will be sufficient to trace the transit of the revered Egyptian triad into the Greco-Roman world. The Ptolemies found the worship in the land of their suzerainty, and Ptolemy Soter undertook to modify it into a form acceptable to Greek and Egyptian alike. By the collaboration of an Egyptian priest and of a Greek Eleusinian priest (so the story goes), both myth and cult were given typically Hellenic artistic embellishment, but especially the ritual took on the form of striking dramatic representations. It was the modified, not the purely Egyptian, worship that came to Rome. The presence of a temple of Serapis at Puteoli testifies to the practice of the cult in southern Italy as early as the second century B.C. Sulla was an Isiac votary, and it seems that he brought the cult to Rome during his dictatorship. At first a private devotion, it struggled against politically motivated persecution for a hundred years. In 59 B.C. a temple of Isis in the city was pulled down by the then authorities. In 43 B.C.

devotees of the Egyptian goddess secured a decree authorizing a state temple to her, but Antony's alliance with Cleopatra prevented the decree's execution. In 29 Augustus took occasion of a scandal among Isiac priests to proscribe the cult. Most serious persecution occurred under the suspicious Tiberius, who banished Isiac votaries, destroyed the temple they had at last erected, and threw the cult-statue into the Tiber. Between this dark year of A.D. 19 and the year 71 the cult was restored and so flourished that Vespasian and Titus spent the night preceding their joint triumph in the new temple of Isis just outside the city. After this the religion of Isis enjoyed official favor, though it was not solemnized within the Pomerium till Caracalla erected the temple of Serapis there. Of the popularity of the cult there is abundant evidence in Lucian, Apuleius, and Martial, as well as in the polemics of Church Fathers.

Heading the Isiac priesthood was the *propheta*. Under him were groups of priests distinguished by functional names, as e.g., *pastofori* or pastors. Distinctive of Isiac worship among mystery-religions was the feature of daily services—two, in fact, each day. Before daybreak the votaries assembled in front of the temple, the door being open but a curtain concealing the cult-statue. The priest removed the curtain, the votaries recited prayers and hymns and were then dismissed by the priest. The second service occurred at two in the afternoon, when the priests chanted hymns, there was the elevation of a vase of sacred Nile water and some form of minor burnt offering. We know of the following seasonal festivals. The fifth of March was the Navigium Isidis, commemorating Isis' journey to Byblos and worshiping her as a patroness of the opening navigation season. Roman worshipers, it would seem, repaired to Ostia, to witness the launching of a bark splendidly adorned and laden with spices. November the first to the third solemnized the Loss and Finding of Osiris. Processions of priests and votaries, shaven-headed and white-

Fig. 39. Serapis

Ancient Egyptian votaries of Osiris would hardly have recognized their darling god in this his Greco-Roman form. Face and torso are those of the Zeus-Jupiter of the Western World, while the modius or corn-measure which serves as a crown suggests Osiris' attribute of patron of agriculture.

Fig. 40. Endless Time, a Divinity Worshiped in Mithraism

He stood in Mithraic genealogies in a position similar to that of Kronos among the Greeks. He was a primordial principle from which all the gods sprang. Key, serpent, and lion's head symbolize eternity and invincibility.

robed, lamented with Isis and the dog-faced god Anubis, to the din of incessant rattling of the cistra. On November the third the finding of Osiris took place in the Heuresis or Hilaria rite, and was followed by unrestrained rejoicing, as on the parallel day in the cult of the Magna Mater.

Every temple of Isis had adjoining it an initiation room and an assembly room, and here were celebrated the more properly mystic rites of the cult. From Apuleuis we know that the initiation consisted of severe fasting and other purificatory ordeals, of the communication of secret formulas, of dramatic representations, finally of the mystic marriage of the initiate to the goddess. Of the doings in the assembly room, which only the fully initiated might enter, we know that they comprised pageantry based upon the myth and modeled upon the Eleusinian Mysteries.

To indicate the faith of the initiates, two short quotations may suffice. As Lucius the hero of Apuleius' *Metamorphoses* enters upon his initiation, the initiates exclaim: "Happy and thrice blessed he who by the innocence and constancy of his former life has won so noble an inheritance from heaven, that he should be reborn and forthwith devoted to the service of the sacred rites." During life Isis would be his protectress, but she further promises him: "When thou shalt have run the course of thy life and passed to the world beneath, there too in the very vault beneath the earth, thou shall see me shining amid the darkness of Acheron and reigning in the secret domains of Styx, and thyself dwelling in the fields of Elysium shalt faithfully adore me as thy protectress."[1]

In the Mithraic monuments of the Roman world, this Persian god of light and truthfulness is pictured in Persian garb of loose trousers, cloak, and peaked cap. He holds in his hand the short Persian sword with which in the myth he slays the bull. The child Mithras is shown holding forth a torch as he is born from a rock. Other divinities who traveled with him

[1] Bk. XI, Chs. 4, 16.

from Iran into the west and were associated with his cult were the lion-headed, snake-girdled Zervan Akarana or Infinite Time, the sky-god Oromazdes who took on the attributes of Jupiter, and a water-god, Apanm Napat, who was similarly identified with Neptune.

The legend of Mithras begins with his birth as above indicated from a rock. His destiny is Promethean, but, unlike the Greek culture hero, he struggles not against the envy of the gods to win blessings for men, but against the agents of Ahriman with whom Iranian dualism chooses to fill the earth. In the progress of the conflict he works his share of the prodigies so dear to the Persian storytellers; for he procures drink for thirsting mortals by shooting his arrow at a rocky cliff, rain for them by piercing the sky with the same weapon. With the sun, who at first opposes him, he engages in battle and debate, but finally cements an alliance with him and thereafter is accompanied in his adventures by the sun's bird the raven as adviser and familiar. Iran's "bull of heaven," whom we have seen figuring in the Avestan episodes of creation, is the final and chief objective of Mithras' earthly work. For the animal must be slain in order that the earth may be made fertile. The monuments show Mithras chasing the bull through the mountains, capturing and dragging it to a cave. There, as the raven looks on approvingly, Mithras drives his sword into the animal's heart. A dog leaps up to the wound, seemingly to catch the soul of the bull as it leaves the body, while a serpent symbolic of the earth drinks in the fertilizing blood. A scorpion sent by Ahriman attempts at the last minute to poison the bull's vital fluid.

The Mithra of the *Avesta* is one of the Venerable Ones or Yazatas and is specifically the spirit of truthfulness. As Yazata, he ranks below Ahura Mazda and below the whole class of the Amesha Spentas. Achemenean domination of the Tigris-Euphrates valley from the sixth to the fourth centuries confronted Avestan religion with the astro-religious system of the Neo-Babylonians, Avestan gods with the ancient divine lords of the valley. Here for the first time Mithras took over from Shamash the attributes of a sun-god, here Iranian religion in general adopted some of the astronomical symbolism which has been explained in previous chapters on Babylonian religion.

The Persians brought Mazdeism and Mithras with them into their satrapies in Asia Minor. Further syncretism resulted, as Ahura Mazda was fused with the sky-god of Doliche, while it is more than probable that Mithras became a "god of the mysteries" in imitation of the several models in that line offered by Asia Minor. But Mazdeism never supplanted the indigenous cults in this western frontier of the Achemenean Empire and itself sank into unimportance when control of Asia Minor was wrested from the descendants of Cyrus. Vestiges of Avestan religion left in the region were the royal names of Pontus, Cappadocia, Commagene, which were frequently compounded from the word Mithras; a bas-relief showing Mithras as sun-god extending his hand to Antiochus I of Commagene; another bas-relief from Daschylium in which a Magian priest, with mouth and nose covered according to the Avestan rubric, extends the holy Barsom bundle toward the altar.

The Near East was lost to the Iranians by the Macedonian conquest, nor was it ever regained even by the Parthian restorers of the Persian Empire. Nevertheless, successors of the Magi managed to maintain Avestan worship in the region west of the Euphrates down to the Christian era. The Greeks knew them as *Magousaioi* and spoke of them as "fire-lighters" and nature-worshipers. Aramaic was first the language of their ritual, afterwards Greek. These *Magousaioi* must be acknowledged as contributors to the Mithraism which Rome was to borrow from the Near East. Other contributors were Iranian feudal lords who maintained their independence in long struggles against Roman expansion in highland strongholds on the borders of Asia Minor and Armenia. They are known to have developed the idea of Mithras as their god of battles and as "the unconquerable."

Plutarch's statement in his *Life of Pompey* that Rome first received Mithraism from the Cilician pirates in the first century B.C. may well be doubted, since the earliest Roman Mithraic inscription is of the second century A.D. As a matter of fact, we have only sketchy knowledge of the causes and occasions of Mithraism's western aggrandizement. What may be said with certainty on the authority of Professor Franz Cumont, is the following. As the first century of our era merged into the second, Rome established her frontier on the Euphrates and built military roads thither, thus effecting contact with Iranian civilization. Oriental merchants and slaves traveled westward as the first missionaries of the modified Avestan religion in which by this time Mithras had become the chief divine figure. Soldiers of the eastern legions, recognizing in the warrior-god Mithras a fit patron of their profession, embraced his religion and carried knowledge of him to every outpost of the empire. The cult's morality emphasized fortitude and fidelity to duty, so doubtless military authorities encouraged its spread among the troops. Along the Rhine and the Danube, at the Roman Wall in Britain, in the deep Sahara, wherever the legions guarded the provinces against restless barbarians, Mithraic monuments have been discovered.

In the second century high functionaries of state and army were embracing Mithraism, and at its end the Emperor Commodus was initiated. The zenith of the cult may be said to have been reached when at the end of the third century Diocletian at Carnuntum on the Danube consecrated a sanctuary to Mithras as "protector" of the restored Empire. Shortly afterwards Mithraism suffered a decline, which was consummated with the overthrow of the Roman legions on the frontier and with the triumph of Christianity. Cumont asserts that the spirit of Mithraism continued on down to the Middle Ages in such oddities as the Cathari and the Manicheans.

The Mithraea are uniformly subterranean rooms reached by stairs from an upper vestibule. The room was long and narrow with a tunnel-vaulted roof which might be pierced by a light shaft, though illumination might be wholly artificial. A stone bench extended along each wall for the accommodation of worshipers. At the entrance was placed a bowl of water, while at the head of the chapel stood the altar with its four sides decorated with carved reliefs of scenes in the cult-legend. Behind the altar on the farthest wall was invariably sculptured Mithras slaying the bull. In this setting the hundred or so Mithraists who made up the individual community worshiped, but of the liturgical actions in which they participated we know really nothing.

On the excellent authority of St. Jerome we can name the seven grades of initiation, which may be likened to "degrees" of Freemasonry both in their mumbo-jumbo of cryptic symbolism and in their progressive enlightenment on the esoteric meaning of the religion. The seven were: Crow, Veiled, Soldier, Lion, Persian, Racer of the Sun, Father. Tertullian supplies a little information on initiation ritual, telling us that the initiandus was dipped in water to be washed of sin, that the Lion took an oath not to reveal the cult's secrets, that honey was placed on the tongues of the Lion and the Persian. At some point in the initiations the candidate was deemed worthy of partaking of a sacred meal of water, perhaps mingled with wine, and bread. A kind of supermystes was the Pater Patrum, who probably resided at Rome and enjoyed a primacy of honor or even of supervision over other communities.

Doctrinally "the Mithraic religion was a compound of

Iranian beliefs, Semitic theology, certain elements borrowed from cults indigenous to Asia Minor."[2] The age-long struggle between Ahura Mazda and Ahriman, which obsesses the Iranian religious mind, was also the fundamental article in the creed of the Mithraist. For the latter, however, Mithras had concentrated in his own person the attributes of all the demigods and heroes who in Avestan and other Iranian legends war against the daevas. In this struggle his devotee was called to take part by fortitude in the difficult experiences of life and, so doing, would find Mithras "an anchor to the soul," a companion and helper, a remunerator in a celestial hereafter. All this is essentially the dualistic theology of Iran. To the Semites western Mithraism owed its concept of Mithras as a sun-god, as well as its body of astroreligious lore whose nature and extent we may only conjecture from the frequent presence of astronomical symbols on the monuments. Finally, Mithraism's "mystery" elements properly so called — its initiations, secret formulas, close companionship with the god, sacred banquet, liturgical drama, and so on — seem to derive from mystery-cults of Asia Minor. In that region there were surely apt prototypes which the Magusans might well have copied during the centuries of their sojourn there. An alternate explanation is a borrowing from Greek, perhaps Eleusinian, sources; however, the known mutual antipathy of the Greek and Iranian spirits seem to render such an explanation improbable. Direct action of Satan establishing in Mithraism caricatures of Christian mysteries is an explanation suggested by some Fathers of the Church, but a wider knowledge of the natural genesis of pagan religious ideas makes this appeal to the preternatural less necessary.

---

[2] Cumont, *Les Religions Orientales dans le Paganisme Romain,* p. 137.

L'ENVOI

RELIGION AND THE STUDY OF RELIGIONS

CHAPTER « 33

RELIGION AND THE STUDY OF RELIGIONS

NO ATTEMPT has been made in the preceding pages to define just what is meant by religion. It was thought better to let concrete religious facts speak for themselves. Peoples of lower and higher culture, of wide geographic distribution, of different eras have been allowed to testify by word and action to their consciousness of dependence upon powers higher than the human. The testimony has embraced actions as simple as the Aryan's offering of flesh upon his grass altar and words as theologic as the Atonic hymns. The priestly caste, or the assumption of sacerdotal functions by the family head as among the early Romans, evidences a social institution whose purpose was to bridge the chasm that man senses between himself and the Overpowers. Origin myths attest everywhere to reason's effort to justify the sense of dependence. The same cosmogonies and theogonies, though grotesque more often than convincing or edifying, receive the submissive adherence of unquestioning faith. Intricate ceremonial observances accompany the changes of the seasons as well as the crises of individual and group life. Injustice, though it meets in the *lex talionis* a social sanction, is understood also, together with other forms of human sin, to lie subject to divine vengeance. The virtuous man, though in some of his lineaments rather a caricature of the true ideal, is the darling of the gods and walks secure under their protection.

The religious manifestations are part of the warp and woof of the life of the peoples we have been studying. What is meant, is that ancient man was religious quite as naturally as he was a builder and wrecker of cities, a giver and taker in marriage, a buyer and seller, a *homo sapiens* and a *homo faber*. He did turn his mind to the religious problem; he imposed upon his intellect beliefs, upon his conduct restrictions, upon his body ceremonial attitudes and gestures, upon his tongue prayer formulas. The whole man testified spontaneously to his dependence on Overpowers. There was question of a life that had to be led, that might not be cast off as some artificial and accidental imposition. Statecraft and priestcraft modified religious forms, but religion itself was natural to man.

Religious observance was marked by a tremendous seriousness. Inviolability of sacred places, of objects used in cult, of the person of the priest attested reverential fear for what belonged to the gods. Scrupulous exactitude in ceremonial and in prayer formula showed how august the persons addressed were thought to be. To the believer, the gods were no childish night-fears, but potent individuals with whom he had to reckon. For the sake of them he sacrificed in fulfillment of various religious devoirs his goods, his affections, and his most dear person. Self-devotion, the test of seriousness, was found abundantly among the votaries of polytheism. Skepticism and dilettantism grew only insofar as philosophy expressed its discontent at the unreasonableness of certain beliefs and sought to base religion anew on sounder foundations.

Vertiginous thinking has been at pains to explain the universality, the spontaneousness, the seriousness with which ancient man sought his God. Superstition and fear, totem and fetish began it all, it is said; then higher forms of cult evolved with the rest of man's advancing culture. If our thought processes be forthright, we shall not be inclined so to define religion as "to exclude the very concepts that constitute the essence of religious thought in the judgment of the human race." Instead, we trust to offend no one's sense of logic in maintaining that the cultual facts arrayed in the foregoing chapters indicate that "Religion is the ensemble of beliefs, dispositions of heart, rules of conduct, ritualistic observances which man himself directs toward, or which are imposed upon man by, that Power which man actually believes to be sovereign and with which man has established personal relations." In briefer phrase, "Religion is the dealing of men, as individuals and as members of society, with their god." These definitions are suggested by Professor Jastrow in *The Study of Religion* and developed by Fr. de Grandmaison in *Christus*.

Does the definition imply monotheism? No! But it does imply that the Power(s) is (are) personal, for believers would not direct the acts mentioned in the definition to the insensate glebe or the lightning. Further, the definition embraces both the interior religious disposition and the act of cult which is its external expression. Finally, by stressing the essential notion of reverent dependence the definition relegates to the penumbra of secondary and derivative features such religious manifestations as magic and mythology. Magic presupposes and follows after the fundamental religious element, inasfar as it is an attempt to control by cabalistic means the powers whom religion reverences. Mythology, for its part, is the embellishment that poetic romance adds to the belief in the Powers — a well-meant attempt, it may be, to furnish a quasi-historical basis for belief or to cherish piety, but not strictly religion.

Religious conviction plunges its roots deep into individual psychology. In possession of a solution that is subjectively satisfactory of the anxious problem of "the one thing necessary," the believer clings to his solution with a tenacity proportionate to his appreciation of the gravity of the matter involved. Loyalty to tradition and to education, contempt for contrary and supposedly erroneous opinions, the very desire for peace and disinclination to further inquiry increase beyond all reason the subjective firmness of conviction. Altogether human is the spectacle of the tumult in the theater at Ephesus, with the people crying down St. Paul's friends by reiterating for two hours the slogan: "Great is Diana of the Ephesians." They had been pricked in the sensitive area of their dearest prejudice and had no mind to bear it patiently. Shrewdly their town clerk employs the only argument capable of quieting them. "Ye men of Ephesus, what man is there that knoweth not that the city of the Ephesians is a worshiper of the great Diana and of Jupiter's offspring? Forasmuch, therefore, as these things cannot be contradicted, you ought to be quiet and to do nothing rashly." It was a case of "the old-time religion being good enough for them," the psychology of the closed mind, a type which has not varied substantially during the two thousand years separating the erection of the famous temple of Ephesian Diana from our own day.

The student of the facts of religions past and present will be inclined to color the facts with his own religious philosophy. His certitude—genuinely such or merely subjective, it really matters little here—determines for him what conclusions religious history ought to support. He will, by consequence, tend to stress every feature which reflects his own mentality. From the aprioristic material furnished by the same mentality he will strive to construct ingenious bridges over the chasms yawning between different segments of evidence. Where evidence proves unfavorable to the desired conclusion, he will seek reasons for disparaging the importance of the nonconformist facts. For the most part, it can readily be believed that such coloring and prejudging are so far unconscious psychological processes as to be attended by only occasional twinges of the historical conscience.

To a scientific study of religions, as Fr. Pinard remarks, the tendency to read one's own religious philosophy into the facts is the greatest psychological obstacle. Still, a personal creed and personal religious experiences are, in the no less worthy opinion of Fr. Schmidt, important aids to the right understanding of other men's religions. For example, the infra-religious and parareligious manifestations of Magic, Mythology, and Totemism will not be confused with the genuine religious *élan vital* by a student who in his own life has known and experienced the meaning of the relation of man to his Maker.

With his faith, then, affording him sympathy and understanding, the student investigates the cults of mankind in the scientific spirit. For him cultual facts are so many chemical substances to be analyzed and studied in relation to other facts and groups of facts. For him, as for the chemist, theories and laws are the ripening or ripened fruit of his investigation. On the acquisition of the totality, morally speaking, of pertinent facts and on the replacement of theories by demonstrated and universal laws which will give coherence to the mass of detail, will progress in the study of religions, as in any other science, be conditioned. As regards the actual state of the scientific study of religions, it must be confessed that, though the pains of labor are passed, the infant still lies in swaddling clothes, an interesting and promising *homunculus,* but demanding an unlimited amount of expert care before it can be expected to reach lusty manhood.

An illustration may clarify these abstractions. Among a number of the retarded civilizations brought to light by European discovery and colonization appeared the phenomenon of Fetishism. The fetish, which might be the teeth, claws, or tail of an animal, a stick or a piece of iron, a lump of clay stuck with nails or a bundle of rags, seemed to receive a certain reverence and to be addressed with prayers and sacrifices for the purpose of obtaining favors. Distribution of the practice was wide enough to embrace Australian Bushmen, Andaman Islanders, African tribes, and Amerindians. Hasty theorizers could not, of course, resist the temptation, so the fact of Fetishism was glorified as the primal religious fact; for man first conceived a fear of these inanimate objects, then made gods of them. Auguste Comte, for instance, made out Poor Lo and his Australian cousins as fetishizing everything they could not explain, even to the sun, the moon, and the earth. Scientific method, however, succeeded in reducing Fetishism to its proper proportions in the religious picture. First, by further ethnological investigation the supposed universality of the practice was disproved: hence, the notion of a primal and essential religious factor became, at least, highly improbable. Next, the supposed worship of the fetishes was subjected to intensive research with the following findings. The "worshipers" attested a vast body of belief and practice apart from and independent of their fetish practices. They emphatically denied that the inanimate fetish as such was their god. They attributed to it the dignity of a lower form of idol, and in many cases they had major idols which outranked the fetish in dignity. To the fetish, as indeed to the major idols, they paid the reverence due to an object which an Overpower had freely chosen to inhabit. They prayed to this Overpower, not to his vesture.

To put Fetishism in its place, use was made of the Comparative Method, which may be roughly defined as: a method for interpreting religious manifestations in the light of the whole cult in which they are found and by comparison with similar manifestations in other cults. Borrowed from the physical sciences where it had ably served, the method has been employed enthusiastically in the study of religions, but unhappily without due regard for the peculiarities of this field. For evidence of the abuse of the comparative method, we need but turn the pages of Reinach's *Orpheus*. "It is possible that the communion rites as understood and practiced throughout the Middle Ages were a survival of this very ancient superstition which consists in fortifying and sanctifying oneself by assimilation of a divine being. If primitive Christianity with its theophagistic practices conquered Europe so rapidly, it was because this idea of the manducation of the god was not new, but simply the presentation of one of the most profound religious instincts of humanity in a more spiritual form."[1] We have here a sample chosen at random from the many remote analogies in which Reinach delights and which he offers as proof positive of the origin of all religion from certain supposed characteristics of a fancifully reconstructed primitive mentality. In the gallery of analogies which amuse the reader of *Orpheus* the Sabbath prohibition of work is painted as a survival of a belief that the seventh day is unlucky; Jewish suophobia, a survival of a taboo on eating the totemic swine; Friday fish eating, a survival of a Syrian ritualistic banquet on sacred fish; the Greek gods, survivals of the sacred animals with which they are associated in mythology (Zeus of the eagle, Athene of the owl, Artemis of the stag).

The derivation of one religion from another is not proved by the argument from similarity unless the similarity is so detailed that it is evidently impossible that two such systems could have originated independently. Why should not different men, striving to express their reverence for the divinity, choose similar rites and prayer formulas? After all, the human mind and heart are constant quantities, whose meditations and aspirations tend naturally to parallel self-expression. The crude comparisons, then, indulged in by Solomon Reinach and by the more erudite Sir John Frazer in *The Golden Bough* are inconclusive. Further, both these writers and their schools are, in general, content to stop at surface resemblances between religion and religion. They do not bother to examine a detected resemblance in the setting of the whole cult where they find it, nor are they concerned to find out just what sense the votaries attached to the rite. Hebrew abstention from pork is no taboo, but an ordinance of a revealed ceremonial law. In Christian thought and preaching the Eucharist has always been immeasurably different from Dionysiac or any other ancient theofagy.

---

[1] Horace Liveright, ed., 1930, p. 19.

When the childhood of Comparative Religions will have passed, the science will look back upon such works as *Orpheus* and *The Golden Bough* as distressing children's diseases. Even now Comparative Religionists are growing up methodologically. Evolutionism, which in its application to the religious field was committed to proving the development of all cults from a few primitive "dawn-concepts," is no longer used as a master key of interpretation. Analogies between religions are still sought and noted, but are not so confidently adduced as proof of interdependence. Together with appreciation of the splendid new information supplied by recent ethnology and archeology, there appears, at least among students whose opinions matter, a healthy realization of the many gaps in our knowledge. In particular, the fogs of nineteenth-century theories have lifted sufficiently to reveal the true goal of the study of religions, described by Fr. H. Pinard de la Boullaye as: "A scientifically documented history of the origin and vicissitudes of the religions, to serve as a basis for a judgement on their relative value and a judgement as to the transcendence of one among them."[2]

As is clear from the treatment of any one of the five religions presented in the book we are now concluding, the groundwork of study must be as comprehensive a catalogue of cultual facts as documents and monuments allow. These beliefs, precepts of conduct and rites cannot, of course, be rightly understood except as interdependent members of the whole organism which is the traditional religion of that particular people; and except, secondly, as considered in their relations to the social and political life of that people. The further duty devolves on the investigator of determining what special causes—teaching of religious leaders, decrees of monarchs, borrowing from other religions—gave origin to the cultual elements.

---

[2] Definition translated from Art. II of the second volume of *L'Étude Comparée des Religions* by H. Pinard de la Boullaye. To this author the present chapter is much in debt.

Only upon a sound knowledge of individual religions can comparative study be based. Many resemblances between religion and religion the cautious student will explain by the mere unity of human nature which expresses itself in parallels. Others, he will be content to leave *sub judice,* reserving his judgment until further discoveries show whether they prove anything or no. Some triumphs in comparative method have, however, already been celebrated, while still more seem definitely on the schedule. We can now speak with certainty of the Orientalization and Hellenization of later Roman religion, as has been shown in foregoing pages. A great group of religions, the Indo-European, has been traced to a parent stock of beliefs. In his *Der Ursprung der Gottesidee* (*The Origin of the Idea of God*), Fr. Wilhelm Schmidt is building a notable historical proof that the first religion was monotheistic. A comprehensive history of the origin and growth of religion will never be written, for too many of the records have perished, but with a soberer method now at hand to coordinate and appraise old and new evidence progress seems assured.

The more one knows about the natural religions of mankind, the more one is impressed by the kinship of fundamental ideas. What was to be expected *a priori* from the unity of human psychology and the identity of the religious object, is verified by empirical examination of the facts. Cardinal in whatever cult we study are a body of doctrine and a moral code. The gods are addressed by prayer and sacrifice, which latter act is performed through the mediation of priests. The sense of guilt moves to some form of ascetical propitiation, while the nisus toward union with the divinity expresses itself in mysticism. A principle of religious authority stands unquestioned, whether it be immemorial tradition, written documents or the living voice of a priesthood. Believers are convinced of the fact of direct divine intervention through revelation, oracle, and prodigy. In all of these the student of Comparative Religions recognizes the functioning of the geniune religious *élan,* though, of course, he is not blind to manifold human corruptions, to perverted moral precepts, for example, to human sacrifice, to spurious oracles.

What may be called the by-products of religion are not found so universally. Their presence or absence is seen on investigation to be accounted for by such factors as race, stage of material culture, social and political organization. Mythology and Magic, whose genesis and prevalence in higher cultures have been explained in preceding pages, are wanting or only rudimentary among truly ethnological primitives or near-primitives. Animism, Fetishism, and Totemism have all had their day as simplicist universal explanations of religion, but progress of knowledge has now refuted their universality and fairly indicated the reasons why they are found as elements of particular religions. Animism and Fetishism seem parented by peculiar race psychology and environment, while Totemism is chiefly a resultant of the social phenomenon of the clan. Caesaropapism, finally, as may be deduced from ancient records and from current news, is a pernicious penchant of the totalitarian state.

Judgments of value occupy the student in the highest stage of his investigation of religions. How suitable is each religion to the needs of man? How coherent in its various parts? How true? Adjudging to each, as he can from the evidence, its due share of suitability, coherence, and truth, he can further determine if among them all there be one which is transcendent in these three regards. If one does so stand out, it is in order to seek the reason for its pre-eminence. Are its beauty and truth to be acclaimed, as we acclaim a sublime work of art, as the triumph of human genius? Or are they such that he must reject human genius as the cause and judge that "the finger of God is here"?

BIBLIOGRAPHY

Dictionaries and Encyclopedias

Corpus Inscriptionum Latinarum.
Dictionnaire Apologetique de la Foi Catholique.
Dictionnaire de Théologie Catholique.
Harper's *Dictionary of Classical Literature and Antiquities.*
Hasting's *Encyclopedia of Religion and Ethics.*
Mythology of All Races, Marshall Jones (Boston, 1916).
Pauly-Wissowa, *Realencyclopedie.*
Schreiber, *Atlas of Classical Antiquities.*

Periodicals

Archiv für Religionswissenschaft.
Biblica.
Classical Journal.
Classical Philology.
Journal of the American Oriental Society.
Journal of University of Pennsylvania Museum.
Oriental Institute Communications of The University of Chicago.
Revue Apologetique.
Revue Biblique.
Revue de l'Histoire des Religions.
Revue des Sciences Philosophiques et Théologiques.

General Works

Chantepie de la Saussaye, P. D., *Lehrbuch der Religionsgeschichte* (Mohr, Tübingen, 1925).
Cumont, F., *Les Religions Orientales dans le Paganisme Romain* (Geuthner, Paris, 1929).
Huby, J., *Christus* (Beauchesne, Paris, 1912).
Jastrow, M., *The Study of Religion* (Scribners, N. Y., 1902).
Lang, A., *Magic and Religion* (Longmans, N. Y., 1901).
——— *Myth, Ritual and Religion* (London, Longmans, Green & Co., 1899).
Messenger, E. C. (ed.), *Studies in Comparative Religion* (C.T.S., London, 1935).

Mills, P. L., *Prehistoric Religion* (Capital Publishers, Washington, 1918).

Pinard de la Boullaye, H., *L'Étude Comparée des Religions-Beauchesne* (Paris, 1929).

Prümm, K., *Der Christliche Glaube und die Alt-Heidnische Welt* (Hegner, Leipzig, 1935).

Schmidt, W., *The Origin and Growth of Religion* (Methuen, London, 1931).

Babylonians and Assyrians

Deimel, A., *Pantheon Babylonicum* (Gregorian University, Rome, 1914).

Jastrow, M., *The Religion of Babylonia and Assyria* (Ginn & Co., Boston, 1898).

——— *Hebrew and Babylonian Traditions* (Scribners, N. Y., 1914).

King, L. W., *A History of Babylon* (Chatto & Windus, London, 1919).

Lagrange, M. J., *La Religion des Semites* (Lecoffre, Paris, 1928).

Langdon, S. H., *Lectures on Babylonia and Palestine* (Stechert, N. Y., 1906).

Luckenbill, D. D., *Ancient Records of Assyria and Babylonia* (The University of Chicago Press, 1926–27).

Olmstead, A. T., *History of Assyria* (Scribners, N. Y., 1923).

Rogers, R. W., *Religion of Babylonia and Assyria* (Eaton & Mains, N. Y., 1908).

Sayce, A., *Assyrians and Babylonians* (Clarke, Edinburgh, 1905).

Persians

Cameron, G. G., *History of Early Iran* (The University of Chicago Press, 1936).

Jackson, A. V. W., *Persia, Past and Present* (Columbia University Press, 1900).

——— *Zoroaster the Prophet of Ancient Iran* (Columbia University Press, 1899).

Mission Archeologique de Perse, *Memoires* (Paris, 1921–1934).

Müller, M., *Sacred Books of the East* (Oxford University Press, 1879–1910).

Pavry, J. D. C., *The Zoroastrian Doctrine of a Future Life* (Columbia University Press, 1926).

Rogers, R. W., *A History of Ancient Persia* (Scribners, N. Y., 1930).

EGYPTIANS

Boylan, P., *Thoth the Hermes of Egypt* (Oxford University Press, 1922).

Breasted, J. A., *Ancient Records of Egypt* (The University of Chicago Press, 1927).

——— *The Dawn of Conscience* (Scribners, N. Y., 1933).

——— *A History of Egypt* (Scribners, N. Y., 1912).

Budge, Sir E. A. W., *Fetish and God in Ancient Egypt* (Oxford University Press, 1934).

——— *The Gods of the Egyptians* (Methuen, London, 1904).

——— *A History of Ethiopia, Nubia and Abyssinia* (Methuen, London, 1928).

——— *Osiris and the Egyptian Resurrection* (Putnam's Sons, N. Y., 1911).

——— *The Teaching of Amen-em-apt* (Hopkinson, London, 1924).

Gauthier, H., *Personnel du Dieu Min* (Institut Francais d'-Archéologie Orientale, Paris, 1931).

Moret, A., *Mysteres Egyptiens* (Colin, Paris, 1913).

Petrie, Sir W. M. F., *Religious Life in Ancient Egypt* (Constable, London, 1924).

Renouf, le Page, *The Egyptian Book of the Dead* (Williams and Norgate, London, 1879).

Sayce, A. H., *The Religions of Ancient Egypt and Babylonia* (Clarke, Edinburgh, 1902).

Steindorff, G., *Religion of Ancient Egyptians* (Putnam's Sons, N. Y., 1905).

Weigall, A., *Tutankhamen* (Doran, N. Y., 1924).

Weynants-Ronday, M., *Les Statues Vivantes* (Fondation Egyptologique Reine Elizabeth, Bruxelles, 1926).

GREEKS

Adams, J., *The Religious Teachers of Greece* (Clark, Edinburgh, 1923).

Butcher & Lang, *The Odyssey of Homer* (transl.) (Macmillan, N. Y., 1888).

Caird, E., *The Evolution of Theology in the Greek Philosophers* (Maclehose, Jackson, Glasgow, 1923).

Evans, Sir A., *The Earlier Religion of Greece in the Light of Cretan Discoveries* (Macmillan, N. Y., 1931).

Keller, A., *Homeric Society* (Longmans, London, 1901).

Kittel & Weinrich, *Pantheon, Religiöse Texte des Griechentums* (Kohlhammer, Stuttgart, 1929).

Lang, Leaf, Myer, *The Iliad of Homer* (transl.), (Macmillan, N. Y., 1907).

McEwan, C., *The Oriental Origin of Hellenistic Kingship* (The University of Chicago Press, 1934).

Myres, J., *Who Were the Greeks?* (University of California Press, 1930).

Nilsson, M., *History of Greek Religion* (Oxford University Press, 1925).

Picard, C., *Les Origines du Polytheisme Hellenique* (Laurens, Paris, 1930, 1932).

Prumm, C., *Introductio in Res Religiosas Hellenicae Aetatis* (Gregorian University, Rome, 1930).

Romans

Axtell, W., *Deified Abstractions* (University of Chicago Press, 1907).

Bailey, C., *Phases in the Religion of Ancient Rome* (University of California Press, 1933).

Carter, J., *Religion of Numa* (Macmillan, London, 1906).

——— *Religious Life of Ancient Rome* (Houghton, Mifflin, Boston, 1911).

Cumont, F., *After Life in Roman Paganism* (Yale University Press, 1922).

——— *Astrology and Religion among the Greeks and Romans* (Putnam's Sons, N. Y., 1912).

——— *Textes et Monuments relatifs aux Mystères de Mithra* (Bruxelles, 1896).

Fowler, W., *Religious Experience of the Roman People* (Macmillan, N. Y., 1911).

——— *Roman Festivals* (Macmillan, N. Y., 1925).

——— *Roman Ideas of Deity* (Macmillan, N. Y., 1914).

Halliday, W., *History of Roman Religion* (Small, Maynard, Boston, 1923).

Jayne, W., *The Healing Gods of Ancient Civilizations* (Yale University Press, 1925).

Roscher, W., *Ausführliches Lexikon der Griechischen und Römichen Mythologie* (Leipzig, 1884).

Showerman, G., *The Great Mother of the Gods* (University of Wisconsin Press, 1901).

Taylor, L., *The Divinity of the Roman Emperor* (Amer. Philol. Assoc., Middleton, Conn., 1931).

Wissowa, G., *Religion und Kultur der Römer* (C. H. Beck, München, 1912).

INDEX